Balham to Bollywood

Chris England

Balham to Bollywood

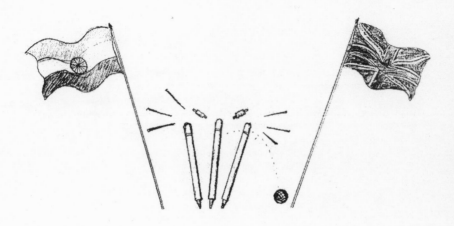

Hodder & Stoughton

Copyright © 2002 by Chris England

First published in Great Britain in 2002 by Hodder and Stoughton
A division of Hodder Headline

The right of Chris England to be identified as the Author
of the Work has been asserted by him in accordance with the
Copyright, Designs and Patents Act 1988.

3 5 7 9 10 8 6 4 2

A CIP catalogue record for this title is
available from the British Library

Hardback ISBN 0 340 81988 X
Trade Paperback ISBN 0 340 82481 6

Typeset in Sabon by Palimpsest Book Production Limited,
Polmont, Stirlingshire
Printed and bound in Great Britain by Clays Ltd, St Ives plc

Hodder and Stoughton
A division of Hodder Headline
338 Euston Road
London NW1 3BH

To the people of Bhuj

Contents

I
A Bit of a Loosener

As long as I can remember I have been a cricket fan, and consequently a sucker for the literary subgenre that is the England cricketer's tour diary.

You know the sort of thing – 'Antigua, 9 March: Got a slight twinge in my back that might rule me out of the one-dayer against the President's XI. Went marlin fishing with Gus, Moose, Chalky, Dazza, Lubes, Minty and the Guvnor, etc. Didn't catch anything but we got more than a little, shall we say, merry, and Pizzer fell overboard . . .'

Every now and then there'd be a cricket match, featuring the same cast, and you'd constantly have to refer to a glossary of the impenetrable nicknames they gave each other to find out who the hell Pizzer was, and why.

I would dearly have loved to have been selected to represent England on an overseas cricket tour, not only because I would have enjoyed the actual cricket, but also to see how my own tour diary measured up. It never happened, though, despite many sterling performances for my own team – which is even called 'An England XI' to give the selectors at Lord's a little nudge – and I had come to believe it never would.

But then, out of the blue, I was selected to go to India, to play the part of 'English cricketer' in a multimillion-rupee-budget Bollywood epic film about cricket. I realised that this was as close as I was ever going to get to the dream, and promptly invested in a Biro and an exercise book.

I toyed, briefly, with the idea of getting some seedy member of the sporting press corps to spend a weekend ghost-writing a diary for me, but there's never one handy when you need one, is there, so I've ended up doing it myself.

First of all I should own up. I don't really live in Balham, but when I was trying to come up with a zippy title I thought a little alliteration wouldn't do any harm, and Balham is the nearest place beginning with B to where I live (unless you count 'betting shop' or 'boozer'). I actually began the journey described in these pages from one stop farther out of London on the Victoria–Epsom Downs line, at Streatham Common.

Bollywood is not a real place, and not just in the sense that Hollywood is unreal. There actually is no such place. No gigantic white letters spelling out Bollywood on the side of a hill overlooking giant sprawling film studios, no Bollywood Boulevard snaking past high-security electric fences protecting the palatial homes of the stars, no Planet Bollywood serving blockbuster-themed curries from a menu selected by Amitabh Bachchan and Shah Rukh Khan.

Bollywood is only a name, a nickname for the Indian film industry. It is a play on the name Hollywood, of course, corrupted by the first letter of Bombay, where the bulk of Indian film-making takes place.

In January 1996 Bombay was renamed Mumbai, which is the old Maratha name for the city. I am all in favour of arbitrarily renaming places. The sooner the local council see sense and rename Streatham 'Islington' the better, at least as far as the price of my house is concerned. When, however, Bombay was renamed Mumbai, surely Bollywood should also have been renamed at the same time. Mullywood, it should be, shouldn't it . . . ? If that had happened, I would have pretended I'd set off from Mitcham.

2
Johnny Player is Very Excited

*Through the sticks, behind in the distance, Bhuvan sees
Arjan followed by a group of fifteen villagers walking
towards him.*

ARJAN
Bhuvan! I am with you now, if I can be of any help! And
so are they!

FAT VILLAGER
Yes! We will play too!

BHUVAN
That's great news!

*Bhuvan is at first happy but now unsure as he sees the
crowd. One of them has a big tummy, one is stick thin,
another is drunk, and some are fairly old . . .*

(*Lagaan* – English translation)

It started on Paddington Rec on a sunny Monday afternoon
in September.

The cricket season was almost over. England had blown
another summer, picking a team of journeymen bits-and-pieces
players in their World Cup squad, and then meekly surrender-
ing a four-Test series to New Zealand.

On this particular September afternoon I had been invited
to play cricket, and turned up at the appointed hour with my
kitbag slung over my shoulder. Sunbathers lounged all over the
outfield, but it's amazing how quickly they can move once you
start whacking a hard lump of leather about the place with a
big bat.

I strolled up to the pavilion, trying to look like a cricketing mercenary. When you're playing with and against people you haven't played with before you can score important psychological points by looking the part. Even something as innocuous as wearing a proper-looking cap can give you a slight edge.

A few other players were already lounging around, a few of whom I knew, most of whom I didn't. I nodded to the ones I knew, and cast a quick appraising glance over the others. A palpable tension hung in the air. They were waiting for something. I waited with them.

This was to be no ordinary game of cricket. Something big was at stake. For this was also an audition for a movie about cricket. None of us knew too much about it at this point, but the one thing we all did know was that it was a Bollywood movie, and we were to be playing for a trip to India.

For us, this match would be like the NatWest final to a nervy England hopeful – a big showpiece game at the very end of the season, one last chance to impress the selectors before the winter tour party is announced.

And the nervy England hopeful knows that if he doesn't take his chance, doesn't get the nod, then he has to look forward to a winter as a plasterer's mate, or window-cleaning, or working as something like an assistant consultant in a property management company, making cups of tea for estate agents. Not dissimilar to an actor's life, in fact.

I had heard about the big match a week or so earlier, when I got a phone call.

'Johnny Player's very excited,' the voice at the other end said.

The speaker was Howard, opening batsman and occasional wicket-keeper of the cricket team of which I am the eponymous captain. He is a slightly bandy-legged Yorkshireman in his early forties, lean as a whippet and fit as a butcher's dog. Something about his demeanour on a cricket field, and something about his venerable and ancient cricket kit, makes him look like a cricketer from another time. A more innocent time, a more honourable time, the time of Hobbs and Sutcliffe, when a batsman walked without waiting for the umpire's decision and shook the bowler's hand on the way to the pavilion, while the fielders all stood and applauded. On the cricket field Howard looks as if he has just stepped straight off a 1930s cigarette card, and I call him Johnny Player. Among other things.

'Now then, Johnny,' I said. 'Tell me all about it . . .'

Howard is an actor (among other things) and a neighbour of his was working at the time for a casting agency. She had come to him, burdened with the task of finding as many actors who could play cricket as possible to audition for a film, and without a clue how to go about it. Howard rubbed his cricket-callused hands together with glee, and directed her to my address book.

I spoke to Urvashi, the girl from the casting agency, and it turned out that she was looking for cricketing actors and comedians in their thirties and forties. As it happens, my team is drawn almost entirely from a vast pool of actors and comedians in their thirties and forties, and so I gave her a couple of dozen suggestions and left her to get on with it.

At this point neither Howard nor I took the idea of the actual film particularly seriously, but the audition was to take the form of a cricket match, and when you spend the entire summer, as I do, organising cricket matches, the prospect of playing in a match that has been organised by somebody else is not to be sniffed at.

For a start, there is the chance of playing for a captain who is unaware of how very very poorly I bowl, and so I might be able to get an over or two. The skipper of our team – that would be me – is only too aware of the mayhem that can ensue when my flighted (lobbed) off-breaks (dead straight balls) fizz and dart (plonk gently) off the track, bamboozling (lighting up the eyes of) the puzzled (delighted) batsman, who is soon trudging off towards the pavilion (to help the fielders look for the ball, which he has clubbed for a massive six).

Then there is the possibility of batting in one of the flashy middle-order positions – four, five, six, once the better bowling has been seen off – rather than having to open again because nobody else wants to. And you have the option of including the innings in your season's official average, or not, depending really on how many you get.

Best of all, though, is avoiding all the admin stuff. Some summer weeks are completely taken up with telephone calls trying to get a team together, waiting for cricket dilettantes to remember to return my nine calls. And no matter how many people I call, plead with and badger to play, I always seem to end up on the morning of the game with precisely ten players in my team, trying desperately to think who might have the phone number of the person at whose party I met someone who said they had a friend who'd really like a game some time.

Then there's tea to make, eggs to hard-boil, sandwiches to spread, individual fruit pies and cricket balls to buy, kitbags to hump, boundaries to mark out, scorers to find, umpires to designate, a batting order to decide on that pleases everyone (impossible), people to shout at and boss around all afternoon, tidying up, collecting money, humping kitbag home . . .

I enjoy it, of course, otherwise I wouldn't do it, but it's nice, once in a while, to be a dilettante myself, and swan along five minutes after the game is supposed to start, read the paper till it's my turn to bat, and let somebody else sort everything out.

As the day of the match approached, however, I found myself drawn into the organisational side of things. I couldn't help it.

'What about kit?' I asked, when they rang to confirm the date and time.

'Everyone will bring their own,' they said, 'and people can just share.'

Well, yes. In a sort of utopian dreamworld cricket match of the future, where everyone shares everything and there is no more war. However, not only was this to be a cricket match where the participants by and large didn't know each other well enough to say hello, let alone ask if they could use each other's protective boxes, it was also an audition. Twenty-two unemployed actors, with a plum job up for grabs in a big film, shooting overseas. The players in this match wouldn't be concerned with bonding, building team spirit and togetherness. They'd be wanting to scratch each other's eyes out.

At the best of times cricket is an individual sport masquerading as a team game. It's great to win, of course, but a gritty half-century in adversity, when the rest of your own team fails ignominiously, can be just as much fun, or maybe even – whisper who dares – *more* fun.

'My big kitbag is in Howard's van,' I said. 'I'd better get him to bring it along.'

Howard's van is big and white. He hires it – and himself – out to people who want to move house, has been known to spend the night in it, and occasionally parks it behind the bowler's arm and uses it as a sight screen.

Six of my team were hanging about at Paddington Rec, besides myself. There was Howard, looking particularly like Johnny Player in his old-style cap. There was Keith, a very tall, very thin Scotsman, who somehow looks as though he couldn't possibly manage sports at all, but who is a pretty good footballer and the best batsman I can call upon. Jon, a tall, slender chap, one of my opening bowlers, was there, and Ray, a medium-pacer with dodgy knees, who comes from the army town of Colchester and has somehow acquired the bearing and build of a typical sergeant-major without ever having been in the army. It must be something in the water.

There was Andy, a comedian, who slogs wildly at everything and insists on playing in an ancient and allegedly lucky torn cricket shirt that is nowadays more tear than shirt. And Paul, a writer, slow bowler and perpetual number eleven, who once went triumphantly through an entire season of 'did not bats', although his prowess is such that if he had made it out to the middle we could still legitimately have written 'did not bat' by his name.

We were all supposed to be at Paddington Rec by four, but at four fifteen there was still no sign of the casting people. Two dozen edgy blokes eyed each other up warily, as actors and cricketers will. Actors will always try to establish their place in a rough hierarchy if they can, trying to work out where the main threat to their getting the job will come from. The eyes scan the assembled company, and the brain is going:

'I don't recognise him . . . him I've seen in *Casualty*, driving a tanker of toxic chemicals that overturned and made his face go orange . . . he is a singing raisin in an advert for Fruit and Fibre . . . he has the same agent as me but I've forgotten his name . . .'

Conversational feelers are ventured, and this sort of thing is heard:

'Would I have seen you in anything?'

'Actually I do a lot of theatre work . . .'

'Yes . . . I did a cricket match once before, in *All Creatures Great and Small* with Chris Timothy . . .'

Classic piece of work. The speaker here has let you know that he has been working in front of the camera for some years, that he expects to be doing so again in this very job, and his abbreviation of the star's name has given him a further leg-up as he tries to undermine your confidence. He could have gone farther still, and cut the show title to *All Creatures*, and the star's name to Chris Tim, but he's judged it quite well, and you only think he's a prat and not a blithering idiot.

One chap, Simon, a stocky fellow around forty, looked very familiar and was getting a lot of quizzical looks from everyone, trying to place him. *The Bill* . . . ? *London's Burning* . . . ?

EastEnders . . . ? It turned out that he was a multiple winner of the daytime quiz show *Fifteen to One*, which explains his very high recognition factor among a bunch of unemployed actors.

Cricketers tend to judge each other on who has the best kit, which is by no means an infallible guide. Players can turn up with immaculate kit, gleaming white, oiled perfection, but when you see them play you discover that this is because the kit, like the scorers in their matches, is rarely troubled.

A coffin, though, is a definite sign. The big, hard, cuboid-shaped cricket bag, with a lock on it, says that the owner is a serious player, with kit worth stealing, or that could possibly be damaged by baggage-handling at airports when travelling to play overseas. Either that or he is a bullshit artist who struck lucky at a car boot sale.

Similar conversational feelers are put out.

'What team do you play for?'

'London Theatres.' Never heard of them, but they don't sound much cop.

'The Gaieties.' A touch embarrassing, frankly. Do they perhaps play in pink . . . ?

The group of players belonging to my team are able to get some intimidation in early, because our team is called 'An England XI'. It's named after me, of course, but we don't have to tell any of them that.

Four young lads are sitting together on the grass. They all have very similar kit, with identical sponsors' logos on the chests of their proper-looking shirts. They have big kitbags – not coffins exactly, but still serious looking, as though they might have coffins at home but didn't think this game important enough to bring them along. They are trim, athletic, confident, and, worst of all for the rest of us thirty/forty somethings wondering where the hell they come from, they are about twenty-three.

Someone tries to draw them into the 'What team do you play for?' conversation.

'Gloucestershire,' one of them says. End of conversation.

All sorts of rumours were flying about concerning the project. It's about a cricket match a hundred years ago between an English army team and an Indian village . . . Sachin Tendulkar and Kapil Dev are making cameo appearances . . . ! The captain of the English team is going to be played by Sting . . . ! Channel 4 are doing a 'Making of . . .' documentary . . . ! In fact there was a bloke there with a camera, claiming to be making a 'Making of . . .' documentary for Channel 4, and most of the rumours were coming from him.

Finally the casting people turned up. Two girls, Urvashi and Danielle, and a tall Indian chap who was fiddling with a camcorder, trying to get it to work. There was a bit of faffing about, and it became clear that nobody was quite sure how to get started. Time was slipping by, and it seemed less and less likely with every passing minute that there'd be time for a proper match before it got dark, particularly as really it was an audition and everyone would expect a fair crack.

I hate to see a vacuum of organisation like this, and even though it was none of my business I couldn't resist volunteering to sort something out. Earlier in the summer I had organised a double-wicket competition, in which teams of two played two-over matches against each other, and so I offered to arrange something along those lines.

A quick roll-call established that there were twenty-four players, so I split us into two teams of twelve. I made one of the Gloucestershire boys skipper of the fielding twelve, and took charge of the batting team myself. Everyone on the fielding side would bowl one over, and each batting pair would face two overs, and when that had run its course we'd swap the teams over. Thus there would be twenty-four overs altogether, which shouldn't take too long, and I reckoned everyone would get a bowl, a field and a bat before the autumn evening closed in.

I called out the names of the first pair to pad up. Ben, a bright-eyed eager beaver, was right at my elbow, and trotted off to oblige, and Barry, a stout chap with a grey moustache, also nodded and unzipped his efficient-looking kitbag. He'd clearly been playing for years and years. I went out to the middle then to stick some stumps in, only to find that the strip was artificial and had no stump holes in it, and so we'd need the sort of stumps which spring back on a little stand. On my way to find the park-keeper to ask if he had any of these, I found that eager Ben, already padded up, was there before me, and was already bringing some out. Very keen . . .

The tall Indian with the camcorder introduced himself as Ash, the director – though whether he meant of the whole movie or just of this day's cricket video wasn't altogether clear.

Ash crouched at mid-on with his camcorder and a little chart which he filled in as we went along. I stayed near by, telling him who was batting and bowling, and sneaking a sly look at his notes every now and then.

Ash's remarks were divided into three columns, headed 'Look', 'Bat' and 'Bowl', like a sort of cricketing Green Cross Code. Using a system presumably inspired by the way fast-food restaurants have eliminated the word 'small', recognising only 'medium', 'large' and 'extra large', Ash predominantly noted that a player's Look, Bat or Bowl was either 'good' or 'excellent', with the most execrable pieces of play earning the scathing comment 'OK'.

Barry and Ben batted out their two overs very smoothly, sportingly sharing the strike, and I wasn't surprised to see that Ash rated them both 'excellent'. He was particularly pleased with their Look, even though they were very different to each other, Barry being a portly fiftyish gentleman and Ben a fresh-faced and sprightly thirty-year-old.

As the next pair – two of the young Gloucestershire lads – made their way out to the middle, Ash explained that the film was set in the 1890s, and he was looking for a wide range of ages and styles for the English cricket team. This was interesting to know, particularly when the Gloucester boys started to smack the bowling to all parts. Perhaps there just might be room for an overweight slogger like me to make the trip along with these cricketing wunderkinds.

Behind the stumps, Howard, as usual, had transformed himself into Johnny Player, and the illusion was so strong that he actually seemed to be keeping wicket in black and white. Ash's director's eye had clocked this.

'Who is that?' he asked me at one point. 'He has an excellent wintage look.'

'I'm sorry?'

'He looks like a real weteran.'

'Ah. I see. Yes.'

Midway through the proceedings it was my turn to bat. I found myself paired with one of the intimidating young pros, and, as chance would have it, facing Jon's bowling. I knew, having seen him bowl often enough over the years from my captain's vantage point at first slip, that Jon could swing the ball nastily and be very difficult to hit. He's a mate, though, so surely he'd be gentle with me . . .

The first couple swung in past the inside edge of my forward defensive prod, thumping into my front pad. Hmmm . . . The next ball was quicker and went the other way, past my outside edge, and slapped into the wicket-keeper's gloves. Hmmm . . . At least I was making Jon look good. Another one fizzed down the leg side and I wafted at it without making contact.

Come on, now, get a grip – only a couple more balls to make an impression, and then I really *have* to give the bloke at the other end some of the strike. Jon, bless him, came up with a big yorker which I only just jammed out with the toe end of the bat.

The last ball came swinging into my pads, and I wound up and had a big lash at it. There was a satisfying smash as bat hit ball, an instant of relief at having actually succeeded in playing a shot, and then a ghastly split second in which I realised that the ball was heading at great and dangerous speed straight for Ash and his camcorder. I had time to think, Oh well, at least he'll be able to flog the tape to Jeremy Beadle, and even time to think, Oh no, hang on, it's not Jeremy Beadle any more, is it, it's that fat lass off of *Emmerdale*, before the ball neatly parted his hair and streaked off to the boundary, off the playing area, over a path, past a kid on a bike, through a flower-bed and in through the open door of a gents' public toilet. For my next trick . . .

Later I was able to steal a glance at Ash's notes, and saw that his brush with death had gratifyingly blinded him to my shortcomings. I knew, though, that I would find it much harder to impress him as a bowler. At least I had the advantage, once the two teams had changed over, of determining when I bowled, and so I brought myself on when Paul, my perennial number eleven, came out to bat. I figured I was doing us both a favour, protecting Paul's batting from some of the other bowling, which was really rather good, and also disguising the guilelessness of my own deliveries.

I lobbed down six of the slowest donkey droppers imaginable, as is my wont, and Paul missed them all. His usual technique, honed over the years, involves not making any movement of any kind until the ball has pitched. This went out of the window towards the end of the over, when he tried to give me the charge and was stumped. Twice.

And then, as the early autumn sun set over Paddington, it was over. I thought my lads had acquitted themselves respectably enough. Howard and Keith looked the part with the bat, and Jon and Ray had bowled well. Some of the other bowling had been pretty good, too, and not just by the professionals. An actor called Neil had been really quite swift, despite claiming to be carrying an injury, but then claiming to be carrying an injury, in my experience, is usually the prelude to a fast bowler ripping all three of my stumps clean out of the ground. There was no denying, I'm afraid, that I had bowled the worst over of the afternoon by some distance, but I saw in his notes that Ash had inexplicably thought my bowling 'good' rather than the dreaded 'OK'. Presumably his wits were still scrambled by my nearly knocking his head off.

We were all asked to describe ourselves into Ash's camcorder before leaving, which gave me and my team-mates the opportunity to say we played for 'An England XI', which I didn't suppose would do our chances any harm.

A few of us went for a quick pint, but it was strange. Normally after a cricket match you have either won, drawn or lost, and can enter into increasingly drunken post-match analysis accordingly. On this occasion there were winners and losers, certainly, but we didn't know who they were yet.

I wasn't even sure, as we talked about it, that I wanted to go to India all that badly. It would be devilishly difficult to arrange childcare, for a start, since I have two small boys and my wife works, and it's often quite handy that I myself am at home most of the time. But cricket brings out the competitive streak in me – actually, buying a Tube ticket or cleaning my teeth can bring out the competitive streak in me – and I knew that even if I didn't end up actually going to India, I damn well wanted to be asked.

Then we went our separate ways preparing to spend the next few days and weeks doing what actors (and writers, for that matter) do if not best then at least most – waiting to hear.

Waiting to hear about acting jobs can be a slow, painful business. You very rarely get rung up to be told that you haven't got a job, so it can be difficult to achieve what the Americans call closure. If you are an optimistic soul, you can find that you are still clinging on to a scrap of hope that the phone just might ring even after eight friends have already heard, and the project in question has already been filmed, and is in the *TV Times*, and is on next week.

Tauntingly, the England party for the tour of South Africa and Zimbabwe was announced. No Thorpe, staying at home to play with his kids, and no Ramprakash, possibly planning to go round to Thorpey's to throw his kids' toys out of his kids' pram. No Hick, either, which made the South Africans cackle with glee, although they may have been taking the piss. And no Crawley, who the Australians rate as our best bat, and whose first-class average has hovered around fifty for his whole career.

I checked the rest of Ceefax for news of the party to go and be in a cricket film in India, but nothing. I explored the only other possible avenue for information that I could think of, which was to look at the website of the Sting fan club. I deliberately tempted fate by putting all my cricket kit away for the winter.

Then, happily just before I cracked and let myself down badly by asking Howard if he'd heard anything yet, I got the call. I was going to India, to be a pretend cricketer.

3
Padding Up

CAPT. RUSSELL
All right . . . I'll cancel the lagaan. But you must defeat
us in this game . . . You. Tell me.
Do you accept the bet?

*Everyone looks at Bhuvan. The farmers, the British,
Elizabeth, Puran Singh and Russell. All eyes are on
Bhuvan.*

BHUVAN
I accept the bet!

(*Lagaan* – English translation)

At first, information about what was being offered was quite
hard to come by. The production would be based in the town
of Bhuj in Gujarat, a long way off the established tourist
routes, near the Rann of Kutch. I'd heard of the Rann of
Kutch, but had no idea in what connection. I had a feeling
it was either in something by Kipling or in a *Goon Show* –
both seemed equally likely.

Filming was due to begin in three months' time, in January.
I would be required for four weeks, or six weeks, or possibly
eight weeks. Then again it might be nine weeks or ten weeks.
And the money would be really quite poor, but then there was
the argument that I would be representing my country at my
favourite sport, however fictionally, and so the money was not
really the point.

The film, *Lagaan*, was apparently set a hundred years ago.
The star, Aamir Khan, was also the producer. The story, I was
told, concerned a fictional cricket match between the British

16

Army and a small Indian village, whose occupants have never played the game before.

At this point, I should admit, I knew very little about Bollywood, about Aamir Khan, or about India altogether. I'd seen the occasional glimpse of Bollywood movies here and there. Occasionally Barry Norman would have mentioned or shown a clip from one, and I knew, from the thriving Indian video store at the end of the road, that there was a market in this country. Vast numbers of videos were on display in this little shop, the boxes of which all seemed to feature an impossibly beautiful and highly decorated girl and a slick-looking individual with a floppy quiff.

I quickly discovered that Mr Khan's fame had spread to these shores, though, and no mistake. Susan, my wife, told an Indian friend of hers at work that I was going to be in a Bollywood film.

'Oh really?' the friend replied, mildly interested. 'Who is the star?'

Susan shrugged, and said: 'He's called Aamir Khan, something like that . . .'

Whereupon her friend let out a scream as though she'd just seen a Bay City Roller. I'm talking twenty-five years ago, obviously. Nowadays catching sight of Les McKeown or Derek Longmuir provokes a quite different sort of scream.

An old school pal of mine is married to an Indian, and when I mentioned the film to him he started grumbling that Bollywood films were the bane of his life. His wife subscribes to the specialist Bollywood movie channel on satellite or cable – B4U, I think it's called – and whenever he wants to watch live football these days Steve finds himself banished to the small black-and-white portable in the spare room. I told him to bring up the name Aamir Khan in conversation, and if a signed photo would get him the fourth round of the Worthington Cup in colour in the comfort of his living room then I'd see what I could do.

I later heard that the very idea of the sudden reduction in the degrees of separation between herself and the Khan to only three – via Steve, to me, to Aamir himself – had brought on, in Steve's wife, an attack of what used to be called the vapours.

So far so glamorous. Howard, I soon discovered, had also got the call, as had Jon and Ray, so there would be at least four members of An England XI on the trip. We immediately and earnestly resolved to keep ourselves in trim with regular nets in the weeks before we were to leave, but this went the way of many an earnest resolution. We'd pretty soon get our eyes in once we were out there, if all we were doing was playing cricket all the time, and anyway, it was film cricket, so if we messed it up we could always have another go. So that was it for the nets, then.

Almost immediately, however, the whole idea of going anywhere near India was thrown into doubt and confusion by news of a military coup in next-door Pakistan. It was a bloodless coup, with the Prime Minister Nawaz Sharif gently overthrown by the army chief, General Pervaiz Musharraf. Nonetheless it caused considerable alarm in India, where Musharraf was suspected of having masterminded guerrilla incursions into Kashmir in the summer. The new Indian Prime Minister, Atal Behari Vajpayee, placed their military forces on high alert.

I was alarmed too, having spotted in my atlas that Bhuj was right by the Pakistan border and was the closest Indian town to Karachi. As if that wasn't enough, the place was also drawing attention to itself by having a military airbase.

I watched the story develop over the next few days, wondering whether there would be a war, or at the very least one of those diplomatic situations where all British personnel are advised to leave the area, but gradually tensions seemed to die down a little. The situation remained quite volatile, though, and I'd have to keep an eye on it.

I thought I'd find out a little bit about Bollywood, fore-warned being forearmed, so first of all I checked out the Aamir Khan fan websites. Among the things I found out about the star – apart from what he looks like with his shirt on and with his shirt off – was that he has a reputation as a serious craftsman, trying in his films to portray naturalistic characters, avoiding as far as possible the over-the-top hysterics of his rivals. The other thing that came up again and again in descriptions of the man was that he shunned publicity, having a particular disregard for award ceremonies, which he made a point of not attending. Good for him, I thought.

Next I nipped down the road to the Asian video shop. This stocks exclusively Bollywood films and Bollywood soundtrack albums, and it thrives, so there is certainly an audience for Bollywood output in my part of South London. I found myself wondering whether I would be stopped in the street once *Lagaan* was released.

The video shop guy was a bit surprised to see a white bloke browsing in his store, and couldn't take his eyes off me. I was probably unshaven – I usually seem to be – and I dare say I looked as if I was preparing to rob the place. I strolled around looking at the film boxes, but I hadn't a clue what I was looking for particularly, which made me look even more suspicious.

I decided to ask for his help and went over to the counter. His eyes flicked nervously from side to side, and he looked like he was sizing up his chances of making a break for the police station on the other side of the road. When I asked him if he had any Aamir Khan films he breathed a huge sigh of relief, and suddenly a little pile of tapes materialised on the counter in front of me. None of them had boxes, and I wondered for a moment whether he'd misunderstood me and thought I wanted porn, but I gathered as he described them that none of the films he was offering me had actually been released for video rental yet. Aha – bootlegs!

The huge global demand for Bollywood output is met, in part at least, by the Indian underworld. The traffic in bootleg films and soundtracks via Karachi and Dubai is reckoned to be worth as much as £6 billion a year. And the gangsters' interest in the movie business doesn't end there. Many Bollywood films have mob money behind them, and they often try to cast the big stars by sending them death threats.

'Which is the best one?' I asked.

'All very good,' he offered, helpfully. Oh well. I picked a couple more or less at random. *Mann* and *Mela*, they were called, and I hoped they would show me what Aamir Khan was all about. I bade the video shop man good day, and left him to recover his composure, poor chap.

Later that evening Susan and I stuck the tape in and gave *Mela* a go. I recognised Aamir from the soft-focus publicity shots on his fan club's website. All I could say after watching a bit of *Mela* was that if he was the naturalistic one, then the rest of Bollywood must be populated with hams that would give Messrs Sinden and Callow a run for their money.

It's hard, at the best of times, to follow a film in a completely unfamiliar language, such as Hindi is to me. Usually, though, the language of film itself gives you a clue as to what is going on. We see a scene in a sort of faded blueish monochrome, for example, and we gather that it is a flashback. We see a small boy in the flashback, and something about the cut back to the present day tells you that the boy and the adult we are now looking at are one and the same.

It also helps that the predominant genre of movie in India is so all embracing. The 'masala' movie – masala in India meaning mixture, whereas in our country it means a sort of bright orange creamy tomato sauce – has a little bit of everything. A wild and exhilarating mix of romance, adventure, tragedy, knockabout comedy, pathos, emotion, musical numbers and dancing is the usual recipe, and the idea is to thrill you, move you and generally excite your envy on every front.

And if you are finding the main love story a little bit too syrupy for your taste, don't worry. There'll be some slapstick along in a moment, knockabout stuff of a calibre that would make even a Norman Wisdom blench.

Within about fifteen minutes of *Mela*, however, I was utterly at sea. Aamir and his mate were involved in a fantastic fight scene, and then we cut away to a musical number. In a Hollywood musical the songs by and large seem to grow out of the story. Characters burst into song, which is not a particularly realistic thing to have happen, but the song takes place in the same location as the surrounding story, and pushes the plot along, or illuminates a character's emotional state in some way.

In this, though, we were wrenched from a countryside scene on to a huge theatrical stage, where the characters were suddenly all clad in black leather, and surrounded by neon lights and a bewildering number of dancers. It was as though the Young Generation, the Younger Generation, the Second Generation, the Nigel Lythgoe dancers, the Jeff Thacker dancers, Pan's People, Legs 'n' Co, Hot Gossip, the lads from Michael Jackson's *Thriller* video and the Kids from Fame had got together to form some kind of almighty synchronised pelvis-thrusting supergroup. They did their funky thing, and then it was back to the plot, and a bit of comic relief.

In front of a camera, I always find the temptation to mug almost irresistible, and consequently always enjoy a bit of Finlayson, the pop-eyed double-taking overreacting king of the Laurel and Hardy sidekicks. Apparently, during the making of *Big Business*, the classic silent in which Stan and Ollie gradually demolish his bungalow while he destroys their car, Finlayson did a double-take so violent that he knocked himself unconscious against the side of the house.

Once the comedy cranked into action in *Mela*, I knew that the spirit of Finlayson was alive and well and flourishing in the subcontinent. One sequence I found particularly enchanting. Aamir and his pal beat a few people up, reason unclear, and then drive away in a truck. As they go along, discussing the scrap they have just been in, Aamir becomes desperate for a piss. He tries to persuade his mate to pull over, but his mate doesn't want to. Instead the mate digs out an empty beer bottle from the glove compartment, and tells Aamir to relieve himself into it, which, after a bit of complaining, he does.

We are then treated to the spectacle of India's leading heartthrob panicking as he realises that one bottle is simply not going to be enough to contain his epic whizz. His chum frantically roots around in the cab of the truck, and to Aamir's considerable relief finds another bottle. Despite the bumpiness of the road, the tricky transition from bottle A to bottle B is successfully concluded, and the crisis is over.

Or is it? Almost immediately the truck is pulled over by a traffic policeman, and the lads are trying to explain why they were weaving all over the road. The policeman is about to give them a ticket, ignoring their protestations, when he spots two beer bottles on the floor of the cab, full to the brim with foamy amber brew. Coyly winking and muttering the word 'baksheesh' – the Indian tradition of greasing the wheels of bureaucracy with, let's face it, open bribery – he gives the boys to understand that he will let them off in exchange for what he takes to be lovely beer. They, of course, perhaps spotting that the curly-moustached policeman is the comic relief, cheerfully oblige.

There then follows one of the most over-the-top pantomime performances I have ever seen. The fact that I couldn't understand a word of the dialogue was immaterial. The traffic cop strolls cockily round behind the truck, chattering away to himself, presumably about how much he is going to enjoy the beer. He takes a good long hearty swig, and then pulls at least fifteen distinct and enormously funny gurning faces as he grabs at the truck for support.

First he does a double-take directly at the camera – 'straight down the bottle', as the technical term goes. Then he blinks, his eyebrows shoot up and down, he goes purple, he slaps his own forehead, he looks at the bottle in disbelief, he pants for air, and he grabs at his throat. His knees give way, he looks straight at the camera again, as if asking for help, he exhales, wafting his hand in front of his mouth as though he has eaten something hot, twitches, shakes his head, and finally holds up the beer bottle and looks quizzically at it, pushing his policeman's cap back so he can scratch his head in what the international dictionary of mime would translate as 'bemusement'.

After a perfectly timed pause, in which we think Aamir and his pal are going to be in serious trouble, our man winks at the beer bottle, mutters something to the effect of 'that's good stuff', and strolls off taking another swig. A genius.

I stopped the tape, satisfied that I had seen enough. If this was the level of comic sophistication that would be required, then I was absolutely certain that I could provide it. No problem.

Around this time I was visiting the doctor with my son John, and I thought while I was there I might as well ask about what jabs I'd need if the India trip came off. I glanced at a chart on the wall behind the doctor's shoulder, which had all the countries of the world listed in alphabetical order on the left-hand side, and then along the top all the diseases you could and should get immunised against before travelling. I checked out India, and there were ticks in virtually every box. Every conceivable illness seemed contractable in the subcontinent, from the ague to zip fever.

I was particularly concerned about malaria, having the sort of tasty pale white flesh that attracts mosquitoes like Elizabeth Hurley attracts photographers. The faintest whiff of mosquito repellent is enough to call up vivid memories of foreign holidays without number, doused in the stuff from head to foot. The charms of the Camargue are reduced in my memory to a frenzy of calf-slapping, ankle-scratching misery; the ancient beauty of Florence and Rome is recalled only as sleepless nights spent trying to smash the blood-gorged little vampire bastards into bloody stains on invariably white hotel room walls. My most recent family holiday had seen the local mosquito population choose my white legs, of the twenty-four legs on offer, as the delicacy of the week, and that was in Suffolk.

The doctor told me I'd need immunising against hepatitis A, typhoid, diphtheria, tetanus, polio, and meningococcal A+C, whatever that is. He said there was no point doing anything about malaria until a couple of weeks before going, because the recommended course of treatment for the area could change at any time.

'Why's that?' I asked.

'The mosquito mutates,' he replied. 'He becomes resistant to one treatment, so we have to try another. And so it goes on . . .'

There was a cheery thought. Mutant mosquitoes. The doc went on to explain that what he meant was there were various strains of malaria, and it would be necessary to find out which was being carried by mosquitoes in the Bhuj area before taking the appropriate precautions, but he'd got me thinking now. What is the lifespan of the mosquito? Is there a possibility that if I'm out there for ten weeks I'll need protecting against another sort of malaria before it's time to leave?

And how many generations of mutating insects would have come and gone in ten weeks? I imagined a mosquito coming into my hotel room on my first day and having a squint in my toilet bag for my malaria tablets.

'Curses! Paludrine!' it would buzz in its buzzy little way, shaking its little mozzy fist in impotent fury at my sleeping form. Then it would root around in my stuff looking for my plane ticket, find I'm going to be there for another ten weeks, and suddenly its little buzz would have a new, triumphant tone.

'You win this time, whitey!' it would be thinking. 'But I'm going to be telling my children – hell, my grandchildren – about you. We can evolve, we can mutate, we can beat your puny Paludrine, we have time. We can even learn to love your Boots own-brand mosquito repellent! Why, in six weeks or so it will be like nectar to us. Ha ha ha ha ha . . . !'

As if this wasn't bad enough, I began to notice stories in the paper about one anti-malaria drug, Lariam, having psychiatric side effects, which had in odd cases led to depression, mood swings, heroin addiction – in short, things normally associated with a career in rock music.

At the end of November the real England team made a dispiriting start to the Test series in South Africa. After a few minutes they were 2 for 4, and duly subsided to defeat by an innings and twenty-one runs. Oh dear.

In December I began to wonder whether the whole thing was actually going to happen. I hadn't heard anything from India or from my agent for weeks, and when I thought about it the idea of me being asked to appear in a Bolly film started to seem extremely far fetched. Then, out of the blue, I got a message that Aamir Khan was in London and wanted to meet us all.

He and his wife, Reena, were staying in a hotel in Knightsbridge, and they invited us to visit them there. Coincidentally, on the day we were to do this, Ray and I were working together on a short film, called *Wonderbait*. Ray played a character called Ray, which had been written especially for him. I played a character called Happy Ron the miserable barman, which had been written especially for Arthur Smith.

In the evening Ray and I made our way down from Elstree to Knightsbridge, expecting a medium-sized party to be in full swing. It turned out, however, that we were coming to the last of a number of small audiences that had been conducted throughout the day.

We knocked on the door of the hotel room, and Aamir himself opened it. At first sight he was a slight figure and I felt I was towering over him, but once he had shown us in, offered us a seat and some coffee, and sat down himself, I could see that he was rather impressively muscled up. He was wearing a sort of skin-tight cycling top, and he clearly looked after himself. Reena was co-producing the film, and she was surrounded by paperwork of all kinds, in little piles on the floor, on the coffee table and in her lap.

Lots of big film stars are a bit on the short side, aren't they? There's something about the film camera that is kinder to short people than it is to tall people, for some reason. Your Bruce Willises and your Tom Cruises look like perfectly balanced male specimens, and of course they are (if any of their lawyers are reading this), and yet if you met Tom Cruise in real life, apparently, you could just pick him up and pop him in your pocket.

Howard was there already, and Simon the *Fifteen to One* champion, whom I remembered from the game at Paddington Rec.

After a little faintly awkward chitchat, Aamir started to tell us a bit more about *Lagaan*. His eyes lit up, and his energy and enthusiasm for the project were unmistakable. We knew a little, already, about the British side of the story – that we were to be a cricket team from the British Army pitted against a humble Indian village. Aamir told us more about the Indian side of the tale.

He was to be the leader of the villagers' team, natch, and in the story none of them have ever played cricket before. Much of the build-up to the match in the film would be concerned with his attempts to mould a team out of the raw material at hand, with the help of Elizabeth, the English captain's beautiful sister.

Bhuvan, Aamir's character, notices, for example, that the village blacksmith pounding his anvil will make a powerful batsman, and that the farmer hurling rocks at the birds who are eating his crops will be handy in the field. He spots the young untouchable with the withered arm, and notices that when the kid throws the ball he makes it spin dramatically, and Bhuvan has his Muralitharan. It began to sound like just the sort of film I'd actually pay to go and watch.

Aamir described the location they had built out in the desert. A whole village from scratch, and a whole cricket ground with its own pavilion. We began to realise that this wasn't just some two-bit operation. For the cricket match sequence in the film, Aamir went on, they were planning to get a crowd of ten thousand. And as if the idea of playing on a purpose-built cricket ground in front of ten thousand people wasn't enough to pump us full of enthusiasm – I saw that Howard had begun to drool slightly – he mentioned that most of the other scenes would be shot at a palace by the seaside with its own private beach.

It wasn't all good news, though. Aamir warned us that Gujarat is a dry state – no bars, no alcohol – and I noticed that Simon in particular had gone pale.

For some cricketers the beer is as important as the game itself. The excuse to have beer at lunch-time, followed by an afternoon drinking beer and then a post-match beer or two, is what some of them play cricket for.

It is remarkable how often, when I find myself in Cricket Captain Hell, trying to get a team together for the weekend, scratching around for players, I come up against someone who is almost keen, who quite fancies it, but he's not sure, he'll have to think about it . . . Then when I mention that there is a pub practically on the boundary he suddenly becomes a definite tick on the list. It happens so regularly, in fact, that – at the risk of blowing one of my secret arts of captaincy once and for all – I admit that I do sometimes say there is a pub practically on the boundary when there isn't.

Simon was clearly going to turn out to be a cricketer of this ilk.

Aamir said that it was possible to get a permit to buy alcohol if you could get a letter from your doctor saying that you required drink to do your job, or that a prolonged period of abstinence might be injurious to your health. He himself is teetotal, but he chuckled at the thought of a film unit arriving *en masse* from Bombay and England applying for a hundred and fifty alcohol permits on day one. We laughed too, but I noticed that Simon had started taking notes.

The conversation turned back to the film, and I asked Aamir again about the cricket match part of the story. It was to be a two-innings-a-side contest, taking place over four fictional days.

'Just so we're clear,' I said, 'who wins the game?'

Aamir smiled. 'I'm afraid the Indian team will win,' he said.

'We'll have to see about that,' I said. 'I'm not going all that way just to lose.'

There was a moment when I thought Aamir hadn't realised that I was joking and perhaps thought that I was demanding major script changes, but then he laughed.

'Of course, we will also play a proper match,' he said, 'and then we will see who will win.'

I was pleased to see a competitive glint in his eye as he said this. A challenge match. Excellent . . .

We left in high spirits. The film sounded good, the locations sounded exciting, and Aamir and Reena were charming and funny. For the first time I felt free to start looking forward to it all.

———

The year 2000 dawned with a slight sense of anticlimax. No computers packed in, not bringing the civilised world to a standstill. No planes fell out of the sky. No river of fire appeared on the Thames. There was, however, another innings defeat for the real England team in the fourth Test down in Cape Town. Hey ho . . .

Word came from India that all the English actors were required to grow their hair and beards – even the women, ho-ho – to give the make-up department as much as possible to work with. I was to be the exception, apparently, as they had 'something special' in mind for me.

I found out what this was one afternoon when a lady – Jean – came to my house for a moustache fitting – and that's not a phrase I ever thought I'd see myself writing.

'Normally we'd have you come to us,' she explained. 'We did have a huge hair workshop in North London, but it just burned down.' Imagine that. All that hair crackling and spitting away . . .

I sat at my kitchen table while Jean prepared the tools of her trade, which turned out to be a felt pen and a roll of cling film. She spread the cling film all over my face, and then quickly drew all my facial features on to it in felt pen before I suffocated. Cunningly, she was then able to transfer a flat map of my face on to paper.

While she did this I managed to sneak a glance at some pictures she had laid out, and found what they were planning to make me look like. I was to have a large droopy handlebar moustache and long sideburns, and it was a good job they were going to be fake because it would have taken me the best part of three years to grow anything remotely like it. The most interesting thing by far was that by my name there was a drawing, and a character name – 'Yardley'.

This was the moment I stopped thinking of myself as 'Cricketer', and began to imagine myself as a Yardley. The drawing of Yardley, with his splendid whiskerage, looked uncannily like Flashman, the ladies' man, coward and unwitting military hero. The eponymous central character of George MacDonald Fraser's novels would surely have found a soul mate in 'Hardly' Yardley, the scornful braggart of the East India rifles, the flamboyant dashing blade of the army cricket team . . .

Or something. I still hadn't seen a script.

A week later I got a small cardboard box in the post. I opened it, and glimpsed a couple of undoubtedly poisonous giant millipedes lurking in some toilet paper. Who had it in for me? Who hated me so violently that they would dream up such a . . . ? Oh yeah, it was the moustaches.

Actually I thought myself lucky to have something so small and inoffensive to stick in my luggage. Ten years ago I had a part in a comedy war film which was being shot in Israel. The production people rang up and asked if I'd pick up a couple of bits and pieces from a costume supplier in London and bring them out with me. The items they wanted me to carry nonchalantly through El Al security, the most rigorous luggage-checkers in the world, were some Nazi regalia, a couple of Nazi uniforms, some SS armbands, a machinegun, and a corset. I politely declined. They didn't seem altogether surprised.

I went into London one wintry afternoon for a costume fitting, bumping into Ray, as luck would have it, on the train. The costume designer, Bhanu, was staying in the same hotel where we had met Aamir and Reena before Christmas, and Aamir had told us on that occasion that Bhanu was the most highly respected costume expert in India. She won an Oscar for *Gandhi*, apparently, and her experience then of clothing vast crowds in period costume would stand her in good stead for *Lagaan*.

Bhanu showed Ray and me into her room, grumbling about the British weather, which was typically unpleasant, and started to measure us up. I can honestly say I have never been so minutely mapped. She found at least half a dozen separate parts of my arm to measure, two different neck measurements (above and below the Adam's apple), and I think three waists, although she might just have had difficulty finding one underneath my spreading beer (and chocolate) gut. This is the sort of attention to detail that wins Oscars, I thought, and I looked forward to wearing clothes cut perfectly to suit my highly individual physique. I always have trouble with shoes on film shoots owing to my large flat plates of meat, but Bhanu drew carefully around our feet and assured us that shoes were being specially made by the finest cobblers in India.

Some instinct told me that she was speaking some of the finest cobblers in India, and the next day, when I went out shopping for essentials, I made sure that I bought about a dozen pairs of cushioned sport socks to protect me from these specially made shoes.

People go to India for many reasons. Some go to find themselves, and then, once they have done that, to immerse these new-found selves in the ancient mystical spirituality of the region. Some go to sample the many divergent cultures that rub along together in this vastly overpopulated country. Some will drive there overland in an old Volkswagen camper with a group of similarly vacant sandal-clad individuals and a guitar to sing 'Hare Krishna' at baffled locals. Some go to visit the tourist landmarks, the Taj Mahal, the temples intricately carved into the sides of mountains. Some go for the mountains themselves, or for the beach resorts like Goa; others stuff a few T-shirts and pants into a backpack and ride around on the trains. All of these, with their different expectations and experiences, will return with one thing in common.

That thing is an anecdote which begins something like: 'Oh God! It was fabulous! What an experience! But I'll tell you what – after we'd been there for about five days I got the shits like you wouldn't believe . . . !'

Figuring that a certain amount of digestive upset was inevitable, I bought a big load of Dioralyte, and then a bit later I became convinced that I hadn't got enough so I bought a load more. I also bought boxes and boxes of water purification tablets, and all the mosquito repellent I could get my hands on. I hoped I'd have enough room in my suitcase for one or two clothes as well as the travelling chemist's I was accumulating.

The other thing I bought was a notebook, in which to keep my diary of the coming weeks, my pretend cricketer's pretend cricket tour diary. I decided to start it right away, to give a flavour of the build-up to the adventure, and then forgot all about it until . . .

18 JANUARY

I'm driving along, having just dropped John, my younger son, off at Wendy's (our childminder, not the burger place), listening to the fifth Test from South Africa on talkSPORT radio. It's still quite new, the cricket being on a commercial station, and it still seems odd hearing Jack Bannister effortfully shoving the phrase 'brought to you by Regus office systems' into otherwise quite straightforward remarks.

The Test has been ruined by the weather, and we're on the final day with South Africa still ploughing along in the first innings of the match. It suddenly dawns on me that the commentators seem to have got wind of an arrangement between Hansie Cronje and Nasser Hussain to forfeit an innings each and effectively play a one-day game. This happens from time to time in county cricket, but not in a Test match surely . . . ?

David 'Bumble' Lloyd is getting quite indignant about the idea, his annoyance brought to you by Regus office systems, but the others are seriously discussing how many Cronje will need on the board before declaring. The consensus seems to be about 275, which sounds about right, and then, just as I'm turning into my driveway, South Africa declare on 248 for 8.

I applaud Cronje's sportsmanship, although I think he's gone quite, quite mad, and a day on which I was vaguely planning to do some work becomes a day pacing up and down in front of the telly, as England inch their way towards the required total. The series has gone, of course, and all that's at stake is whether England will lose 3–0 or a face-saving 2–1, but still . . .

On the radio they are saying that as long as Atherton can stay there, brought to you by Regus office systems, England have a chance to pinch it. Atherton is promptly out for seven. Hussain and Butcher have a bit of a stand, and then Stewart and Vaughan put on a hundred together. It seems to be going our way, but then both of them are out, along with Maddy and Caddick, and we are eight wickets down with nine runs to win.

The stage is set for a real nail-biter, but then suddenly Gough and Silverwood have biffed the remaining runs and it's all over. Hussain is triumphant, and Cronje is remarkably good natured about it all, I must say. Especially considering he himself got a duck.

22 JANUARY

It was my thirty-ninth birthday a couple of days ago. Susan bought and gift-wrapped for me another huge box of Dioralyte, among other things. I celebrated the occasion – the birthday, not the big box of Dioralyte – by having some friends over for a meal. Knowing that the following weekend I was going to start ten weeks of exclusively Indian food, I decided that it might be a good idea to get my gastric system into training. I've never really been a big fan of curry, preferring to stick to cuisine that doesn't actually cause me physical pain, either on the way in or on the way out again. I don't eat much broken glass either – similar reason.

Every day leaflets from all kinds of takeaway restaurants drip relentlessly on to our doormat, and I shuffled through the latest fistful waiting to be recycled to see whether there was a promising Indian among them.

As it happened there was one for a nearby Punjabi place that we hadn't tried. OK, so half the Punjab is in Pakistan, but Bhuj is closer to Pakistan than it is to most of India, so I thought it might be representative of what was in store. The clincher was that the leaflet featured a recommendation from no less a figure than Javed Miandad, the well-padded international cricketer. To look at him, you'd certainly reckon Miandad could stick his grub away – he's like the Pakistani Mike Gatting – but would he turn out to be a discerning scoffer or merely interested in volume? Well, the perfect appropriateness of eating an Asian meal recommended by a top cricketer was too much to pass up, so I gave them a call.

The food was good, actually, and the evening very enjoyable. The next day, however, I got the shits like you wouldn't believe, which didn't bode particularly well.

Luckily I had about two tons of Dioralyte on hand. I'd better buy some more . . .

24 JANUARY
Urvashi has been on to me – she is working for the production now – and she needs various bits and pieces, including passport, photographs and my contract in order to apply for a work permit. Time is very short, now, and so I've had to sign the contract and effectively agree to do the film without seeing a script. I'm sure proper actors reading this will throw their hands up in horror, but what the hell.

Actually I'm not too bothered about what I will be asked to do. I acquitted myself reasonably well with the bat in the audition game, and so I am presuming that I will be asked to unbuckle a couple of cover drives, maybe a hook or two, the odd forward defensive. No problem. Just as long as I don't have to bowl, everything will be fine.

27 JANUARY
Leaving tomorrow.

Packing my kitbag for India, I am careful to root out my own box, my abdominal protector, guardian of the family jewels. It hardly seems possible that anyone could contemplate making a film about cricket without being prepared to supply these vital items, but it's not the sort of thing you want to leave to chance.

I find it and stick it in the bag, along with – to be on the safe side – the spare box, which I never use, never would use, never would dream of using, because it's only in my bag in case, horror of horrors, anyone ever sidles up to me at a match and says:

'You haven't got a . . . um . . . box . . . I could . . . um . . . borrow . . . have you?'

It's colour coded, so I never get it muddled up with my own box, because if someone is so unprepared, so ill equipped, so damn casual about abdominal protection, you know for bloody certain that they won't have any sort of athletic support to slip your box into. No, it will be thrust down between pubic hair and Y-front, cradling the tackle next the skin.

And another thing. If ever anyone borrows your box you know with the grim certainty of the Law of Sod that they are then going to score at least fifty, with lots of really sweaty running between the wickets, and possibly a couple of really nervy close run-out appeals, the sort that get the adrenalin pumping and the sweat flowing, particularly in that pivotal groin area, that awesomely well-lubricated fulcrum of the batsman's technique.

And you know, equally certainly, that it's going to be tossed back to you at teatime with a nonchalant 'Cheers!', arcing moistly through the air to where you will instinctively, unerringly, make your best catch of the season, despite having a Bakewell slice in one hand and a corned-beef-and-pickle bap in the other.

The one urgent task which has been preoccupying me is sorting out a fixture list for the cricket season. Ordinarily I would be doing this in February and March, but I fancy it will prove difficult to arrange from the Rann of Kutch, so I have been trying to force my feckless fellow captains to commit to definite dates before I leave.

I have run my cricket team for the last eleven years. It started in response to a challenge from the comedian Arthur Smith, with whom I wrote a play called *An Evening with Gary Lineker* around that time. We each got a team together to play a couple of matches, and they were successful and enjoyable enough for us to do it again the following summer, and we have played a 'Test' series against each other every year since.

My team, as I have said, is called 'An England XI', a simple and tinily amusing play on the fact that my surname is England – do you get it . . . ? Despite the feebleness of this quarter-joke, Arthur was jealous of it, and also wanted a comedy name for his team. He is not a man to be satisfied with 'The Arthur Smith XI' or 'Arthur's Team', anything like that. Not with worlds of obliqueness and obscurity out there to plunder. For one early match he named his side after Arthur Cravan, a little-known nephew of Oscar Wilde who was a pretty much unsuccessful pre-Dadaist philosopher/poet/boxer, but this only led to confusion in his ranks and a consequent lowering of morale. As Arthur was casting around for new inspiration, an advert on the television caught his eye.

In it a beautiful girl with long hair is running along a beach. She is panicking, splashing through the surf, and we quickly see that she is being chased by a black helicopter. A man is leaning out with a rifle to gun her down. She stumbles, she sprawls in the sand and spray, the helicopter roars overhead, the gale from its mighty rotors lashing her dark hair this way and that, and . . . a voice shouts 'Cut!'

The girl picks herself up and plucks unhappily at her hairdo, and we see that the whole set-up is a location shoot for a movie. The director calls for the star's hair to be fixed, and a man in a suede bomber jacket sprints urgently out from among the film crew.

The picture freezes on a close-up of this man, a caption appears and a voice-over tells us the same information. We are looking at:

'Dusty Fleming, International Hairstylist'.

CUT TO: Dusty fixing the star's seemingly impossibly snagged hair, with the help of the product, Sunsilk Hairspray. She smiles, and says:

'Dusty, you've done it again!'

He smiles back. 'Now it's *your* turn to do it again!'

Dusty and the girl hold their cheesy smiles for several beats longer, as though they had both accidentally sprayed their faces with Sunsilk holding mousse, and then there's a pack shot, and it's over.

There was another one, around the same time, involving a girl falling from a juggernaut into a safety net and consequently needing her hair fixing. It also had the key element which tickled Arthur so, to wit the freeze-frame on Dusty, and the caption: 'Dusty Fleming, International Hairstylist'. Like he was some sort of impossibly glamorous superhero, ready to fly off at a moment's notice to solve a hair-related crisis anywhere in the world.

The tagline – 'Dusty, you're a star!'

'Well, that makes two of us!'

– was, if anything, even more cheesy.

Enchanted, Arthur decided to call his cricket team the Dusty Fleming International Hairstylists XI, and a B-list celeb amateur part-time cricket legend was born.

With this summer's England–Dusty dates in the diary, I finally feel able to leave the country.

4
Going Out to Bat

*A bearded man with long unkempt hair looks intently at
the last rank of troops, spits, and mutters to himself.*

GURAN
One day you're going back to your frozen little island . . .
whimpering . . .

(*Lagaan* – English translation)

28 JANUARY
The flight to Bombay is not until 22.20, so as on almost every
Friday for the last ten years I go to play football. Howard, Ray
and Jon also play a valedictory match, sporting their alarming
Lagaan facial hair. Howard is flying out with me this evening
– Ray and Jon fly out next week.

The rest of the day is spent trying to cram T-shirts and boxes
of Dioralyte into my biggest suitcase.

In the evening, Susan and the boys drive me to Heathrow
to see me off. Susan is quite apprehensive about the coming
weeks, but the boys run around excitedly, and don't really
understand that I'm going away.

We try to find somewhere to watch planes landing and
taking off, but there isn't really anywhere to do this at the
world's busiest airport, which strikes me as a bit crap. I think
I'd like to buy Peter and Johnny a little goodbye present, but
brilliantly there's not really anywhere to do that either, unless I
can interest two pre-school boys in the works of John Grisham
or expensive leather hand luggage.

Who buys luggage at the airport? What sort of disorganised
fool turns up with all their stuff in a few Sainsbury's carrier

bags, pairs of pants sticking out of every available pocket, thinking: I really wish I had some proper expensive leather hand luggage to bung all this lot in – ah, the very thing . . . ? You can imagine that happening once every six months or so, but that surely should not be enough to keep an outlet going in Heathrow's departure mall.

In the end I get the lads some socks with pictures of Dalmatians on them from Sock Shop. They put them on when they are strapped into their little car seats, and I say a slightly tearful goodbye to my little family in the short-stay carpark.

In the departure lounge I hook up with Howard, and we look out for the other two English cricketers who are supposed to be flying out with us. These turn out to be Ben – the eager beaver who sorted out the springy stumps back at Paddington Rec – and Jamie, one of the lads from Gloucestershire.

My initial scheme for spotting them was to watch for the most improbably bearded men on the flight, but as it happens Ben has a neat little goatee in the Sheriff of Nottingham style, while Jamie has a tiny little beard on his bottom lip of the kind sometimes sported by trumpeters, for some reason.

Howard has a nice turn of phrase to describe the way actors behave when they meet a group of new colleagues for the first time.

'They're like a bunch of dogs sniffing each other's arses,' he says.

A couple of early sniffs occur, and Ben, a dapper thirty something dressed all in black, manages to give the impression that he knows everyone or else knows someone else who knows everyone who comes up in conversation.

I am a little more interested in Jamie's experiences, as this is my first trip to play cricket overseas. He, fifteen years younger than me, has already been on proper cricket tours to the West Indies, South Africa, Zimbabwe and Australia, the lucky pup.

We are chatting away, waiting for the flight to be called, and

I ask Howard how he has got on in court the previous week, knowing that he has been doing a bit of jury service. He starts relating the details of a particularly nasty case of aggravated rape under the influence of vodka, and we slowly twig that Ben and Jamie believe Howard, a man they have only just met, and who they are to be stuck with for a ten-hour flight, not to mention a ten-week stay in India, to have been the defendant. This passes the time very agreeably, as we crank this wind-up tighter and tighter until it begins to fray and finally snaps.

Then first-class passengers are called, and Ben stands up and says: 'I seem to have been bumped up to first class, I can't think why . . .'

I can. He clearly has a much better agent than we have.

On the plane I am pleased to see that there is a little video screen set in the back of the seat in front. Even though the flight is an overnight I know I won't be able to sleep, so I may as well watch all the films going. One of the channels is showing a view from a camera mounted in the nose of the plane. I've always thought something like this would be a good idea, as you can never really see much out of the little side windows. I watched this channel as the plane charged down the runway and lurched into the air, and then all you could see was darkness. It was interesting for about fifteen seconds.

One of the movies on offer was *Mickey Blue Eyes*, starring Hugh Grant. Before he became one of the most famous men on the planet, Hugh used to turn out from time to time for An England XI. On one such occasion, a needle Test match against the Dusty Fleming International Hairstylists, Arthur, the Dusty's skipper, was surprised and delighted to be approached in the pub beforehand by a group of attractive young girls.

'Excuse me,' one of them said to him. 'Aren't you Arthur Smith?'

Arthur beamed that this was indeed the case, and casually assumed a louche chatting-up posture leaning against the bar.

'It is him,' the girl said to her friends, 'I told you it was. We're very pleased to meet you, Arthur – can you get us Hugh Grant's autograph . . . ?'

Another time, Arthur brought in a ringer, a girl who had played 'ladies cricket at a high standard'. He brought her on just before tea to bowl at Hugh, who hit her two overs for 43 runs, and then, as he strolled in for his sandwiches, was heard to mutter:

'I feel such a cad . . .'

The stewardesses turn out the lights as the Emirates jet drones over eastern Europe, Turkey, Saudi Arabia . . . I marvel at how people can sleep, packed in so closely together. I've never been able to manage that – I'd have been hopeless at public school.

29 JANUARY

The horse thing first comes up while we are waiting for the connecting flight to Mumbai at Dubai airport. The place is being renovated, and is consequently even more mind-numbingly horrible than I expect it is normally. Grey temporary ceilings and walls, decorated only by apologies for any inconvenience in about eight different languages, and not even a decent view of any planes landing and taking off. Once we've taken a shambling plane-tired turn around the duty-free shop there's nothing to do but sit.

There are actually plenty of comfy seats, bolted together in threes, but each three is covered by a dozing Arab businessman with his shoes and socks off. Being too polite to whack a couple of them on the soles of the feet with a rolled-up newspaper and get the selfish bastards to move over, we spend quite a long time pretending still to be drinking the Cokes we'd ordered some hours ago so that we could stay sitting on the really uncomfortable hard wooden sub-Ikea upright chairs in the café.

After our success at leading Jamie and Ben to believe that

Howard had spent the previous week in court on a charge of aggravated rape, Howard and I decide to pass the time by winding them up about the film itself. Ben realises early on what is happening and joins in, but Jamie knows even less about Bollywood than we do and is horribly prepared to believe anything.

'Now you know, don't you, that all Bollywood films are musicals?'

'Erm . . . yeah. Yeah, I knew that.'

'And that everyone is liable to break into song-and-dance routines at any moment?'

'Really?'

'It doesn't really concern us, of course, it's mostly the Indian actors who'll be doing the songs.'

'Phew!'

'Oh yeah. Apart from the Bowlers' Dance.'

'Eh? Bowlers' Dance? What's that?'

'Oh, I'm not really sure. I'm a batsman, you see. And you're batsmen, as well, aren't you? Howard? Ben . . . ?'

Howard and Ben confirm that they are, indeed, batsmen. Jamie's eyes grow wider with apprehension. He, of course, is a bowler. We chip in suggestions until Jamie has compiled in his mind a nightmarish picture of what will be required of him.

There will be at least a dozen wickets, you see, all laid side by side. When the music starts, all the bowlers will run up simultaneously alongside each other, singing in Hindi, and do an elaborate kung-fu-style pirouette before all simultaneously delivering their balls. These will, naturally, all have to land exactly on a length, otherwise the take will be ruined, but Bollywood film-makers are quite happy to film the same shot over and over again for several days until they get precisely what they want.

Jamie, unsure whether to believe any of this, pulls out the clutch of papers the production have sent him to see if he can find any reference to the Bowlers' Dance. He can't, of course, but he stumbles across an insurance document. To save money, the production has insured three of us – Ben, Jamie and me – on the same policy and sent it to Jamie to bring out to India, so this is the first time Ben or I have seen this particular item.

It looks pretty standard, until we catch sight of the box headed 'Special Considerations', and I see one line of type-writing which chills my blood.

'Horse-riding (not jumping)' is what it says.

I experience a cinematic moment. The sounds of Dubai airport retreat into the far distance, and all I can hear is the blood thundering across my eardrums. Thundering, thundering, like . . . why, like the hoofbeats of a thousand crazed horses, galloping, frothing, rearing, stamping, crushing, biting, crapping . . .

I don't like horses much.

At a distance I merely dislike them. For years I have resented horse-racing for wantonly interrupting the Test match on the television. Richie Benaud will be summing up the match situation, and suddenly there will be a shift, a sigh, in the tone of his voice that you register in your central nervous system even before your brain makes sense of what he's saying, which will be something like:

'And now, with England needing seven runs to win and one wicket standing, it's time to go over to the 3.05 at Wincanton . . .'

With luck you suffer the bare minimum, which involves a bit of watching identical snorting horsey beasts shambling around a paddock, each with a tiny Irishman on its back, and then an incomprehensible mêlée hurtling along in a cloud of clods while a very posh commentator pretends he can tell which one is which.

Unless it's Ascot. Then you're in for hours and hours of watching identical snorting horsey beasts shambling around a paddock, each with a fruit-and-veg stall on her head, while a very posh commentator accompanied by hat expert Eve

Pollard will eventually take you over to see a bit of the actual race if you're lucky, before handing you back to Lord's, where the man of the match presentation is already under way.

This is why I was glad when the BBC lost the rights to Test match cricket to Channel 4. They didn't deserve to hang on to them, that's what I thought, but then bugger me if Channel 4 don't nip off to the racing with equal abandon. Bloody horses.

Up close, I have a real problem with them.

The front end has a big swinging, nodding head, with which to knock you to the floor, where it can finish you off by trampling you underfoot, and dozens of razor-sharp brown teeth set in a huge jaw, with which to bite your hands off if you are foolish enough to go within reach.

We mustn't make any sudden movements, of course, or loud noises, in case we startle the horse into standing up ten feet high on its huge hind legs and smashing our heads in with its hooves.

The back end features the stupendously powerful hind-quarters, with more big hooves for suddenly lashing out with. I wouldn't walk round the back end of a horse any more than I'd walk round the front end of a tiger.

It isn't the fearsome array of physical characteristics alone which unsettles me, though. It is that, coupled with the fact that horses are plainly all mad.

We shouldn't be surprised, given the extent to which the animal is prized according to its lineage. You've only to look at the human upper classes, with whom it has to be said the horse shares a good number of facial characteristics, to see that generations of carefully managed inbreeding aren't exactly a guarantee of mental stability.

Horses are the only creature you ever see wearing blinkers, aren't they? And why? Because, unlike any other of God's beasts, they haven't the mental fortitude to gaze upon the real world without rearing up and mashing somebody's skull with their heavy metal-shod kickers.

Look at the thoroughbred racehorse, with its mad eyes swivelling about, trying to decide who to kick first. It's as if it knows that if it stumbles and cracks one of its spindly shins we're going to shoot it in the head, and it's planning to get its retaliation in first.

People feed them sugar lumps, too, recklessly, not even put off by the stupid animal's inability to distinguish between a lump of sugar and a finger. Have they never seen what effect a sugar lump or two will have on a three-year-old person? And at least you can manhandle one of those up to its room until it's calmed down.

Years ago a friend of mine worked on the television series *Black Beauty*, the winning tale of the gorgeous black horse, with its lustrous coat and its almost intelligent rapport with its human counterparts. He told me that the horses they used were so stupid that they had to have seven Black Beauties for the filming, because you couldn't tell from one day to the next which ones were going to be too barmy to work with. And two of them were brown.

I missed the point of *Gulliver's Travels* altogether, because I thought the reader was supposed to be terrified of the crazed destructive power of the Houyhnhnms.

I have always been one of those people who says:

'There's no way you'll ever get me on a horse.'

I've been quite determined about that. A horse's eyes point sideways, like some gigantic two-ton fish, so how does it see where the hell it's going? It weighs as much as a van, and you can't take the key out of the ignition.

Now, in Dubai airport, more than halfway to India and way, way too late to back out, I find I'm going to have to give it a go.

We complete the second, shorter, leg of our journey to Mumbai on a rather less swish aircraft. Ben is again whisked off into the luxury zone, shrugging with genial incomprehension. Right at the back of the plane, I have a seat that slopes forward to such a degree that only the seat belt, strapped tightly and lodged beneath my ribs, prevents me from sliding slowly under the seat in front.

The approach to Mumbai is spectacular. Great red outcrops of rock thrust into the sky, lit up by the late-afternoon sun, and the plane swings lazily round them. As we head for the runway, we swoop so low over an enormous shantytown of huts made from sheets of corrugated metal that it seems the plane's wheels must brush away their flimsy-looking roofs and gather up the casually strung lines of laundry.

As the mad scramble to retrieve hand luggage from overhead lockers drowns out the stewardesses' requests for people to remain seated until the plane reaches the terminal, an elderly lady beside me struggles with a carrier bag full of duty-free Famous Grouse. She finds that the only way she can get sufficient leverage to manoeuvre the bag down is by leaning on the top of my head with the point of her bony elbow, grinding my neck down into my shoulders.

I'm too surprised to complain, but resolve to tread on her foot later. She is, however, as nippy as she is insensitive, and is already barging people aside as she burrows to the front of the plane. I can no longer see her diminutive figure, but I can follow her progress by watching other passengers suddenly lurching out of her way, hand luggage suspended precariously above their heads, or crashing down on to those of their neighbours.

As soon as the plane comes to a standstill, the exit door opens at the back of the plane, right next to where she had been sitting. Ha!

———

Bhuj is only an hour from Mumbai by plane, but there is only one daily flight and that leaves in the morning. It's now late afternoon, so we are due to spend the night in India's largest city. We step out of the terminal into the warm but not unpleasant air and are met by a couple of drivers with a rough approximation of our names written on a piece of cardboard. After a brief discussion, for Ben's benefit, about which is the first-class seat in the car, we set off.

My first impressions of India flash by outside the car windows on the hair-raising drive to the hotel. Hundreds of people are on the streets, and many of them are holding their hands out to beg from the traffic as it whizzes by. I wonder whether this means that all the really good begging spots are taken, places where you could beg from pedestrians, for example, because I'm sure if you hurl a coin from the window of a car at the lick we're going you could easily brain somebody.

All around us, flicking from side to side across the windscreen, is a buzzing cloud of little black-and-yellow round-nosed auto-rickshaws. They make a noise like a moped trapped inside a Reliant Robin, and they weave around at incredible perilous speed, and yet never seem to hit one another. Perhaps they hit each other all the time, and I just didn't see it happen. Perhaps they all started out life as brand-new square-fronted auto-rickshaws, and have all become rounded off by repeated impact with one another.

I catch little glimpses here and there of the life of the place, where many of the signs and shop names are written in English. A bar called the Fancy Saloon, a shop with hundreds of large glass jars arranged on shelves from floor to ceiling called World of Dried Fruit, a huge billboard advertisement offering a night out with a smiling Aamir Khan as a Valentine's Day competition prize.

The hotel we're taken to is one of a chain, and is very Western and familiar. I notice that they offer a continental breakfast, and ask the receptionist:

'Excuse me? I see you do a continental breakfast.'

'Yes, sir.'

'I was wondering . . . is that a breakfast like you would

expect to have in this continent, i.e. the continent we are stand-ing in, or the continent that I have just come here from?'

'It is a continental breakfast.'

It is a phrase that completely lost its meaning when it was absorbed into chain-hotel-speak, that's what it is. I wonder whether, if they lined up a proper Indian breakfast which gave the unsuspecting European traveller the shits like you wouldn't believe, they might call that an incontinental breakfast. Just a thought . . .

Once in my room – which is just like any other chain hotel room anywhere in the world, really – I do all the things you do to mark out your territory. I have a shower, put on clean clothes, strew other clothes all over the place, nick the little bottles of shampoo, eat the complimentary biscuits, look at all the television channels, and flick through the hotel brochure.

After a while, bored, I hear a familiar voice in the corridor and go to the door. Howard, tired and plane-sticky, and his plane-sticker-sticky luggage are still outside the room opposite, and the hotel manager is trying every key on a huge ring, waggling his head from side to side in an eloquent gesture of apology and disappointment as each successive key fails to open the door.

Later I went for a meal in the alfresco restaurant on the hotel roof, and found that Ben was there already. A veteran of many a film shoot, he was trusting in the beneficence of the film company's per diems – the daily allowance actors are tra-ditionally given for living expenses while away from home – to such an extent that he had only brought fifteen quid with him for the entire trip. Of course, as we were staying in a dry state, it's not as if he'd be buying rounds of beers every night.

A notice proudly advertised live music from a jazz trio. As it turned out this was disappointing on almost every front. The trio only had two people in it, and they played neither jazz nor strictly speaking live. Whether you could call it music was a matter of opinion.

The combo consisted of a big busty girl in a tight zebra-print top and jeans, and a fat, miserable-looking male accompanist. While she massacred 'Woman In Love', he nonchalantly plonked away on a keyboard, gazing around the rooftop as though providing a suspiciously full orchestral backing was a piece of cake for someone of his great musical ability. Every melancholy twitch of his sad moustache managed to convey the definite impression that he thought he was way too good for this place, for this singer, as his fingers glided expertly over the ivories. Literally, as it turned out. Midway through the sad demise of 'Eternal Flame' we noticed that the lugubrious one's keyboard wasn't actually plugged into anything, and that his job principally consisted of switching a karaoke machine on and off.

Effortlessly assimilating myself into the local culture with vim and enthusiasm, I ordered *spaghetti carbonara* and garlic bread.

30 JANUARY

In the morning we are taken from the hotel to Mumbai airport to get the flight to Bhuj. Jamie keeps us all waiting, as he has set his watch to Dubai time and thinks he has another hour and a half in bed.

On the harum-scarum return drive to the airport the thing that really catches my eye is that on every bit of open ground, every side street, every space between two houses, there seems to be a group of kids playing a scratch game of cricket. And this is before nine o'clock in the morning.

It reminds me of the summer holidays when I was a boy – skip to the end of this bit if I start sounding like Michael Parkinson. I used to play cricket with my mate Steve all day all summer long. Hour after hour we'd bash a tennis ball about, down the narrow alley alongside his house, or in my dad's driveway, perhaps sneaking into the school playground through a hole in the fence, or using the one dilapidated net down by the tennis courts where we could use a proper corky ball.

We never had cricket lessons at our school, even though Yorkshire was only a couple of miles away, and so all our shots and our wonky bowling actions were telly taught, copied from the likes of Frank Hayes and Derek Underwood.

Despite the school's shortcomings, one local lad and neighbour of mine, known as Johnny Ack-Ack, did make it into Nottinghamshire seconds. This was nothing to do with the school, though, it was entirely down to the drive and competitive spirit of his cricket-mad dad.

'Hey!' he'd shout to us. 'Do you want to come and play cricket with me and John in the park?'

We'd pile into his car and go out into Clumber Park, outside town, where we'd find that the three key elements of the game had been equally and fairly divided between the participants. Johnny Ack-Ack would bat, Mr Ack-Ack would bowl, and we poor saps would be fielding. On and on Johnny would bat, and on and on his dad would bowl. And then it was time to go home. Not too many made that mistake more than once.

You don't see kids just playing knockabout cricket in the street any more, except in the title sequence to *Neighbours*. All the side streets round where I live now are death-traps patrolled by maniac minicab drivers and commuters looking for short cuts, and on what playing fields are left unbulldozed and undeveloped football is king. It's as if the very base level of participation in the game of cricket for kids now involves the whole daunting business of joining proper clubs and getting all the expensive paraphernalia, and how are they going to find out they like the sport in the first place?

Here in Bombay I must have seen a hundred kids of all sizes just bashing a ball about first thing in the morning for the sheer happy fun of it. No wonder everyone's better at the damn game than we are . . .

At the airport we find that the one-hour flight to Bhuj

is delayed, but fortunately Ben, to his surprise and embarrassment, discovers that he has once again been elevated to super-business-luxury class, and he is able to smuggle us all into a fiercely air-conditioned special executive lounge where there is free coffee and cake. We lower the tone considerably.

5
Bhuj

Bhuj airport, when we arrive, turns out to be a military airbase. As soon as we step from the plane we are hustled urgently over to a waiting bus in case we see something militarily sensitive.

Actually there isn't much to see. A couple of low buildings that have been camouflage painted, and that is about it. The camouflage itself is interesting, as it isn't done in the traditional irregular and random lines intended to break up the form of the buildings so much as in the shapes of giant puzzle pieces in beige, pale green and dark green. It's as if they hope that a Pakistani bomber pilot, if he notices it at all, might think:

'No, I won't drop a bomb on that, it's just a jigsaw factory.'

As the bus pulls up at the airport terminal – a small building with a small tin shack alongside it – it is surrounded by an energetic crowd of people selling at the top of their voices. Mostly they are taxi-drivers, I think, but as we push our way through them Jamie remarks out of the side of his mouth that he's just been offered some dope. I am just wondering what the legal position on this is – is selling dope allowed here where selling alcohol is not? Can you just stand among a load of taxi-drivers and shout 'Dope?!' at the top of your voice? Or is somebody making a snap character judgment about Jamie himself, perhaps? – when a charming and unruffled chap from the *Lagaan* film unit introduces himself.

'Welcome to Bhuj,' he says. 'I am Ashish.'

I see.

The tin shack alongside the terminal is the luggage carousel. A bloke drives up with a load of bags on the back of a truck, and he puts them all on the floor. You go and get yours. It works fine.

Some of the Indian actors have flown in from Mumbai on the same flight, and we meet Suhasini, the actress playing Yashodamai, mother of Bhuvan (Aamir) in the film. She is particularly pleased to meet Howard for some reason. Maybe she has a thing for the older gentleman . . . ?

We are all driven to the town, which is about ten miles from the airbase. As you approach Bhuj the main road is lined with shacks that look as though they have just been put up today and might very well fall down tomorrow. Some of them have no fronts, and are little more than bus shelters, but they clearly have whole families living in them.

Then you are suddenly confronted by the dark walls of the old city. We skirt round this through slightly more up-market residential areas – ones that actually have whole houses in. As in Mumbai, kids are playing cricket on any available space. Here as well there are big black hairy bald-bellied pigs snuffling around, and donkeys, and great big-horned cows strolling around as though they own the place. Perhaps they do.

Our big film unit cars, with white faces pressed to the windows, excite quite a bit of attention, and there is plenty of good-natured gawping, pointing, grinning and waving going on out there.

We arrive at the place which will be home for the next ten weeks – Sahajanand Tower. It is a brand-new apartment building, seven storeys high, that dwarfs all the buildings around it. Bhuj is a small town, off the tourist routes, and there isn't a hotel capable of dealing with a film unit of the size of the *Lagaan* operation, so the production has taken the

top three floors of Sahajanand Tower and made it into a kind
of hotel, importing cleaners and waiters both locally and from
Mumbai to run a sort of rudimentary room service.

The building is like a seven-story doughnut, with eight
apartments on each floor set around an open centre which
has the staircases and lifts in it. Each apartment has three
bedrooms, a living room, a hallway and a kitchen, with
bathrooms off some of the bedrooms.

At the production office Howard and I are put in the same
apartment, number 503. We lug our bags in, and endure a
forty-minute-long reprise of the rigmarole at the hotel yesterday as they cannot find the key that opens the bedroom
door. Still, there's a living room with a telly in it, and a
kitchen which doesn't seem to be finished yet. Two other
bedrooms in the apartment are padlocked, evidently waiting
for occupants who haven't arrived yet, and there are a couple
of toilets – one an unappealing hole in the floor with two
helpful porcelain footprints to show where you should squat,
the other the sort we are used to, so there's one unspoken fear
banished.

Finally they manage to get the door open, and an awful truth
dawns on Howard and me. The bedroom is tiny, and has two
single beds pushed together. We are supposed to share this
little space. For ten weeks.

'Well,' I say after an awkward pause, 'this is going to be
cosy . . .'

Howard and I have been partners for a number of years, it's
true, but in the opening-the-batting sense, not in the sharing-
a-double-bed sense. And while it's also true that Howard bats
for the other side, that is on the one summer afternoon each
year when An England XI takes on the Howard Lee Yorkshire
XI at cricket. And neither of us is good enough at bowling to
legitimately claim to swing both ways.

Mind you, if we had genuinely come to India to represent our country at cricket, then the chances are we would

be sharing hotel rooms across the subcontinent, gradually becoming immune to each other's irritating little ways and the rank stink of used sporting equipment. I've never quite understood why grown-up international sportsmen put up with the room-sharing thing. I mean, if the team hotel really can't cope with the numbers, find another hotel.

There's no time to worry about this now, however, as we are to be taken straight to the film location, so we shrug off our bags and go back to the ground floor.

———

It is a Sunday and a day off for the cast and crew. They have decided to spend this day off, from working on a film about cricket, playing cricket. That's how much they all love cricket. Apparently a full-scale tournament is in progress, and if we're lucky we might even be in time to join in.

The film began shooting three weeks ago, and a couple of Brits are already out here. One of them, Rachel, is playing Elizabeth, the young English girl who helps the Indian villagers to learn to play the game. She has refused to spend an entire day off watching everyone else playing cricket, but decides to join us out at the location for the afternoon.

A production Jeep takes us out of Bhuj again, and once clear of the town, the potholes, the cows and pigs, and the little yellow-and-black auto-rickshaws darting in front of him, the driver revels in the freedom of the open road and ventures up into third gear for a heady minute or two. The main road north past the airbase is reasonably well surfaced, like a poor-standard British country lane. After about half an hour, though, we turn off this and on to a dirt track into the desert. Some of the lurches and bumps on this are enough to send your spine through your hat, even in a reasonably well-suspensioned vehicle. Later, coming back in the big team bus, this road really loosens our fillings.

We bump and bounce out into the rocky brown desert,

through scrubby-looking trees and cacti that grow to no more than about shoulder high, and suddenly happen upon a bloke in the middle of nowhere dressed as a security guard with a walkie-talkie in his fist. He flags us down and gives us the once-over, although it must have been pretty obvious that we belong to the film unit. We haven't seen any other traffic for at least twenty-five minutes, and I'm sure there wasn't even this dirt track to drive down until the production came location hunting. I shouldn't think he has a lot of troublesome passing sightseers to keep at bay out here – nonetheless, more than his job's worth not to check.

He waves us through. The road, such as it is, sweeps down past a flat dusty area which has been cleared of vegetation. As we pass, we can make out a pale brown cricket strip with stumps in, and a little boundary fence. Beyond this basic arena are some concrete outbuildings, which form the location base, and we are dropped off here.

Ashutosh and Aamir are there when we arrive, and we are also introduced to Apoorva – 'Apu' – the first assistant director. The first AD's job on any film shoot is to bully, chivvy and generally order people around, and Apu seems ideally suited to the role. He is a powerfully built chap with a loud voice and a bit of a swagger to him, and even though this is technically his day off, he is spending it telling everyone what to do and where to go, organising the cricket tournament.

Another Brit, Paul, is playing Captain Russell, the swinish English officer who is Elizabeth's brother. We meet him out at the set, and he clearly hasn't done any shooting yet as the hair department haven't been let loose on the incredible mane and beardage he has produced for them. He looks like Robinson Crusoe.

A large canvas canopy has been erected on the boundary for a bit of shade, and in front of it is a small table positively heaving with shiny metal trophies.

We have arrived in the middle of the competition, and so

it looks as though we won't get to play ourselves today. Part of me is disappointed – any opportunity for a game gratefully accepted – but part of me is quite content to keep my powder dry for the time being. I haven't forgotten the gauntlet Aamir threw down when we met in London, and I sit under the canopy, taking the opportunity to weigh up the strength of what will be our opposition.

The next match is between a cast team, led by Aamir, naturally, and a team from the crew. In their ten overs the cast make seventy-four, and Apu, who is skippering the crew, makes it clear that he believes this is not nearly enough. His cohorts punch the air and cheer him as he swaggers cockily out to the middle to open the reply.

One thing I notice straight away is that everywhere I look on the field there seems to be an incredibly agile fielder with a great throw. Apu can clearly bat a bit, slogging the bowling to all parts. As often happens when one player is much better than his team-mates, however, he finds himself expecting them to live up to his own high standards, and, at least when it comes to running between the wickets, they aren't able to do this. Apu's crew team reach the last over with their captain on fifty-odd and seven wickets down. Every single one of them has been run out – a performance that Sir Geoffrey himself would be proud of.

It seems as though the crew team must win from here – they only need a couple of runs – but Aamir himself is bowling the last over. His gentle spin looks friendly enough, but he is the boss – not only the star of the film but also its producer and consequently the employer of everyone present – and three of the crew surrender their wickets to him in successive balls to give him a hat-trick. The cast team have won.

Now then. Is Aamir really a demon match-winning tweaker, or has the crew tanked the match like Terry Scott would tank a golf match with 'Sir' in *Terry and June*? Certainly there is a deference in the way everyone deals with Aamir, and while he himself is charming and joking around with everyone it is a little bit like having a laugh with a member of the Royal Family.

As if to reinforce the princely impression, Aamir rides majestically around the cricket pitch on a huge black horse while everything is packed away at the end of the day.

We drive back to Bhuj in a big coach, and the Indians chatter excitedly about the cricket all the way back. Who should have bowled instead of who did bowl, who dropped a simple catch, who was in good nick – the atmosphere is extremely competitive, which is great. Apu stands in the central aisle holding court. He cannot believe he is on the losing side, having whacked fifty-seven out of his side's seventy-two – he is clearly going to be one to watch out for when the time comes.

As we skirt the town, the bus attracts a little following of locals on scooters, who buzz alongside trying to spot Aamir through the windows. Each little scooter has at least two people on it, and there is not a crash helmet in sight. They take their lives in their hands trying to catch a glimpse of the star, and the fact that he is in town is plainly a very poorly kept secret indeed.

Another little crowd is waiting at Sahajanand Tower, kept back by some massive security men, hoping for a sight of Aamir stepping from the coach. He waves genially at them all, and takes the time to shake a few by the hand, before disappearing inside.

Upstairs, Howard and I contemplate our little room. H is very unhappy with the arrangement, muttering that he is a creature of habits and none of them involves me sleeping a foot away from him.

After consideration, we move one of the single beds into the defunct kitchen and he sets up camp in there. He pesters the production to put a mosquito screen up for him, and rigs a curtain using a blanket and some clothes-pegs he has brought along himself.

Then we go down for dinner. Sahajanand Tower is built on a number of great concrete piles, so that the ground floor is effectively an open-air carpark. The production have partitioned some of this off to make a communal canteen dining room, and the catering there is done by the same unit caterers who do food at the location. The evening meal is not especially appetising, but I am very hungry by this time and don't care.

A table tennis table is set up around the corner, so some of us have a game or two, and meet some of the Indian actors for the first time. Rachel has brought a Scrabble set along and starts a game up after dinner. I don't join in, but watch as Paul, scratching his big leonine head like the Wild Man of Borneo with nits, tries to clear his mind of the reams of Hindi dialogue he has been learning phonetically so he can think of some English words.

Apparently, when he arrived at Mumbai airport a couple of days ago, Paul had the bright idea of trying out some of his Hindi on his taxi-driver.

'*Tum gulam log hamesha joota ke neeche rahogey!*' he bellowed, grinning at the poor chap in his rear-view mirror from behind an amount of facial hair that Brian Blessed would consider excessive, and expecting a cheery nod of approval. The driver stared straight ahead and put his foot down, clearly wanting this crazy fellow out of his cab as soon as possible. Perhaps the fact that the Hindi line translates as: 'You slaves will always have to live beneath our boots!' had something to do with it. Still, just wait till *Lagaan* comes out – he'll be going around saying: 'You'll never guess who I had in the back of my cab . . .'

The end of the first day – I feel like I've been here for a week.

31 JANUARY
The first pleasant surprise of the morning is that the English-language *Times of India* has been delivered to the apartment.

I find a short summarising paragraph at the back about European football, which – surprise, surprise – doesn't include any mention of my team, Oldham Athletic, or their result on Saturday.

After breakfast we spend the morning mired in Indian bureaucracy at first the police station, then a local government administration office, and then the police station again, getting permits to visit the villages of Mandvi and Kunariya. While we wait for forms to be filled in by hand in triplicate, I check out a large map of Kutch on the wall, and as far as I can make out we are applying for permits to visit the place we visited yesterday.

The official doing my form runs into the usual fun and games I always have with my surname overseas. When he hands the form to me I see that he has read 'England' in my passport and assumed that was my country rather than my name, and so the permit is made out for a Mr Christopher William. I manage to explain, eventually, and he slowly screws up the permit and begins the whole painstaking process again from the beginning, fixing me with a glare that lets me know it is all my fault.

At least he didn't laugh his head off – that's what I usually get. The lads in my local Chinese takeaway never fail to get a kick out of my name, and once, in my InterRail backpacking youth, I thought one German youth hostel manager was going to have a mirth-induced seizure. What a heartbreaker that would have been.

And I have quite enough trouble with my name in my own country, thank you very much. One lad at my school used to enjoy taunting me by singing 'There'll always be an England' whenever he caught sight of me, seemingly unaware of the affirmatory nature of the lyric. And his name was A. Burke.

A pair of enormous ginger sisters used to follow me around, sneering 'England versus Wales!' over and over again, which never made a great deal of sense to me, until, years later, it occurred to me that they might have actually been sneering 'whales', and that their little slogan might thus have been referring to the enormous ginger sisters themselves.

Once, to amuse myself, I went into one of those fancy kilt shops in Edinburgh where they claim to be able to connect any surname to its proper clan, in order to be able to flog you the appropriate tartan. The man behind the counter asked me my surname, and I told him. He tilted his head to one side and fixed me with a malevolent glare, much in the manner of Mr Mackay out of *Porridge*.

'Well?' I said. 'Is there a tartan for me?'

'Aye,' the man hissed. 'Plain blood red for the dead at Culloden.'

The local government administration office, where we have to get our permits stamped, is a dark, dusty room that has never been penetrated by sunlight or computer science. Shelves and pigeonholes cover the walls from floor to ceiling, haphazardly stacked with fading ledgers and bulging files tied together with string. Desks are covered with still more two or three-foot-high piles of paperwork, arranged around the edges like sandbags in a gun emplacement, and more piles have begun to build up on the remaining floor space. It is like something out of *Gormenghast*.

It takes a moment or two for my eyes to adjust to the murk, and I make my way through the maze of accumulated bureaucracy to where an old man is sitting in a kind of paperwork nest. He takes my permit, ever so carefully rubber-stamps it with a little green stamp, and hands it back. As I make my way out again, I realise that our little bit of business has left no new paper for him to file, stack or otherwise accommodate. So where has it all come from?

In the afternoon Howard, Ben, Jamie and I go for a walk into Bhuj. That was the plan, at any rate. Yesterday, coming back from the cricket tournament, Ben and Jamie had got off the coach in the town with Rachel, who knew her way back to Sahajanand Tower on foot. They were confident they could retrace their steps, and Howard and I, fools that we are, believed them.

At the end of the little road that leads up to Sahajanand they lead us left and we start to walk. The road is a main road, with plenty of traffic, and four white lads walking along in the dust alongside it attract quite a bit of attention. Every few seconds a lorry growls past, and the driver parps his horn or shouts something cheerily at us, and we wave back. All very friendly and good natured.

On and on we walk, on and on, dust in our throats and the sun in our eyes, and every few seconds another parp or another cheery shout and a wave. The residential area we are in starts to look less and less residential, with more and more wasteland on either side of the road.

I stop.

'Are you absolutely sure we're going the right way?' I say, wearily.

'Oh yes. There's a turning somewhere here,' Ben says. 'There's a sign just up ahead, maybe that will help.'

We carry on until we reach the sign, which has nothing written on it. On the back, however, is the legend 'WELCOME TO BHUJ'. We have walked straight out of town. Presumably cheery lorry-driver after cheery lorry-driver has been yelling: 'Where the hell do you think you're going?'.

We traipse all the way back, and find, of course, that if we'd turned right instead of left about an hour earlier we'd have found the town centre in about fifteen minutes. By the time we do find it we haven't the energy to look around much, and finally settle in a small café for a drink. Soft drinks only, of course, in dry old Bhuj, so we order four bottles of Thums Up (sic) cola.

I'd heard of this cola-flavoured beverage via a story on a Bollywood internet site, about the cola promotion wars currently raging in India. The three hottest film stars in India are all advertising rival brands. Aamir Khan is the face of Coca-Cola, Shah Rukh Khan (no relation) is fronting the Pepsi campaign, while Salman Khan (no relation either) is pulling out all the stops for Thums Up, a local concoction that is a distant relative of Tesco's own-brand cola-coloured carbonated pop-style drink. There is no doubt in my mind, having now tried it, that Salman got the bum job of the three of them. In fact, if there'd been anything else at all on sale it would have been Thums Down for Thums Up, but we are thirsty and have walked a sod of a long way, so we order four more.

The old bloke takes away our empties, cracks open four more, and then cleans out our straws by spitting through them before popping them into our new bottles. Dysentery here we come. Thums Up (sic).

We are back at Sahajanand in time to see the coach return from the day's filming. The crowd waiting for Aamir is even larger – there are about sixty people and two bored-looking cows nonchalantly munching litter. Many of the fans are young girls, who have put on their fanciest frocks and make-up to catch Aamir's eye.

Howard doesn't see a crowd of Bollywood movie fans, however. He sees a captive audience for some good old-fashioned street entertainment. I've known Howard a long time, and last year hired his one-man 'Mister Spill-it' show ('spill it, he mustn't spill it . . .') for Peter's fourth birthday party. His fingers start to twitch, and I strongly suspect some juggling is in the offing . . .

I don't have long to wait. We venture out in the evening, and are quickly surrounded by a group of local children, who want to shake our hands and then follow us wherever we go. One of the kids is riding a chopper bike – it is a bit bashed about but we are definitely looking at the bike that defined the seventies (along with slinkies, Kevin Keegan, and the curly-wurly).

Using the international language of mime, Howard arranges the children into an audience, persuades the kid to let him borrow his precious bike, and then with a flourish hoists it up in the air. For a glorious moment or two he holds their rapt attention as he balances the chopper on his chin – now there's something I never thought I'd catch myself writing – before catching it neatly and bringing it safely to earth. Da daah!

Except the seat comes off in his hands, the bike crashes to the floor, and when the kid picks it up the front wheel is 'L'-shaped. Poor little chap. His little face falls, and you can see he's upset, but he's also desperately trying not to blame the funny white man. Howard sheepishly takes the kid by the hand and goes to find a twenty-four-hour cycle repair shop.

At dinner I learn why Suhasini had been so pleased to meet Howard. Gujarat is a dry state, but the rumour is it is possible to get a permit to buy alcohol if you are over forty. Howard thus has the opportunity to become a sort of beer baron, while I, at thirty-nine, am the oldest under-age drinker in town.

1 FEBRUARY

No work to do today, although I've been threatened with a haircut tomorrow.

Bhuj is a vibrant and vital little town. Everyone has somewhere to go in a hurry, and there's none of the sense of 'mañana' that you often get in hot countries – everyone seems very busy. Sometimes what they are busy at is a little odd. Just along the track from Sahajanand Tower we pass a mechanic at work in front of a motorcycle repair shop. He is up to his elbows in oil and grease and has clearly been working on a faulty bike for some time. He tries the engine again – no joy. He steps back, looks at it thoughtfully, scratches his chin, then suddenly lunges forward and begins bashing the machine violently with a big hammer. Pretty much the same approach as I have to anything going wrong with my computer at home.

By the roadside, as we stroll into town, there are various people trying to sell their wares. One chap has set up a little display of loads of home-made cricket bats, all sizes from full to tiny. On closer inspection we can see that they are hewn, blade and handle, from a single piece of wood, and the rubber grip is a cycle tyre inner tube. Indeed, we can see the fellow energetically hewing away at a fantastic rate, and it seems possible that the dozens of bats on offer represent a mere morning's work for him. You wouldn't want to face a proper cricket ball with one of these in your hands, but they'd be all right for bashing a tennis ball around, and they cost less than a quid, so we'll be back later.

Next to him an old woman has spread out some carved wooden elephants that seem to have taken rather longer to make, and farther along another enterprising fellow is selling toilets. Toilets, by the side of the road. He sees us coming, and becomes very animated, beckoning us over to look at his toilets. He has toilets in many colours, whatever you want. And bidets.

Now it seems to me that a toilet is pretty much not an impulse buy. Perhaps after a few more days of Indian food I'll come to see things differently, but realistically I'm not going to see a toilet, however splendid, decide I simply must have it, and snap it up at once while I'm walking along the side of the road. This doesn't deter the toilet-seller, a thoroughly game individual, from giving me his hardest hard sell and beginning the full-on haggling process as though I was actually joining in.

I wonder how this chap manages to keep body and soul together. Every sale he makes must be the most fantastic fluke. Imagine his business plan:

TOILET CHAP:
I'm looking to start up a business selling toilets by the
side of the road.

FRIENDLY BANK MANAGER:
Really, and what sort of sales figures are you
projecting?

TOILET CHAP:
I'm thinking if I can shift one every five years or so to
random nutters I'll be doing well . . .

Is this more or less bonkers than selling luggage at the airport?
A toss-up, I reckon.

The road itself is tarmac, but by the side where we are
walking the desert sand and dust have taken over. This pale
brown dust is everywhere, and seems to have permeated
everything, giving the whole place a sort of beige tint. The
effect is as though everything – the buildings, the vehicles, the
cows that wander everywhere, the people's skin and clothes
– is the same colour it started out, only with the word 'off'
stuck in front of it. An off-green truck hurtles past off-white
buildings, while even a cow chewing lazily on a plastic bottle,
which probably started out as a beige cow, you would have to
say was off-beige.

Howard and I have only been in town a couple of days, but
already we're looking tanned. The sun isn't that hot or fierce,
in fact; we are simply acquiring the tones of the place as the
beige desert dust works its way into our pores.

The exception to this rule is the clothes worn by the local
women, some of which are dazzling. Bright reds, greens and
yellows, in beautiful floaty-patterned garments, that really
stand out startlingly from all the beige and worn-down
dust-engrained off-colours everywhere else, like super-colours.
Some of them must change their clothes several times a day to
stay looking so bright.

The Lonely Planet guide led me to believe that there would be internet cafés in Bhuj. I had taken this with a pinch of salt, but had got myself a Hotmail address just in case, and Susan was sending daily bulletins from home if I could only find a way of reading them out here.

Our wanderings lead us under a squat old archway, a remnant of the old town wall, along to the reservoir, the Hamirsar tank. Pictures suggest that this is usually full of water, but the levels are clearly right down, and there are large flat stretches of dried beige mud between the reservoir walls and the water's edge. A little way off some women, in bright blood-red saris, are washing some clothes by bashing them against a rock. As we watch it feels faintly ridiculous to be looking for an internet café in this place. We give up and go back to Sahajanand for lunch.

We are causing quite a stir here in Bhuj. As we walk whitely around the place, the dazzling bright sun flashing off our pale flesh makes us into beacons of interest for the local population. Every few yards somebody hails us or parps the horn of their car or truck or moped, and the atmosphere is so cheery and so jolly that it's hard to be bothered by it – in fact we become super cheery and super jolly ourselves, waving, nodding, and shaking hands like some demented royal.

Bhuj is a destination for only the most determined of tourists, or the most lost, and as we explore we don't see any other Europeans at all, unless we bump into someone else from *Lagaan*. Everyone here knows about the film, of course, and the news that Aamir Khan is in town has spread like wildfire. This only adds to people's interest in us, as we are not only foreign but boasting an extra Bollywood sheen.

Suhasini, with her Mumbai big-city cynicism, reckons that Bhuj is looking at us as 'fat ducks waiting to be plucked', but that doesn't seem quite fair. No one seems to be trying to rip us off, there is none of the aggressive hard selling of useless trinkets and souvenirs that you find on the better-trodden tourist routes, and hardly any begging. They are just really friendly, and want to watch us as we walk about their home-town, trying to commit our faces to memory for when the film comes out.

The children that flock around us, galloping from their yards and alleys as we approach, interrupting their dawn-to-dusk scratch cricket games to gawp at us, all have a little routine which becomes very familiar very quickly.

They will gather in our path, smiling, and the boldest of them will be shoved forward with his or her grubby mitt outstretched. Then they will quickly rap out their little questionnaire, in a blur, always the same three things:

'What-is-your-name?' (we reply)

'What-is-your-country?' (we reply)

and then, immediately:

'OK-bye!'

Once, only once, has a small child departed from this routine so far. I was striding along by myself when a little cloud of smiling teenagers gathered in the dust alongside me. A hand was proffered – I shook it – and its owner began the usual interrogation.

'What-is-your-name?' he rapped out.

I told him.

'What-is-your-country?'

I told him that too. There was a beat, and the 'OK-bye!' which I knew was coming and which would end the conversation was right on the tip of his tongue, but then, with a huge effort, the lad summoned up another question, and suddenly blurted out:

'What-is-your . . . *purpose*?!'

I was rather thrown by the philosophical nature of the enquiry, but the lad was so pleased with himself for coming up with it that I tried to answer as best I could.

'Ah, well, now you're asking. I mean, what *is* my purpose? What is *your* purpose? What are *any* of us doing here? I suppose one way of looking at it is if you think of life as a journey, in which . . .'

'OK-bye!'

For someone with my particular name, of course, the brief rallies of the 'What-is-your-name-what-is-your-country-OK-bye' game offered a particular opportunity to tease, which after a day or two I became bored enough to try.

'What-is-your-name?'

'England.'

'What-is-your-country?'

'England.'

Naturally this should have been followed by gales of unrestrained laughter and the universal acknowledgment of me as their new king of comedy, but in fact it brought merely a puzzled frown and reset the process to the beginning.

'What-is-your-*name*?'

'England.'

Another frown. 'What-is-your-*country*?'

'England.'

A small discussion now, with some shrugging and waving of hands, and the spokesman was urged to try one more time.

'*What-is-your-name*?' (unspoken: *you-utter-simpleton*!)

'England.'

Turns to his friends, and mutters something which clearly means 'See? It's nothing I'm doing wrong – this chap is an idiot! Watch, I'll ask him one more time, but I know *exactly* what he's going to say. Ready?': '*What-is-your-country*?'

'England.'

Looks skywards, tuts: 'Coh!' Then: 'OK-bye!'

Served me right.

I was reminded of the conspicuously unsuccessful hit rate of my grandfather's favourite joke, which I continue to use in his memory whenever possible. It was a quickfire response to the question:

'Are you hungry?'

'No, I'm England, how do you do,' he would flash back, holding out his hand, waiting for the other person to catch up. Hungary, you see . . . ? It works with 'Are you chilly (Chile)?' too, but people don't tend to ask that quite so often. Once (and once only) I managed to pull off another variation on the theme, when answering the telephone of a friend whose surname is Jordan.

———————

According to the guidebook, there are only a couple of places to change money and traveller's cheques, and both are on Station Road. In the afternoon, Howard and I walk the entire length of Station Road without spotting either of these places – the Hotel Prince or Globex. On the way back we check out a murky little alcove, and almost accidentally find Globex, a tiny little office, tucked away in the gloom.

There is a certain amount of form-filling-in to do, involving my passport, and I spot that Mr Globex has agreed a money-changing transaction with a Mr Christopher William from England. I decide to say nothing. Mr Globex has a little pile of business-card-sized photocopied slips from an operation called PeeGee Enterprises, advertising itself as an Internet facility, so I pick up a couple.

Minutes later Howard and I stand on Station Road looking at PeeGee Enterprises' address on one of these slips. It is on Station Road, as we are, but we have just walked the entire length of that without finding the town's premier hotel, let alone a small business premises. The address has a number, which should have been helpful, but none of the buildings we could see have numbers.

As we stand there without a clue how to proceed, a small child approaches us. We brace ourselves for another quick bout of 'What is your name? What is your country?', but instead the child sticks out his hand and says:

'You are looking for me.'

His certainty is disarming. If I had trekked overland across Afghanistan and Pakistan on a quest for spiritual enlightenment and then met a mystical child who was so clearly expecting me I might have followed him anywhere. As it is I am a cynical old hack who's flown in from London, so I say:

'Oh, really?'

'Yes,' the child replies. 'I am Purvesh Ganatra, PeeGee Enterprises. Follow.'

We follow him round a corner, down an alleyway, up some stairs, along a walkway, and down to the end of a corridor. He stops at an unremarkable doorway to remove his shoes, and, as our sun-dazzled eyes adjust to the gloom, we can just make out 'PeeGee Enterprises' painted in tiny letters above the door frame. If the lad hadn't spotted us squinting at his card in the street, we'd never have found him in a month of Sundays. Make that a year of Sundays.

Purvesh Ganatra's office is tiny, like Purvesh himself. He quietly and courteously invites us in and offers us the only two seats in the place. As he cranks his computer into action, I see the wispy beginnings of a very fine moustache just starting to shade his top lip, so maybe he isn't quite as young as he appears to be (i.e.: twelve).

I had great plans to check out English football results on the Internet, and generally muck about like I would do at home. First of all, though, Howard and I thought we'd look at our e-mail, so we get Purvesh to dial up Hotmail for us.

Purvesh explains that the nearest server is in Ahmadabad, which is a good few hours away towards the east. Sometimes it takes a little while to get connected, he says calmly, and that turns out to be the understatement of the week. Time and time again the connection crashes, and after an hour and ten minutes we finally get through to my inbox, and I learn that Oldham had beaten Oxford at the weekend, and that Peter had had a nosebleed. Then the thing breaks down again, and we decide that life is too short for any further adventures in cutting-edge technology today.

––––––––––

In the evening we get some impressions from the location, from those who have been out there today. Ben has had his beard removed, leaving only a neat little moustache which makes him look like Terry-Thomas. I remember Arthur once presenting some holiday programme showing viewers around a villa that had once belonged to the great posh comic actor, leading the camera into the bathroom and saying:

'And this . . . is the absolute shower.'

I can't quite manage to find a way to pass this joke off as my own, but it still gets a laugh.

Rachel has been a little unsettled by having had a 'moment' on set, where she has let some little prop or costume mishap get on top of her, through being nervous, I think, and has spoken too sharply to someone. Aamir has taken her to one side and given her a little ticking off, apparently.

We spend some time chatting to three of the Indian cricketers from the film, Raj, Adi and Amin. They are great anglophiles and speak very good English.

Amin is very jolly, ever so slightly camp, and could talk for India. I'm not sure exactly where he lives, but there won't be too many donkeys with their hind legs still attached round his neck of the woods, I'll tell you that for nothing. He has known Aamir for some time, has worked with him before, and clearly worships him. He gives us our first real inklings of how the filming is going.

'Aamir is doing really well. He's hardly moving at all.'

He tells us that this is the first Bollywood film to be shot using synchronised sound, which is what we are used to in

Western film and television work. The norm out here is to post-synch all the dialogue four or five months after the filming, which explains the spaghetti western look of so much of Bollywood's output. The Indian actors are finding that using synchronised sound enables them to give slightly more subtle performances than they are usually asked for, and they are relishing the opportunity to try doing very little in front of the camera.

Raj and Adi exchange a glance when Amin says this, and it is difficult to imagine Amin, who is very flamboyant and speaks with his whole body, 'doing very little'.

Amin is very excited about *Lagaan*, saying that it is huge, and 'Bollywood's *Titanic*', to boot. I hope this is true, and that it is not going to turn out to be Bollywood's *Raising the Titanic*, starring Michael Caine . . .

2 FEBRUARY

We were supposed to go to the location today for hair and make-up things but it didn't happen. This meant we were hanging around Sahajanand Tower most of the day on stand-by, reading, playing table tennis.

Mid-morning I am half watching a Test match on the television between Australia and Pakistan. There seems to be live or recorded cricket on the box every single day, by the way. Suddenly an air-raid siren goes off – a pretty alarming occurrence considering we are only about thirty miles from the Pakistan border and so close to an airbase that the whole town might as well have a big target painted on it, and doubly so when it happens just as a disembodied voice on the television in the living room is saying that 'Waugh's declared'.

I run out to the little balcony outside my room and scour the horizon for incoming. Down below, Bhuj is calmly going about its business, remarkably unconcerned, so I quickly gather that this is a regular thing. Apparently it happens at ten thirty most mornings, so that would seem to be a good time for Pakistan to strike if they wanted to catch the Kutchis out.

Because of having to hang around, Howard and I are in the apartment when the cleaning men whisk through. We have a chat with one of them – Zakir – who says:

'Shah Rukh Khan is India's number-one actor. Aamir Khan is number two.'

'Don't let the boss hear you say that,' we say. I ask him about Thums Up cola man, but he is nowhere, apparently.

Aamir's Coca-Cola connection means that there is free Coca-Cola available in Sahajanand on room service. In fact that's more or less all there is. Aamir's ad crops up all the time, too. He is chatting with a beautiful girl on the internet, they agree to meet. But how will I recognise you? I'll be drinking Coke. They both turn up at a café . . . where everybody is drinking Coke! Doh! But they manage to meet up anyway (in case you were wondering), just before the insidious mind-filling jingle – 'Jo Chaho Ho Jai, Coca-Cola, enjoy!'

The Coke is infinitely preferable to the alternatives, which are coffee- and tea-flavoured chai, which don't particularly taste of anything. It's mostly hot milk and water, and Howard has bought some instant coffee which he is experimenting with adding to the chai to beef it up a bit. He also has one of those little one-cup-of-water heating elements that you can stick into the cigarette lighter of your car if you're a cop on a long surveillance job, for instance, or if you fancy a last cuppa before driving off Beachy Head.

By the end of the afternoon it is clear we aren't going to be used, so Howard and I visit Purvesh Ganatra again. Again it takes an age to connect properly, and we only manage to receive and reply to one of Howard's e-mails before we lose the will to carry on.

This time young Purvesh, not one of the great conversationalists, is joined in the office by his outstandingly chatty mother. Mrs Ganatra is thrilled to meet some English film stars, as she insists on calling us. Ha! If only she knew. I haven't even been on *The Bill*, and am consequently under constant threat of being thrown out of Equity altogether. Howard and I have to sign her diary, and she gleefully Sellotapes a 2p piece which I give her on to the same page.

We catch an auto-rickshaw back, saying to the driver, 'Sahajanand Tower.' He nods knowingly, and a few minutes later deposits us outside a travel agent's in a part of town we've never seen before. We can't make the driver understand where we want to go, until we say the magic words 'Aamir' and 'Khan', whereupon he brings us straight back to our building. It seems that everyone knows the movies have come to town.

In the evening Aamir introduces me to Bhatti, the representative from Coca-Cola, who is the only person I have seen in India with a mobile phone. He says that all Bollywood films are two and a half to three hours long, with a built-in interval for people to buy Coke. Howard, like me, had checked out an Aamir film before we came out, and he says that the one he saw was so long that he'd grown a beard by the end.

'Who? Me or you?' Aamir asks.

'Both of us,' says Howard.

3 FEBRUARY

Last night I got hold of a copy of the script of *Lagaan* – that is to say, the English translation of the script – for the first time, and read it through quickly. I mostly resisted the temptation to skip through it looking for references to Yardley, which was just as well since he doesn't figure by name until page 91 (although there are sequences of British cricketers playing cricket before then). Let's just say there was a surprise in store . . .

6
The Story of Lagaan

---

*The year is 1893 . . . The British protected the Rajah's
domain from attacks by neighbouring rulers. They also
promised the other Rajahs protection from this Rajah.
Thanks to this double dealing, the British collected a tax
from the Rajahs, which was paid by every farmer in the
country . . . Lagaan.*

(*Lagaan* – English translation)

This is the story of the film. If you don't want to know how
it turns out, then – as they say on the news – look away now.
It was written by Ashutosh Gowariker, the film's director.

Lagaan – Once Upon a Time in India by Ashutosh Gowariker

It is 1893, and the village of Champaner is suffering a drought. It
is two months into the monsoon season and there is still no sign
of a cloud.

The *lagaan* of the title is the tax that the villagers owe to the
British, who govern the province from the nearby cantonment,
and the drought has made it very difficult for them to pay the
full amount.

The maharaj, Puran Singh, tries to intercede on their behalf with
the British commander, the unpleasant Captain Russell. Russell's
sister Elizabeth has just arrived from England, and his deputy,
Smith, is clearly smitten. Russell tries, for the sheer nasty hell
of it, to make the vegetarian maharaj eat a meat sandwich, and
when Puran Singh refuses, Russell doubles the *lagaan*.

Our hero, Bhuvan, is a fiery young villager, and he has already

76

had one run-in with Captain Russell, when he disrupted a hunt by scaring away the deer that the British officers were trying to shoot.

The villagers are distraught when they hear about the double *lagaan*. They look for Puran Singh, hoping to plead with him, and they find him at the cantonment watching a game of cricket between two British teams. They are amazed that the 'Angrez' waste time playing a silly child's game, which is similar to their game of 'gilli-danda', and Bhuvan is particularly scathing.

Captain Russell comes over, and hears Bhuvan mocking cricket. He says that if the villagers can beat the army at 'this silly game', Russell will cancel *lagaan* for the whole province. If they lose, however, then the tax will be tripled. Bhuvan, goaded by his enemy, accepts the bet, to the fury of the other villagers.

Bhuvan makes himself a cricket bat and begins to recruit his team, in a sequence reminiscent of *The Magnificent Seven*. To begin with he doesn't have much success. Only a small child, Tipu, will play with him, along with the two village weirdos – Bagha, a mute who communicates by banging a drum, and Guran, a wild and extremely hairy mystic.

The four of them secretly watch the British play cricket, trying to pick up a few tips. They are spotted by Elizabeth, Russell's sister, who comes over with her servant Ram Singh, who translates for her. She says that she believes the wager is unfair and wants to help them.

Elizabeth begins to coach Bhuvan's cricketers, which makes Gauri, a local girl who is in love with him, more and more jealous as time goes on. Gauri is being courted by Lakha, the wood-cutter, but she rejects his proposal, believing she can win Bhuvan.

Bhuvan's dream of winning the match and freeing the province from the burden of *lagaan* begins to spread to the other villagers, and his team expands. He recruits Goli, whose skill with the *gofan*, a kind of long sling which he whirls about above his head to hurl stones, will surely translate into a useful bowling action. Bhura, a chicken farmer, puts his feud with Goli aside to join, and his reflexes, honed by chasing chickens, will make him an excellent fielder. And Ishwar, one of the village elders who has opposed Bhuvan, also sees the light.

Meanwhile Captain Russell is carpeted by his superiors, Colonel Boyer, Major Cotton and Major Warren. They tell him that if he loses the match he will pay three years' *lagaan* from his own pocket and be sent to Africa. Russell, steaming, comes back to the cantonment and has a run-in with the blacksmith, Arjan, taking out his frustration by beating the villager mercilessly. Arjan is so stirred up that he immediately joins Bhuvan's team. He should be a mighty bat. Ismail, the potter, also agrees to take part.

Elizabeth gives them another lesson, and Bhuvan's enterprise gathers momentum. Gauri is jealous of their friendship, and Lakha, whom she has spurned, decides to put a spanner in the works. He goes to the cantonment and tells Russell that his sister is training Bhuvan's team in secret.

Russell angrily confines Elizabeth to the cantonment, and persuades Lakha to join the cricket team as his informer.

By now Elizabeth is motivated not only by her sense of fair play but also by her growing love for Bhuvan. She risks her brother's wrath by sneaking out to see Bhuvan, and tells him how she feels – but in English. He doesn't understand, and she rides away.

The watching Gauri misinterprets their conversation and is upset. Bhuvan goes after her, and tells her that he loves her. At this point there is a love song, half in Hindi and half in English. The Hindi parts express Bhuvan and Gauri's love for each other, while the English verses tell of a fantasy Elizabeth is having about Bhuvan being an English lord, and consequently available.

Russell and his team are confident, and practising hard. Yardley, a maniac fast bowler, loses his temper and knocks Burton to the ground with a bouncer, and Russell tells him to save his energy for the match. The English team consists of Russell, Smith (his deputy), Burton, Brooks, Wesson, North, Benson, Flynn, Harrison, Willis, and Yardley.

Deva, a big Sikh who was formerly in the British Army, arrives at the villagers' practice and begs to be in the team to battle the 'Angrez'. He turns out to be a demon fast bowler. With Lakha, this makes ten, and the Indians are almost ready. While everyone in the village is watching the team practising, the ball is at one point thrown back to Bhuvan by Kachra, the untouchable, who has a deformed arm. The ball spins alarmingly as it bounces, and Bhuvan recognises that this would be a big asset. He recruits Kachra as number eleven.

The rest of the team refuse to play because Kachra is an untouchable, but Bhuvan makes an impassioned speech and wins them round. Captain Russell rides up and sees the team lined up defiantly – he is getting a little apprehensive.

The first day of the four-day match dawns. In the pavilion all the British officers and gentry have gathered to watch the humbling of the locals, while opposite them all the important elders of the province have come to support Bhuvan and his boys.

Smith and Burton open the English innings. Deva, the big Sikh, bowls to Smith, who hits the ball, and immediately all the fielders run after it at once. The openers put on sixty or so, dealing particularly harshly with Kachra's bowling, before Smith is run out, bringing Captain Russell into the fray.

Almost straight away there is controversy. Burton is complaining about the curious windmill bowling action of Goli, which he has adapted from his technique with the *gofan*. Elizabeth intervenes on the villagers' behalf with the umpires, who allow Goli to continue, and he immediately gets Burton's wicket.

Otherwise the English team progress smoothly to 182 for 3 at the end of the first day. Kachra has not been successful with the new ball, being a spinner, and Russell is 'dropped' by Lakha.

After the close of play, Elizabeth overhears Lakha reporting to Russell, and she shops the traitor to the villagers. They chase Lakha to the temple, where he allows Bhuvan in to talk. Bhuvan says that he will give him the chance to redeem himself.

The second day of the match sees the Brits move on to 320 all out. At one point Lakha makes a difficult diving catch to dismiss Russell for 122. The Indians begin their innings, and Yardley, the terrifying fast bowler, baffles the Indian openers with his extreme pace.

At the end of the day the villagers are 90 for 5. Russell and the British officers condescendingly admit that the Indians are putting up quite a decent show.

On day three Bhuvan is left stranded as the English spinners bowl his team out for 160. In the English second innings a big breakthrough is made by Deva, who takes a hat-trick. His pace is difficult to handle, so the nasty Brits decide to take him out, Yardley barging him 'accidentally' to the ground while taking a run, and injuring him badly. Bhuvan brings on Kachra to bowl, in despair, having no other bowler to turn to.

Kachra comes into his own with the old ball and becomes a Muralitharan-style hero, as England are bowled out for 210. The villagers promptly lose five wickets, and finish needing 371 on the last day with Bhuvan not out.

On the night before the concluding day the villagers gather, and a song expresses their loss of hope. Gradually the song transforms their mood from gloom, through prayer, to charged hope and grim determination.

Day four. Russell tells Yardley to bowl bodyline, and Indians start to get hurt. There is a fight back, with runs for Deva, the redeemed Lakha and Arjan, but the game swings England's way with the dastardly and unsporting run-out of the child Tipu, who is acting as a runner for the damaged Ismail, by the bowler Willis. Bhuvan is again left high and dry, with only the crippled Kachra left. The two of them mount a heroic last stand, and come to Yardley's last over needing ten to win.

Yardley, the maniacal quickie, paws the ground. One delivery smashes Bhuvan on the head, and he baffles poor little Kachra with his extreme pace. Come the last ball, they still need six, and Kachra, in despair, can only call Bhuvan through for a bye.

The last ball is called a no-ball, however, so Bhuvan has one more chance to snatch victory. The final delivery is a fiesta of slow motion – Yardley thunders in, Bhuvan wipes sweat from his eyes and blood from his ear – intercut with flashbacks of the weeks of preparation. Bhuvan hits the ball high to long on. Russell is the fielder, and he gleefully pouches the catch, but he has stepped over the boundary, and the Indians have won.

A huge pitch invasion follows, as the English fielders scoot for the pavilion, and then, all of a sudden, the rains begin to fall. Russell, enraged, and sporting to the last, tries to shoot Bhuvan, but Elizabeth stands in the way.

The English, beaten, humiliated, and seriously wet, pull out of the region altogether, and there is great rejoicing.

The End.

7
Cow Corner

---

*The whole village cheers. Suddenly they hear the sounds
of neighing horses. They turn to see a party of half a
dozen horses headed by Russell and Smith beyond the
boundary line . . .*

(*Lagaan* – English translation)

3 FEBRUARY (STILL)

I started reading at bedtime, and I didn't get much sleep,
for a couple of reasons. For one thing, the story is actually
rather good, and I wanted to know how it finished. The other
thing . . . well, I couldn't help noticing, and I wonder if you
spotted this too, that Yardley, good old 'Hardly' Yardley, my
character . . . IS A BOWLER!

Not only that, he's a bloody fast bowler, a dangerous
maniac, who comes hurtling in and tries to hurt, maim, or
otherwise injure the batsmen.

Now I don't know whether I've already made this suffi-
ciently clear, but I am not a bowler. I think I demonstrated
during the audition match at Paddington Rec that I can bat a
bit, but I am sure that I bowled absolutely the worst over that
afternoon, six high, wide, non-spinning, over-flighted donkey
droppers, which succeeded in bamboozling my friend Paul –
one of the worst batsmen I have ever seen – only by their
extravagant slowness.

I gave up trying to bowl any quicker than that years ago,
partly because my left knee is not really up to the pounding,
partly because my right shoulder is not all it should be either,
but mostly because I'm simply no good at it.

And I'm playing the main strike bowler. I really need to get some practice in, and fast.

———————

Howard, Jamie and I are taken out to the location today for the first time since the day we got here. The concrete buildings that make up the location base have been built specially for the film, we are told. It seems logical, when I think about it, since they are in the middle of the desert with no readily apparent purpose. There is a large communal canteen/dining area, open on two sides, a costume room, a hair and make-up room, and a couple of production offices.

I wonder whether perhaps the building would be left standing after the shoot if anyone from the nearby village was interested in keeping it, but what would they use it for?

Suhasini says: 'They'd use it for weddings, knowing Indians. Everything is bloody weddings!'

Actually it turns out that it will all probably be demolished, because this is such a sensitive military area. The fear, apparently, is that invading troops or spies could hide out in these buildings, though what they'd be spying on out here in the desert isn't entirely clear.

We have lunch, anyway, with the Indian actors, who are filming a scene on the side of a nearby hill, and then we try on some costumes.

I had been for a costume fitting in London, you may remember, with the costume designer, Bhanu, who they proudly told us had won an Oscar for her work on *Gandhi*. I had never been so thoroughly and minutely measured in my life – upper and lower neck measurements, inside arm, back of leg, circumference of gut – and was quite looking forward to having clothes cut to my own unique physique.

Disappointingly, though, on set there is a sort of lucky-bag approach to the costume side of things. I end up with a pair of riding breeches in which the crotch is virtually between my knees, and a button-burstingly tight tunic, combining into an overall look that Alexei Sayle would dismiss as over the top.

Jamie, on the other hand, a taller, slimmer and, let's face it, much younger man, is in a big baggy uniform comfortably large enough to fit at least three of him.

When it comes to the footwear, the Indian costume lads start out by offering me a pair of riding boots that are far too small. I try to show, using the international language of mime, that I need larger ones. Smaller ones yet duly arrive, so I change my mime accordingly. This goes on for some time, with ever smaller pairs of boots being brought whatever gesture I make, until finally I demonstrate to them that I can only just get my toes into their latest suggestion by prancing about in them like a ballerina. Eventually we settle on a pair of massive square boots that are like a couple of house bricks, together with substantial extra sockage, and I am left wondering why Bhanu had bothered drawing round my feet in such detail.

Then we meet Nicole and Pina, in charge of make-up and hair respectively. They are Canadians, which is a little surprising at first, but apparently quite a few Bollywood films use Canadian locations and that's how Aamir met them. Swiss and Scottish locations are also relatively common in Bollywood features, apparently, because they get to use picturesque mountain scenery without the hassles and harassment of shooting in northern India.

Pina gives me a centre parting, and then the two of them plaster glue all over my face and give a first outing to my magnificent mutton-chop sideboards and moustache. Jamie is also transformed, by the addition of a fancy little tache, but Howard, who's grown his own, looks barely any different when they've finished with him.

When they're satisfied, we're marched up the hill for Ashutosh to have a look at us. Raj says he thinks the facial hair makes me look grumpy, but the fact is the glue keeps my face more or less rigid and I can't smile.

Ashutosh says to me; 'As I remember, you are a batsman, and Jamie, you are more of a bowler . . .'

I stop myself from saying: 'So why have you cast me as the main fast bowler, then?' and begin to wonder whether, once we get round to showing what we could do, all the parts might be shuffled around. I might get the chop – the mutton chop, even – from the starting line-up and be relegated to a makeweight with funny whiskers rather than the fearsome spearhead of the British attack, who is, after all, crucial to the exciting dénouement of the film.

Perhaps, like the fringe member of an England touring squad who needs a good showing in the warm-up games against the President's XI and such like, I need to show well in the opening cricket scenes, and that will decide whether I figure in the first team or spend the winter carting a drinks tray around for everyone else.

I really need to get some practice in . . .

––––––––––

In the evening Amin is holding court again. He and the other Indians were enchanted by Rachel's performance today in a chaste love scene with Aamir, in which she tells him she loves him but he doesn't understand the English. She was very emotional, apparently, and they loved that. I fear this is another score on which I may prove a grave disappointment to them, as the only emotional stuff I am happy doing is grumpy. Or perhaps dopey. Actually, I'll have crack at pretty much anything the seven dwarfs can do . . .

A bit of table tennis doubles with H, Raj and Adi. We swap the teams around, but whoever is paired with Adi seems to win.

4 FEBRUARY
On stand-by again today. I have come to know what that means – a day kicking our heels at Sahajanand Tower – so I

reckon I have time to slip out and pay my pal Purvesh Ganatra another visit. It's Susan's birthday tomorrow, so I want to send her a message.

I am waiting outside his office when he arrives, and so I am privy to his little opening-up rituals. Before he lets me in – and before he speaks a word to me – he spends a few minutes lighting joss-sticks, and wafting the aromatic smoke over the computer, over his desk, into each drawer of his desk, and in front of his colourful pictures of Ganesh, the elephant-headed god.

This is a religious ritual, clearly, but I say to myself: 'If only more computer nerds would take the trouble to make sure their rooms smelled nice perhaps they wouldn't have such a bad reputation . . .'

While he's doing this I see that there is a swastika on his computer which I haven't noticed before. This is a Hindu sign of propitious fortune, which is why the Nazis adapted and adopted it, but when you walk along the roadside and see the sign daubed on every other archway and doorpost it does give you the occasional momentary flashback to away games at Millwall's old Den.

Mission accomplished, I go back to Sahajanand to find that we have been released for the day. Paul, Ben and Jamie are heading for the beach at Mandvi, but Howard and I decide to try and find somewhere to get a bit of practice in.

The town's cricket ground, the Jubli, is a short walk away. It is brown and hard, the same beige, dusty colour as everything in Bhuj, and there isn't a blade of grass on the entire playing area. We have seen some nets there, though, and once the hottest part of the day is past we grab a bat and ball that Ben has bought from the roadside bat-maker and set off to have a knock-up.

One charming feature of the Jubli ground is that, from one end, if you hit a huge agricultural mow over long on to what any English cricket follower might describe as 'cow corner', there is a chance – a faint chance, but a chance nonetheless – that the ball could bounce all the way along Jubli Road to a big corner that has a load of cows sitting at it. Very pleasing.

Whenever we pass the Jubli there is a game of some sort going on. Even in the evening a game of some description is being played under some pitifully inadequate floodlights – droughtlights, you might call them. There had been a game in progress at eight in the morning, when I headed into town to PeeGee Enterprises, and there is a game in progress when Howard and I get there this afternoon.

It looks like a schools match, and the whole place is heaving with schoolkids watching. The nets are empty, and Howard and I foolishly imagine we can just slip in unnoticed, stroll around the boundary, and knock the ball about languidly to our hearts' content.

As soon as we set foot in the place, however, we are swamped. Hundreds of kids come running from all directions, the little grandstand empties, and Howard and I begin 'What-is-your-name-what-is-your-country'-ing as though our lives depended on it.

We shuffle over to the boundary, thinking that if we just stand and watch the game for a minute or two then they'll all get bored, but the whole mass stays with us, and it is growing all the time. In fact they stand in a great crowd on the outfield with their backs to the game, just watching us watching the cricket, and those at the back must be more than halfway to the wicket.

The players in the middle are looking understandably miffed, but actually I reckon they are put out to be stuck playing cricket when their classmates have two white strangers to look at, and if they could drop their bats and come running over I think they would do so.

I try to move the swarm off the playing area, saying that I can't see the game properly, but they all then arrange themselves into the sort of viewing corridor that Nick Faldo sees more and more of nowadays as more and more of his shots skew off among the punters.

Howard and I begin to walk around towards the small concrete grandstand, heading for the nets, but we never stand a chance. Suddenly the mood of the crowd changes. Evidently we aren't being quite entertaining enough. A couple ask for our autographs and we smilingly oblige, until we realise that the autograph hunters are trying to distract us from their mates, who are tying our shoelaces together, planning to bundle us over backwards in a time-honoured St Trinian's-style manoeuvre.

When this doesn't work they start pelting us with fruit to see what we do. What we do is we leave with our tails between our legs. I have my taste of the pressures of Indian film stardom without having even been in front of the camera yet, and I don't particularly enjoy it.

Later I watch England lose to South Africa in a one-dayer – the whole thing live on Star Sports, part of the Murdoch empire. Nick Knight hits 64, and South Africa need seven from the last four balls. It looks as if it might be exciting, but then Mark Ealham bowls two leg-side full tosses and Richie Cunningham out of *Happy Days* hits them both for four.

5 FEBRUARY
Finally, after several days confined to Sahajanand Tower on 'stand-by', I get to make my first appearance in front of the camera today.

Howard, Ben, Jamie, Paul and I are picked up in one of the company 'Sumos' – large eight-seater Jeeps – at midday and driven out into the desert to the location. I can hear these Sumos manoeuvring in the mornings, and each of them has a distinctive sound which plays as a warning when it reverses. One of them has the straightforward beeping you would hear on a reversing British dustcart, for example, but one plays the 'Marseillaise', and the third one has an alarming taped farmyard effect featuring a wild cacophony of pigs, dogs and chickens all making exactly the kind of racket you'd expect them to be making if they were being run over by a reversing Sumo.

We are dropped at the concrete location base in the desert just in time for lunch – hurrah – and mingle with the Indian actors in their sundry fake beards and villagey garb, who have been filming all morning up on the side of the hill.

The food is the same as that on offer back at the Tower, and served by the same smiling faces. Rice, dall, and some suspicious-looking mutton is about the size of it, and I don't exactly feel like tucking in. I fear the beginnings of a dodgy tummy, not helped by the prospect of having to get on a horse this afternoon. Still, perhaps they'll have changed their minds about that . . .

Ashutosh, our director, eating his lunch on the move, greets us with a big cheery grin.

'Your first scene today, eh?'

We grin back.

'This is the scene where the willagers are practising, and they think they are finally getting the hang of cricket, and they look up to see Captain Russell and his men galloping over the hill to watch them.'

'On horses?' I ask.

'Of course on horses!' he laughs.

'We'll get to practise that first, won't we?'

Ashutosh thinks about this, and rather worryingly it looks to me as if it is the first time it has occurred to him.

'Mmm, good idea,' he nods, and wanders away to deal with a million other more important things.

So after lunch, while the rest of the unit are off back up the hill to carry on filming the villagers practising scene, five pale English lads are introduced to their soon-to-be co-stars.

It is the middle of the afternoon, and the heat is making me drowsy, so hopefully it is having the same effect on the horses. Our instructor is a wiry little old chap with a big gappy grin, his remaining teeth stained by a lifetime of chewing and spitting *paan*. He doesn't speak any English, but one of the lads with him can get by, and he explains that these horses are ex-police horses, and consequently very docile. As he says this, a big black brute takes exception to the look in somebody's eye and begins flailing away with its back legs, while one of the handlers hangs grimly to its bridle, his feet scraping up clouds of dust as the horse drags him along. Howard glances at me, and my dinner churns around a little bit more.

The horses are led out on to the outfield of the practice cricket pitch, and we are allocated a mount each. I stay as far away from the crazy black one as possible, hoping for one of the only mildly mad-seeming brown animals. Happily Paul, who's done this sort of thing before, is put aboard Batman, as the black one is called, and I am shown to a distinctly quieter fellow.

The instructor shows me that I should stroke and pat my horse, and gives me a biscuit to feed to it, so that it thinks I am its friend. Outwardly the beast seems placid enough, but as I move in to pat its neck, its big brown stupid eye – the only one I can see – is swivelling crazily in its socket, sweeping the group of us over and over again, watching for the slightest hint of provocation so it can justify rearing up and pounding us into a pulp, which is clearly its dearest wish. God alone knows what the other eye is doing. Scanning the horizon on the lookout for Pakistani fighters, probably.

My horse's handler encourages me to speak loudly and confidently to the horse, so I do, expanding its English vocabulary as I go. Once the horse knows me – though if it understood what I had been saying to it it would immediately have tipped me into the dirt – I am encouraged to hoist myself aboard, and shown how to hold the reins properly.

We are walked slowly around for a minute or two, getting used to the lurching of the beasts, and then encouraged to start riding for real. Our only tuition in this is the gappy-toothed instructor shouting 'Heels!', which seems to be the only English word he is confident with, over and over.

I dutifully bang my heels into the horse's flank, although it seems to lumber along just the same whether I do or not. Gappy waves his arms about to indicate we should go faster, and shouts 'Heels!' even more furiously, so I kick the horse harder with my heels, and it lurches into a desultory trot.

This isn't so bad, and I begin to feel that this is going to be manageable. We circle slowly round the outfield, until Gappy waves his arms around again, evidently suggesting we should stop.

I am feeling on top of things now, and so I loudly and confidently say 'Woah!' – which I take to be international equestrian language for stop – to my new friend the horse. Whereupon it sets off towards the far side of the field at considerably greater speed than it has hitherto displayed. I have no chance to settle into the horse's rhythm, even if I had been shown how to do such a thing, and I am thrown up and down on the horse's back, each bounce trapping my testicles with unerring accuracy between the rest of my body and the saddle. I won't say my life passes before my eyes, but the specific recent part of it in which I had been eating rice, dall and suspicious-looking mutton very nearly puts in an appearance.

It's over in a couple of seconds, but it feels much longer. Gappy and his lads are shouting 'Halt!', and one of them is making a grab for my horse's bridle, and the docile brute finally comes to a standstill.

What they had neglected to mention, you see, was that these horses are trained to stop only at the word 'halt', so effectively I had been having my first driving lesson without being told where the brake was.

'Woah!', to an ex-Indian police horse, means 'head for the far distant horizon with all possible haste', and may well have connotations of 'civic disturbance in progress' or 'sub-post office being robbed'.

I've given Gappy and his lads a moment's amusement, but when Pina, the Canadian head of hairdressing and horse fan, had the same misunderstanding on board the crazy Batman, she set off like a black streak, kicking up the sort of dust cloud you'd expect from a good-sized posse. No one could get close enough to tell her to shout 'Halt!', until she broke into the undergrowth that fringed the film location, and the horse was gamely trying to plough through four-foot-high thorn bushes.

Personally I feel I still have much to learn before I can claim to be a horseman of even the most rudimentary kind, but suddenly that's that. We're hauled off to costume and make-up, and the next time I sit astride the animal will be on-camera.

A short while later we are tramping across the desert in our ill-fitting one-hundred-year-old army costumes. I can see the film unit, clinging to the side of a hill a short way off. Little clumps of brightly coloured umbrellas shield the camera crew and the main actors from the fierce mid-afternoon sunshine. Farther up the hill some local villagers, who are being used as extras, are fending for themselves, pulling their pale white-brown robes over their heads and eyes as they squat in what little shade they can find.

As we approach, I am surprised to notice that the ground all around us seems to be ploughed. Surely no crops would grow in this desert . . . but then I realise that all this land will be in shot and has to look as though it is being farmed.

They are filming a scene in which Elizabeth, Captain Russell's sister, is showing the villagers some of the finer points of the game of cricket. The last shot of the scene will take in the hillside, and Russell and his men will be seen there, on horseback, looking on in a sinister and threatening fashion.

Ashutosh has abandoned his original plan, which was to have us gallop over the brow of the hill, and when we see the place we can see why. The slope is steep and strewn with rocks of all sizes, and the horses are having trouble standing on the hillside, let alone galloping on it.

Now we are to sit perfectly still on our horses, watching the cricket practice, and the camera will come up to find us. That suits me just fine.

When the time comes, we make our way up the hill to where the horses are being held for us. I find the horse with which I had made friends earlier, but now I am wearing a huge false handlebar moustache and sideburns and a large pointy helmet. If that horse recognises me it is a whole lot smarter than I think it is.

Embarrassingly, I find that in my ludicrous low-slung breeches I can't get my leg up high enough to put my foot into the stirrup. I smile at the bloke holding the horse and try to indicate that I needed a leg-up. He isn't having any of it, so I shove a small boulder over a little closer to the horse and perch precariously on it. Now I can reach the stirrup but my ludicrous big-toed army boot won't fit into the thing. I point this out to the handler, but he pretends to ignore me, until the spectacle of me balancing on one leg on a boulder wafting the other leg in the general direction of the horse becomes too embarrassing for him to bear, and he suddenly reaches down and launches me over the beast's back.

Now we're perched on the side of the hill. I can hear my horse's hooves sliding on the scree as it adjusts its weight slightly, and feel more than a little insecure. Howard is alongside me on a black horse, and Paul, Ben and Jamie are a little way down the slope on their horses. All we have to do in the shot is sit still and look forbidding as the camera pans up the hill from the end of the scene being played out in the foreground below.

Apu, the first assistant director, explains that they will not shout 'Action!', because all these horses have been in a film before and believe that this is the cue to gallop away into the sunset. He even whispers the word 'Action!' as he tells us this, in case the horses take off. What they will do, he says, is they will wave a little flag next to the camera when the shot is starting. He scuttles back behind the camera and we are all set for a take.

Now my horse reveals its true talent. It is an upstaging horse, the equine equivalent of the fat bloke in the chorus of the amateur operatic's *HMS Pinafore* who won't stop winking.

As everyone settles down, my horse is stock still. Then Apu waves his little flag in the far-off distance to start the shot, and suddenly my horse starts vigorously nodding its head up and down. We go for take two, and again the horse is like a statue. Apu waves his flag, and my horse starts walking backwards up the hill, sending little avalanches of gravel down round the feet of the other horses, who completely ignore this.

Take three, and my scene-stealing nag decides to eat a bush. I tug at the bridle, but to no avail. The horse's handler hisses to me from behind a rock: 'Tell him to stop eating bush!'

'Oi! Horse! Stop eating bush!' I say, firmly. Predictably this has no effect, other than corpsing me, until Ashutosh shouts 'Cut!', whereupon the horse withdraws from the bush and stands stock still, awaiting further instructions.

We get the shot eventually, persuading my horse to stop larking about in the background by tying its head to the floor with a bit of rope, which you won't be able to see in the finished film. Ah, the magic of cinema . . .

The Indian actors – Aamir, Raj, Adi, Amin, Pradeep, Suhasini, Yashpal – had all painstakingly wished each of us good luck with our first shot in the film, and now – even though all we've had to do is sit as still as possible in the background – they break into applause. It seems this is one of their on-set traditions, and very friendly it is too.

Howard and I take pictures of each other as the sunset turns the red ridge orange, trying not to think about how easily they could have done that shot with absolutely anybody silhouetted against the skyline in the back of shot wearing our silly helmets.

———————

In the evening there's a right result. I'm preparing to trawl the shortwave frequencies for the World Service, when I find that Liverpool v Leeds is live on telly on a channel called ESPN.

I get the Second Division results from the radio (Millwall 1 Oldham 0), and then go upstairs to another apartment, where the Indian cast and crew are having a musical evening. They are taking it in turns to sing *ghazaals*, lushly romantic songs from Indian myth and legend. Rachel is in the middle, having spurned the Liverpool v Leeds game altogether for some reason, and Apu, the first assistant director, is breathing a translation of the lyrics into her ear.

The whole gathering looks somewhat overwhelming, and I don't stay long, but later on Ben apparently sings something from *Cabaret*.

Rang Susan to wish her happy birthday. I'd given her her present before I left, but we spent a moment or two at cross-purposes while she tried to thank me for the surprise I'd left for her. It turned out that Peter had led her to the cast-iron casserole I'd wrapped up and hidden for a wedding anniversary present which she wasn't supposed to get until April 2.

8

The Squad Begins to Take Shape

BHUVAN
We are coming together to form a fist.

(*Lagaan* – English translation)

6 FEBRUARY

Mandvi

Sunday, and a day off. I go to Mandvi with Howard, Ben, Paul, Rachel and Pina.

Mandvi is on the coast about sixty kilometres – an hour by taxi – south of Bhuj. About halfway down the scenery undergoes a complete change. Where northern Kutch is dry, dusty desert, with scrubby, small spiky trees and cacti, the southern district is lush and green. Huge thick palms flourish, and rich green foliage arcs over the road. This part of the world is known as Banni, and it was once one of India's most fertile areas. It is drier nowadays but still supports many different kinds of crops, which we can see waving in the sea breezes, green and thriving in every direction, and heaped precariously on the brightly painted goods wagons that rattle up and down the Mandvi Road. The contrast between green Banni and beige Bhuj could hardly be more dramatic. It's like going from Kansas to the mystical land of Oz.

As the road reaches the town, it swings right to cross a wide river estuary which creates a small natural harbour. For centuries Kutch was cut off from the rest of India, surrounded by inaccessible mountains and desert to the north, the treacherous salt flats of the Ranns of Kutch, and the sea. The Kutchis became great seafarers, establishing trade links with Africa and Arabia, and Mandvi was the port from which Gujarat exported its goods to the rest of the world. A fleet of four hundred dhows traded out of this once-thriving little port, and wealthy merchants built some pretty fancy gaffs here once upon a time.

Its importance as a port has dwindled away to nothing, and as we cross the estuary we catch sight of the huge wooden skeleton of a single dhow beached to one side. It is impossible to tell whether this is halfway to being built or slowly falling to bits. The tide is out, and in front of the dhow skeleton half a dozen flamingos are picking for food in the mud.

Our taxi is too wide to negotiate the narrow alleys of the old port, so we get out and walk through the town to the beach. Paul, who was here on Thursday, is very enthusiastic. He's very enthusiastic about everything. Everything is fantastic. He takes us by way of a fruit-and-veg market he found on Thursday, and buys all sorts of fruit.

'Here,' he says, 'you've got to try some of this – it's fantastic!'

He buys a big pineapple, some fruit that looks like a potato and tastes like a gingery kiwi fruit, and then catches sight of a slab of dates. It is absolutely heaving with flies. In fact, to look at, the slab is more fly than date.

'Fantastic!' cries Paul. 'I'll have some of that . . .'

He cheerfully offers some to me as we walk on through the little town, but I am just feeling a little bit delicate and don't risk it.

Alongside the sandy track that leads down to the beach, Paul leads us into a basic little hut, which seems mostly to be made from woven twigs. It belongs to a tall bearded chap dressed in orange, with long hair in rasta-like ringlets.

'This is the Sadhu,' says Paul. 'I met him the other day. He's fantastic.'

Sadhu is a name for a kind of spiritual fellow, and unless I'm very much mistaken this guy is nothing more than a spaced-out beach bum. Still, he and his mates make us welcome, and offer us chai. This is a milky tea mixture which they keep more or less constantly bubbling away on a small camping stove, and they sieve out a small glass for each of us. The Sadhu then vouchsafes to us the source of his great spirituality, by rolling a huge joint.

We then head down to the beach, which is spectacular. Golden sand stretching as far as the eye can see, with the sparkling blue Arabian Sea lapping gently away. There are those who want to turn Mandvi into a top holiday resort to rival Goa, and while you'd have to say they've got a long long way to go in terms of facilities – there are none of any kind whatsoever – they certainly have the natural resources. If you want beach, just beach, reduced to its two most basic components – sand and sea – then you couldn't do much better than Mandvi.

Stretching away from us along the back of the beach is a long line of gigantic windmills, like aeroplane propellers on sticks, which provide electric power for the area. Just now they are still and silent, but later, when the sea breeze picks up, the place does start to sound as if there is an airport near by.

Paul says that the place was deserted a couple of days ago, but this is Sunday, and there are plenty of families and children running around. I am offered rides on fancily dressed camels and horses, but I had enough of that yesterday, thank you ever so much.

We set off down the beach to find a quiet spot. It should have been possible – the beach is miles long, sand as far as the eye can see – but the word is out – how? – that some English 'film stars' are here and we rapidly attract a little gaggle of hangers-on.

One lad strolls alongside me; others attach themselves variously to Howard, Ben, Paul, Pina and Rachel. Mine is telling me that he runs a health club in Gandhidham, about 105 kilometres away. He is very keen that I should visit it, but 105 kilometres seems to me a long way to go for some health. I ask him why people are following us around, and he says:

'Indian people are crazy about actors, crazy. Any actors, it doesn't matter. They just want to watch you to see what you do. They are crazy.'

And you too, son. He is a friendly chap, gently spoken and reasonably interesting, but I am desperate to shake him off. The fact is that, after a week in India, I can feel the unmistakable rumblings of my first major gastrointestinal incident.

How can I put this delicately? I am within maybe fifteen minutes of the end of *The China Syndrome*, with meltdown imminent.

I manage to free myself of my companion by taking his business card, and promising to go to Gandhidham, and write to him from England, and get him and his family jobs in the health-club industry, preferably somewhere in Kent.

I look around anxiously. Mandvi's chances of being taken seriously as an international holiday resort would be greatly improved, there's no doubt about it, by even a single solitary portaloo. There are no cafés on the shoreline, no bars (naturally), no hotels, no houses or buildings of any kind. There are the blokes with the camels and horses, and a chap selling coconuts from a barrow, and I'm not at all certain he'd stand still long enough for me to squat behind it. I wouldn't, in his place.

No, there's only two dozen gigantic bloody windmills, and half the population of Gujarat watching my every movement – in more senses than one if I'm not careful.

Suddenly Howard shows me the way. To the left is Mandvi, and to the right miles of more or less deserted beach. He darts out from the crowd of watchers and sprints away into the distance to the right, his bandy little legs pumping for all they're worth. One or two of the cinema fans look his way, but he's caught them on the hop, and he's a good hundred yards away before any of them think to follow him.

I watch his little silhouetted figure curve around the water line, until he thinks we can't see him any more, and then he stops, wades in a couple of yards, and relieves himself ecstatically into the sea.

This course of action won't quite suit my purposes, unfortunately, but as the beach slopes inland from the sea it becomes dunes, with a fair covering of head-high bushes more or less where the row of cafés and ice-cream parlours should be. Needs must . . .

I set off along the beach, but sadly my guts insist that I affect a casual stroll with unusually small strides rather than emulating Howard's speedy burst for privacy. This means that when I look back I see to my horror that a group of nine or ten film fans has broken away from the main group to see where on earth I think I'm going.

I stop. They stop, twenty yards away, watching me. I set off again, they set off again. I go a bit faster, they go a bit faster. I stop and look thoughtfully out to sea, hoping that this spectacle will be so dull that they'll head back to see whether the others are doing something more interesting. They stop and look thoughtfully at me looking thoughtfully out to sea.

I am seriously thinking that the only way I'm going to get the private moment my churning bowels crave ever more urgently is by standing in the Arabian Sea up to my waist, when suddenly salvation appears. Howard returns, jogging comfortably, damn his eyes, and confusion spreads over the faces of the film fans. What to do? Which one to follow . . . ?

As Howard passes me I try to use this moment to make a break for it, and head away up the beach as fast as I dare. Howard reaches my nine or ten pursuers, and they break. Some head in my direction, others start to wheel around and go with Howard. There is a little argument, a split, and they all stop. Excellent! I scuttle away across the beach, looking for a suitable gap in the bushes. I glance over my shoulder, and . . . hell! The entire group has reassembled, having democratically decided to ignore Howard, and they are trotting along in my wake, trying to catch me up. It is a *Butch Cassidy and the Sundance Kid* moment – who *are* those guys?

It's now or never. I dash as quickly as my condition will allow into the bushes, and as soon as I reckon I'm out of sight I double back through the undergrowth on my belly like a commando until I'm satisfied that they can't possibly find me. Snarling, and spitting sand, I finally reckon I can risk it. The facilities leave something to be desired, particularly in the toilet paper department – but let's just say I manage.

A few moments later, greatly relieved, I step out from my hiding place, and . . . aaargh! There they all are!

'What are you doing?' one of them asks. I suddenly feel a great responsibility – is it really my place to tarnish the magic of the cinema for these lads, to shatter their illusions that film actors are wonderful, brilliant, god-like creatures . . . ?

'Having a crap,' I growl, and stride off back to the others. I'm moving a little more freely now, and leave them trailing in my wake.

Later in the afternoon the Sadhu and his little gang turn up, re-emphasising their great spiritual depth by ogling the girls' backsides, and we strike up a conversation with a Scottish woman whose husband, it seems, is building the dhow we saw in the estuary along with a team of locals. He worked in a Glasgow shipyard until that was no longer an option, and has sold up and come out here determined to build a ship. It has taken eighteen months for him to get as far as he has, and his wife seems resigned to waiting at least as long again.

We play some cricket at last – a hotly contested, five-over, five-a-side game against some of the locals on the beach. The wicket is nice and flat, if a little sandy, and I am encouraged by bowling a not too unrespectable over, with only a couple of wides in it. The home team make 34, which we knock off without too many alarms. Ben hits a six over to the giant propellers, and then holes out trying to repeat the shot, which takes a bit of doing as only three of the thirty or so people scattered on the outfield are bona fide fielders.

As we leave the beach to head back into town, three young American girls, who are travelling around India, come over to chat to us, probably hoping that we are American too, as Americans do. Almost the first thing they tell us is that they met a couple of guys in Mumbai who had been extras in some bar scene in a Bollywood movie. When they find out that all six of us are working on a film nearby they go goggle eyed with excitement:

'You are in the *movies*?! That is *way* cool!'

This is a reminder that Americans are just as crazy about the glamour of cinema as the Indians, only in more of a jumping on the spot, pissing themselves with excitement, screaming kind of a way, as opposed to a silently following people around to see if they are going to have a crap kind of a way.

Ben gives them the phone number of Sahajanand Tower, and tells them he can get them into the movies, baby . . .

If I was thinking that Mandvi's chances of becoming a top resort were hampered by the absence of a thrilling amusement park ride, I needn't have worried on their account. We take two auto-rickshaws into the little town, three of us in each, and the drivers spontaneously decide to have a race. They take different routes, screaming along through the maze of little alleys and roads, suddenly coming face to face with some cattle, turning, and buzzing off in another direction. At one point we are tearing along an alleyway towards a little crossroads, when the auto-rickshaw with the other three in it suddenly zips across the junction at right angles to us. Our driver shakes his fist at them and floors it into the marketplace, and we arrive neck and neck with the other guy. Very hairy . . .

The drive back to Bhuj is a little more sedate, in a low-slung old Austin Ambassador taxi. A cab company in West London, apparently, uses these vehicles as a nostalgia novelty for Indian customers.

Later, having placated the film production security guys, who thought we'd been abducted, I go down to make a phone call.

There is just one public phone for the whole building. It is on the ground floor by the lifts, and like the pay-phones in the town, it is not coin operated. It is connected to a cash register in the adjoining room, where a man sits and gives you a bill when you are finished.

Because it is the only phone, there is usually someone using it, but it is quite agreeable waiting in the office with the man who operates the cash register, whose name is Mahesh. He makes out that he is like a local 'don', and says he can get me beer. Tonight he has a friend with him who is called Omar Sharif. This guy is a student, doing an MA, and he is planning a Valentine's Day coup.

'Three girls are in my eyes,' he tells me gleefully. I ask him which one he hopes to get off with, and he insists he is trying for the hat-trick. He is under the impression that England is very free, sexually, and badgers me for details of my many conquests. I am afraid I must be sadly disappointing to him. He is convinced that if he lived in London he'd have had at least forty women by now.

When I get through to Susan she tells me that Peter tapped on the double glazing in our front room with a little plastic fishing rod, no bigger than a pencil, whereupon the whole window shattered into a million pieces, showering the boy in broken glass. Happily he was unhurt, but you don't want that sort of thing happening, do you . . . ?

7 FEBRUARY

No *Times of India* delivered to the apartment this morning. When I get hold of one later on I find out why. Pakistan have threatened to nuke India, and Indian PM Atal Behari Vajpayee is posturing that he will respond in kind. This is a continuation of the long-standing dispute over Pakistan-occupied Kashmir, and evidently the production team thought we'd head straight for the airport if we saw the story.

There is another story about three twelve-year-old schoolgirls who bunked off school at playtime and travelled 300 kilometres to see Aamir Khan. They found their way to the location in the desert, got his autograph, and then disappeared. Now they've turned up safe and sound after a state-wide search. The story goes on to describe Aamir living in a 'posh bungalow' in Bhuj – it's seven storeys high, guys – and travelling around in luxury buses.

Also news of another big Bollywood film in production at the moment, called *Water*, directed by Deepa Mehta. In fact, the full title of the film seems to be *Deepa Mehta's Controversial Film Water* whenever it gets a mention in the paper. She has offended the Shiv Sena, a Hindu fundamentalist party, and activists are protesting to have the filming stopped. One of them took poison, and then tied a boulder to his waist and jumped into the Ganges. It was supposedly a suicide protest, but apparently he didn't jump until he saw the police frogmen arrive, and they got him out in time.

I spend the day, on and off, racking my brains, trying to remember where all the home insurance stuff is, feeling guilty about kicking my heels out here while Susan has windows shattering on the kids. When I get her on the phone she's dealt with the whole matter calmly and efficiently without me. The double glazing company rather sniffily explained to her that it was all her fault, and there was nothing they could do unless she paid for the whole thing to be installed again. So she rang a friend at a well-known TV consumer programme, and he faxed the chief executive, saying that they were about to run a story about our window and giving him the opportunity to respond. Within half an hour the chief exec had rung Susan personally offering to replace the window free of charge. She doesn't really need me there at all . . .

This evening there is a blackout at Sahajanand Tower. The guidebooks warned that this might happen, so I have a torch with me. Howard, however, cackling with glee, has gone one better. Out of his knapsack he brings three juggling balls with batteries and little red lights in them, and he proceeds to wander about the darkened building, startling everyone he meets with his little display.

Down in the canteen we find Ashutosh and Aamir, eating their dinner in the dark having got back late from the set. Howard does his little party piece, and Aamir cries:

'Howard, this is deadly!'

Not meaning that it is extremely dull, you understand, but that it is extremely impressive. Lots of things can be 'deadly' here – bowling, batting, a funny story, a shot in table tennis. The little red balls light up the dining room, and you can just make out the smiles on people's faces. Howard juggles on and on, though, and is in danger of outstaying his welcome. The next time Aamir says: 'Howard, this is deadly . . .' his meaning is a little more ambiguous. I take Howard by the arm and lead him away, still juggling.

8 FEBRUARY

Another day with no filming – beginning to get cheesed off now.

Another opportunity to familiarise myself with pedestrian tactics here in Bhuj. You are at a busy traffic junction and you want to cross. There are no traffic lights here, or pedestrian crossings, and the traffic is a constant breakneck flow in all directions. Take a deep breath – mind you, it is as likely to be the deep breath that kills you – shut your eyes, and step out into the road. Miraculously the trucks, bikes, mopeds, and auto-rickshaws snake and veer around you and carry on their merry way.

The cows and pigs and dogs that roam the streets seem to subsist mainly on litter. It's common to see a cow lazily chomping up a plastic bottle, and Jamie was highly delighted to discover a dog turd that was nothing more than an undigested oily rag. In the shape of a turd.

A large British contingent arrived today, along with another clutch of Indian actors, and Ray and Jon from my An England XI, both looking well, Jon swinging his guitar. They were whisked off to the location as soon as they arrived, along with Simon and Barry, and Jamie disappeared with his girlfriend, Katkin, and his sister, Charlotte, to show them around.

Howard and I were left wondering why on earth we had been brought out here so early, and showing the two remaining Brits, Alex and Neil, where to get lunch.

Alex is a tall, pale student, and as far as he knows his role is 'extra'. Neil is playing Harrison, and I remembered him bowling pretty fast at the audition. He told us he plays for an actors' XI, and also for a side in the Essex League, and I found myself thinking he could be quite an asset when it comes to the big-crunch challenge game against the Indians.

Harrison has no lines in the script 'at the moment', and I got the definite impression that here was a lad who would be looking to impress the selectors, in the hope of snagging the opening-bowler role, which is currently Yardley's, of course. I shall have to keep an eye on him . . .

Neil lets us know how busy he is – he's been unable to grow his hair or beard too much 'because he's had so many castings'. This is one of many variations on the actor behaviour which Howard eloquently characterises as 'dogs sniffing each other's arses'. In his analogy, the dog's arse represents his career – a particularly apt way of describing my own professional life, actually – and I suppose what Neil is doing is less to do with sniffing our arses as showing us that his own arse is doing very nicely.

Later, when the others returned from the set, where they were hair-and-make-upped, I met Simon again, and Barry. Simon is playing Brooks, and he was the chap who looked so dismayed when Aamir told us, back in London, that there was no alcohol here. After that meeting I did vaguely ask my doctor, as Aamir suggested, about writing me a letter saying I needed to drink for my work, so that I could apply for a permit, but my doctor refused point blank, saying that no reputable physician would ever write such a letter. Simon is more dogged, and has managed to blag himself one.

Barry, who is playing Benson, is more cricketer than actor. He is the middle-aged chap with the moustache who kicked off the audition match, and he plays for a village side in Kent, is a member of the MCC, and has also played for Kent over-50s. He could be handy, too, once the serious stuff starts . . .

Ray, as a lifelong fan of the Ruby Murray, is keen to wrap himself around some of the local cuisine, and is certain that years of training have prepared his insides for the challenge that lies ahead. I break it to him that what we have had so far is quite different to the dishes on offer at your typical flock-wallpapered, illuminated-aquariumed, Tiger-beered British high-street establishment.

The food provided by the caterers both at Sahajanand Tower and at the location is fine, if a little samey. Rice, roti, dall, and then dry and spicy dishes of chicken or mutton – which actually doesn't look too trustworthy – and various curry-flavoured desserts make up the usual choice. There's no sign of the creamy-sauced milder dishes I would usually plump for in an Indian restaurant in Britain, and there's certainly no chicken tikka masala. Apparently this dish, the market-leading curry in the UK, accounts for one in seven meals ordered in British Indian restaurants, but is totally unknown in Indian cuisine. Now, hysterically, it is being exported from Britain to India and Bangladesh to satisy the demands of frustrated British holidaymakers. The same is happening to the balti, another British-based Indian creation which began in Birmingham.

There is some confusion over the genesis of the chicken tikka masala. One theory is that an Indian chef was asked for some gravy for a straightforward chicken tikka, and whipped one up using a can of tomato soup and some cream. Now a considerable number of chefs are claiming credit for its invention, and there are something like forty-eight separate and distinct recipes in circulation in the UK. The version favoured in Glasgow is supposed to glow in the dark, so God only knows what it does to your insides.

9 FEBRUARY

In Varanasi the filming of Deepa Mehta's controversial film *Water* has been halted completely by public protests. Although the film script has been approved by the government, it is still too sensitive for the Shiv Sena, apparently. These are the guys whose Valentine's Day disco for the people of Mumbai – the 'Mumbaikers' – forbids any dance in which the participants touch.

Yet another day off – went down to Mandvi again, this time by public transport. The bus was a bit of an old boneshaker, but still more comfortable than six of us in a taxi. Once we passed from the desert north to the lush green south of Kutch, we passed a brightly painted lorry which had been piled high with hay. Too high, it seems, because it had turned completely upside down trying to go round quite a gentle bend.

Took an auto-rickshaw to the beach. These little farty yellow-and-black machines – known also as 'put-puts', 'fut-futs' or 'tuc-tucs' – combine all the manoeuvrability of a shopping trolley with the pulling power of a Lego train set. At one point Howard and I had to get out to shove the thing up a slight incline.

Paul, bless him, is still besotted with the place. He decided that the little pale brown scabby dogs that frisk around on the beach are 'amazing', and he wanted to take one home to London. I don't really see him getting away with one of these flea-ridden mongrels in his hand luggage. Anyway, he changed his mind somewhat about the dogs later when he found them munching on something that was floating in a bin-bag in the shallows, which when he looked more closely was one of their dead brothers.

Back to Bhuj on the bus as well, this time having to stand all the way. The only slight difficulty with using the buses is that the timetables in the bus station are all in Gujarati, and everyone I asked for information turned out to be a taxi-driver who started ushering me off to his car.

Later had a game with Ray's *Who Wants to Be a Millionaire?* book. Ray was Chris Tarrant, providing all the little quirks and musical stings, and Simon, who has been a winner on *Fifteen to One*, was the definite favourite. Ray got the million, however, with Jon muttering darkly about how it was Ray's book, and how Ray'd been reading it on the plane out here . . .

10 FEBRUARY

The 10.30 air-raid siren reminds me of the proximity of still-aggressively-posturing Pakistan. Madeleine Albright has offered the US as a mediator in the ongoing Kashmir dispute, saying that the situation makes South Asia too unstable for comfort. Here, she means . . .

I heard a charming tale of border tension from nearby. Indian border farmers grow crops right up to the frontier, while on the Pakistan side the ground is left as wasteland. The farmers till their fields during the daylight hours under armed supervision, but they are finding that during the night their crops are trampled by wild boar from across the border.

The Indians, naturally, accuse the Pakistanis of shooing these creatures over from their side on purpose, and to get their own back they have been making atta bombs (not atom bombs, thank God). They conceal explosives in balls of tasty atta, whatever that is, and these attract the boars. When the boars bite into them, the bombs blow their snouts off. Now the Pakistanis accuse the Indians of wantonly exploding stray farm animals, which of course they deny furiously. The atta-bomb scheme is not entirely successful, however, as several farmers have been savaged by crazed and snoutless bomb-damaged wild pigs, only escaping by feigning death. A crazy everyday story of border folk.

I have more or less given up on Purvesh and his interminable crashing internet link to Ahmadabad, and have sent Susan a couple of faxes instead. She has replied, asking me to leave a message to the boys on the answer machine – her suggestion is something along the lines of: 'Will you stop making that bloody noise!'

Simon, Ray and Jon disappeared for the whole day. Late in the afternoon they returned to Sahajanand Tower in triumph (actually in a tuc-tuc), having waded through miles of Gujarati red tape and been vouchsafed some permits to buy small amounts of alcohol. They then went straight to Hotel Prince, which houses the only off-licence in town, and bought as much beer as they could carry in one auto-rickshaw. They are allowed some more next month, apparently, and the way they were splashing out the stuff – which was warm and tasted rather nasty – they'll have run out long before then.

Neil and Barry went down to Mandvi today. While they were waiting in a queue at the bus station for the bus back to Bhuj, all the locals who were waiting with them suddenly scattered. They looked around, and saw a cow lolloping madly towards them. Barry, sensibly, reckoned that the Mandvians maybe knew this cow and what the odd look in its eye was about, and he scarpered with them. Neil, however, was tired after a long day on the beach, and not inclined to move, so he stood his ground. The cow looked at Neil, and from the cover of the bus station the locals yelled to him that he should run for it, but he was adamant that no dumb cow was going to . . .

Suddenly the beast lurched forward, scooped Neil up with its horns, and jolted and buffeted him along for a few yards. To great cackling mirth from the unsympathetic spectators, it dumped him on his feet, and butted him again, and again, until he finally did what he should have done to start with, and took to his heels with howls of derision ringing in his ears.

Fortunately he was only bruised, in the nether and pride regions – this is our main strike bowler we're talking about, don't forget. I don't suppose you'll ever hear that Darren Gough is going to miss a Test match because he's been butted by a mad cow. Not unless he finds himself sitting next to Margaret Thatcher at one of his testimonial dinners . . .

11 FEBRUARY
Found another internet place and thought I might give it a try. It uses a server in Gandhidham, apparently, and so I'm hoping that if the Ahmadabad server can't get me through to Hotmail, then the Gandhidham can. The Gandhidham can, 'cos it mixes it with love and makes the world seem right . . .

Opened the *Times of India* at the sports page this morning, planning to check its cursory coverage of European football, and, to my utter astonishment, found a huge match report about a midweek game between Bury reserves and Oldham reserves. Any snippets of news about the Latics have been so hard to come by, either via hours waiting for an internet connection or the distant cracklings of the World Service, that I just sat and stared for a moment or two.

The explanation soon presented itself. Oldham had won the game 3–2, and Bury's two goals had been scored by Baichung Bhutia, India's top football star, who is trying to make it as a pro in the English Second Division.

Football is nothing like as big as cricket over here, but even though Bhutia was only playing as a semi-professional for East

Bengal, he would sometimes play in front of 100,000 people in their Salt Lake Stadium. European and South American football has only been available via satellite television for about three years on the Star channels and ESPN. If the game ever took off properly here you have to think that the population is so huge that sheer weight of numbers would make them a force to be reckoned with. It doesn't always work out that way, though, as they found when they were knocked out of the 1998 World Cup by Qatar.

Also, the ref in the Liverpool–Leeds game is in trouble for punching the air when Patrik Berger scored. He claims he was celebrating his successful application of the advantage rule, and denies that he is a Liverpool fan, saying: 'Calm down, calm down . . . Eh, dey do, doh, don't dey doh . . . ?'

I thought I was finally going to do some work today. They were filming a big night scene, where the Indian cricket team are practising by torchlight before the start of the big match. It promised to be spectacular stuff. I was taken out to the location in the middle of the afternoon, and it was quite obvious as soon as I arrived that nothing was going to happen for ages. I had nothing to do but wait around, and so I decided to explore a little. The unit was filming about half a mile away – I could see the brightly coloured sun umbrellas clinging to the side of a hill – and so I wandered over in that general direction. As I came round behind the production building the well-trodden path to the left led across some pretend-ploughed fields, an area of barren desert masquerading as drought-ravaged farmland. To the right and down the hill was the pretend village of Champaner.

I strolled down to have a first look at the village, and I must say it struck me as pretty impressive. There was a main street leading straight through, with an open square in the middle, and other streets leading off to either side. The houses were all round and made from the same-coloured mud as the surrounding area, with neat little conical thatched roofs.

Each had a cattle stall or a chicken hut round the back, or something to indicate the livelihood of the particular character who lived there, and the huts had door holes and window holes, but no doors and windows. Of course, this was an 1890s village, so there were no even vaguely mod cons. I poked my head into one, and it was wonderfully cool, compared with the desert outside. I could see that the set builders, mostly local villagers, had used strictly traditional methods – there were no hidden scaffolding bars and stage weights holding the thing up; the mud-and-dung walls were authentically thrown up on to a lattice of interwoven sticks. It must have taken them quite a while to build the whole place.

When the unit first arrived, back in early January, the Indian actors fell in love with the place, and some of them seriously wanted to live in the village for the duration of the shoot. The idea was quickly shelved, though, partly because the desert floor heaves with scorpions and snakes at night, and partly because the rooms back at Sahajanand have tellies. And toilets. And there's a ping-pong table.

As I walked round, Champaner was completely, eerily deserted, and although I'd never seen it before there was definitely something familiar about it.

It wasn't that I'd seen anything like it in India, that was for sure, because if I had it would have been clogged up with litter and cows, and cows eating litter. This village, though, was almost supernaturally clean and tidy. Even one rogue plastic bottle in the corner of a shot would presumably be picked up on by some Indian Denis Norden, allowing him to hold the whole enterprise up to ponderous, laboured ridicule, repeated over and over again every Bank Holiday until the last syllable of recorded time.

Suddenly it came to me. I'd seen this village, or one just like it, on *Star Trek*. There, in the main square, under the spreading boughs of that shady tree, that's where Captain Kirk would beam down, with Spock and Doctor Leonard 'Bones' McCoy.

The villagers would be tall and beautiful, strolling slowly and serenely around in carefully basic, stylishly frayed, pastel-coloured clothing. They would calmly welcome Kirk, and offer him the fruits of their honest labours, perfect fruit and delicious home-baked bread, saying: 'It is but simple fare,' and Kirk would look at Spock, who'd raise an eyebrow quizzically.

Then McCoy would notice something, and hiss urgently: 'Jim! Where are all the little children?'

The lead villager, a tall, good-looking man in his early forties, would say: 'Our children are at learning, stranger, and will be here presently.' Sure enough, a crowd of perfect multiracial kids would then suddenly bustle in and ask embarrassingly direct questions about Spock's ears, which would make everyone laugh.

Kirk, Spock and McCoy would then tuck in, and speculate about this being the perfect society. They have returned to the basics of life, a very popular sixties notion, and abolished stuff like war and hatred and so on. And they prove endearingly unable to pronounce the names of the *Enterprise* crew, calling them Kirrok and Maccacoy.

Then a huge klaxon would go off, and all the villagers would start to move like zombies, out into the street, where they would join with a load more similarly dressed extras, and head inexorably towards a temple on top of a nearby hill.

I turned a corner, and sure enough, there, on top of a nearby hill, was a temple, with a steep curving staircase leading up to the front door.

Kirk and the others would try to communicate with the villagers as they walk, but to no avail. McCoy would consult some sort of hand-held cassette recorder, and solemnly pronounce: 'They seem to be in some sort of trance, Jim.'

The villagers would file into the temple, and Kirk, Spock and McCoy would nip in and hang around at the back. The villagers would make some sort of offering, and then a deep, booming voice would order them to kill the strangers, or else assimilate them into the village society and its simple ways.

The *Enterprise* crew would want to get to the bottom of all this, and there would be time for Kirk – or possibly Chekhov – to fall for a local girl, before Spock discovers that the whole society is run by a giant super-computer left over from a previous mechanised age, or a race that has long since died out. Kirk would decide to free the villagers from the tyranny of the machine so that they can rediscover the virtues of standing on your own two feet in an American kind of way.

The *Enterprise* would then leave, and within six months the villagers would all have died of some plague, or a famine, or something, thanks to the busybodying of the *Star Trek* crew, who by this time are grappling with a giant pulsating tarpaulin several light-years away.

That was why Champaner looked so familiar, and from then on I couldn't look at it without thinking of Captain Kirk. I don't think this is entirely a coincidence, either. Idly flicking through my Lonely Planet guide, I frequently come across names or places that have clearly been borrowed by *Star Trek* and its various generations – foreigners are *feringhee*, for example, then there's *jemadar*, or the prefix *Gul* that they have given their Cardassian soldiers, or the term *Vedek* for the holy leaders of the planet Bajor, which is similar to the word Vedic, which refers to the study practised by the holy sadhus of Hinduism. Interesting? Well, maybe, maybe not . . .

When I wandered back up to the base they had decided that Yardley wasn't in this bit after all and sent me back to Bhuj. All of the other Brits figured at some stage today, though, which means that of all of us I have been used the least. The most frustrating thing is being on 'stand-by' every day, because if they'd told me I was going to work for one day in the first two weeks I'd have taken off and had a look round farther afield, in Mumbai, say, or Agra. I resolved to get hold of a shooting schedule in case there are any other long periods of inactivity coming up, so I can make plans to get away . . .

12 FEBRUARY

No filming today, because everybody else was up all night doing the torchlight practice scene. Apparently it was quite spectacular, but absolutely freezing cold out in the desert. Ha!

At least there is English football to look forward to on the telly, or there was, until I found that ESPN has disappeared, because they are in dispute with the cable company. Apparently it has been off in Mumbai for six weeks. I listen to Newcastle beating Manchester United 3–0 on the scratchy World Service, which changes frequency to one I can't get at the very second that the classified results rundown ends. I think I can just make out that Oldham have lost at home to Gillingham.

We have a new flatmate. Farhan is the director of the film Aamir will do next. He tells us a little more about Deepa Mehta's controversial film *Water*. The story is set in the sixteenth century, and concerns a house of widows. These widows, who in more extravagant times would have thrown themselves on their husbands' funeral pyres, are social outcasts. Their heads are shaved, and they may not allow their shadow to fall upon anyone else. The two main characters are upset when a ten-year-old widow arrives, and they begin to consider that there is more to life than the house of widows, if not for them then for the child. They plot to help the girl escape, in a story about the women asserting their freedom to choose, and developing a sense of hope, but they fall foul of the matron, who has been making a huge profit from prostituting the widows secretly to rich clients.

The system in India required that the script be submitted to the Ministry of Information and Broadcasting, who cleared it for shooting. However, right-wing Hindu extremists are protesting that the story is insulting to Indian culture, and they have broken down the set and disrupted the shooting, as well as poisoning themselves and tying boulders to their waists before jumping into the Ganges. The bloke who did that is still ill, apparently – not from the poison he took or his near-drowning, but from having swallowed some of the river.

The state government of Uttar Pradesh have blocked the filming now, saying that this is because of 'law and order concerns'. Their solution is not to arrest the protesters for civil disobedience but to stop the film-makers from provoking the protesters by working. It seems odd, to say the least, that the protesters have a right to free speech, which they can then use to prevent the same right being extended to Deepa Mehta, even though the national government has given her the go-ahead.

One side effect of the suspension of filming on *Water* is that our meals have improved. The same catering company is doing both *Water* and *Lagaan*, and, now that *Water* has closed down, the head man has shown up here and his cooks have bucked their ideas up a bit. Bakshi, his name is, a tall, slender gentleman, very polite and charming. Despite this improvement, however, Ray, the lifelong curry fan, has inevitably succumbed almost immediately to a bout of the shits like you wouldn't believe. In fact, he was ruefully telling us, they began after he ate the curry on the plane out here.

———

On Saturday evening there is a performance on the flat roof of Sahajanand Tower by a group of local Bhuj musicians. If they are not already called 'Bhujie Nights', then that is something they should perhaps consider. They are very well respected, and this special recital is in honour of Aamir and his production coming to Bhuj, so everyone dutifully gathers to listen.

The musicians sit on rugs on the floor. There are half a

dozen of them, and arranged behind the main singer they prepare to play a variety of traditional instruments. A couple of percussionists play on tabla, drums played with the fingers, there's a recorder-like whistle, one has a squeeze-box, and one has a quite swish-looking Casio keyboard.

Even though they are going to play us a selection of traditional Kutchi music, and they are all wearing traditional embroidered local costume, they have a fat roadie with his arse hanging out of his filthy jeans who shambles across in front of them tapping on the microphones going: 'Two . . . ! Two . . . !' I suppose that's traditional as well, come to think of it.

The music is very distinctive, and unlike anything I have heard here so far. The rhythm that the tabla guys are playing is very difficult to get into. It is very complicated and doesn't seem to be in repeating patterns that I can pick out. I look around, and some of the senior Indian actors are listening intently, rapt, eyes shut, heads back. Jamie, who is a drummer in a band back home, is frowning, trying to pick up what the rhythm guys are doing as well.

Gradually it dawns on me that the percussion is not driving the song in the way that my musical ear is used to, and it's not supposed to be. It is more like texture, giving the music body, but the structure of the song is being dictated by the singer. I am a little surprised to find it is quite so alien, but by the end of the recital I have more or less got the hang of it. Up on the roof, with the cloudless night sky twinkling overhead, and the little town of Bhuj twinkling down below, the whole effect is very atmospheric and foreign, somehow.

After the group have finished – I didn't catch their name, but I reckon Bhujie Nights would be a good one – Aamir takes the microphone and begins to MC a musical soirée. He sings a hit from his film *Ghulam*, which he himself, unusually, sang on the actual soundtrack of the film. The more normal way of the Bollywood world is for the star to mime to a track provided by one of a number of specialist movie singers. There is no deception involved, no one is hard done by like Debbie Reynolds in *Singin' in the Rain*, that's just the way it is. At their film award ceremonies one of the most fiercely contested categories is that of best unseen soundtrack singer, and the best ones are celebrities in their own right. Aamir has got quite a bit of kudos, apparently, from singing this particular song, 'Aati Kya Khandela' (I think), and his performance here is greeted warmly, naturally.

After Aamir there is no shortage of volunteers. Ishwar and Bhura, particularly, two of the senior Indian character actors, take the lead in a number of folk songs, and all the Indians join in, slapping the rhythm out on their thighs. The songs are vibrant folk tales of love, romance and heroism, and the striking thing is that all of the Indians know these tunes, know all the words, and have clearly grown up with them and a strong shared culture which lives in their memories.

After a few of these vigorous and vital numbers, Aamir, as ever the soul of politeness, grabs the microphone and says:

'We mustn't hog the evening. Let's have a song from one of our British guests. Paul . . . ?'

Everyone cheers enthusiastically, and Paul shambles forward. He jokes along for a minute or two, but it is clear that he has nothing, no idea at all what he can do. His mind is full of the Hindi dialogue that he has been learning, and in desperation he suggests singing that to the tune of 'God Save The Queen'. The Indians think he's joking, and will soon start singing something properly, but I can see that he really is drowning.

I start frantically racking my brains for a song, any song, that I could do myself, partly to rescue Paul from this horrible buttock-clenching moment, and partly just to hold the English end up, but under pressure I can't call to mind a single thing that I know all the way through. Paul's squirming is becoming unbearable, and out of sheer fellow feeling I take a deep breath and steel myself to step in and join him – surely something will pop into my head . . .

Suddenly Jon appears at the top of the stairs. He has nipped down to his room and grabbed his guitar, and he strums his way confidently up to the microphone and goes into an Elvis number. Paul's relief is palpable, and clearly this is a debt of gratitude which Jon will be able to call in any number of times for the rest of his life, if he is so inclined.

Jon segues into some early Beatles, and pretty soon has acquired a little backing group. There is one hilarious and bizarre cultural crossover moment, when Nakul, the sound man and the coolest dude on the set, wanders up with a harmonica and says: 'Say, have you guys heard of a cat named Bo Diddley . . . ?'

The rest of the evening rattles by in a jolly fashion, and Jon is a big and charismatic hit, but I can't help feeling a little envious of what the Indians have shared earlier on. Their songs were expressing truths about the world and the human condition that are passed on from generation to generation, solid, rich and life enhancing. Their singing to us was a gesture of welcome and friendship. And to return the compliment, what did we have to offer?

I just wanna be your te-heddy bear . . .

9
The PCG

---

*After the echoes of the gunfire die down, an English
voice roars in disappointment.*

CAPT. RUSSELL
Bloody hell, missed it again!

(*Lagaan* – English translation)

13 FEBRUARY
There are a load of English extras involved in the film, and I
came across many of them for the first time today. They are
mostly staying at a hotel in town, the Hotel Abha, which is a
pretty bog-standard hole, by all accounts. Rob and Andrew,
who are mates of Alex's – the three of them plan to go
travelling around the country once the filming is finished –
often come up to Sahajanand for their meals, which gives us
some idea of what the Abha's kitchens must be like.

The extras fall into two camps. There are the ones who've
flown out from the UK, like the students Rob and Andrew,
and Katkin and Charlotte, who are staying here with us,
and there's a contingent of India-based Brits, who have been
recruited from Mumbai and points east.

Today is a day off, but all the extras have been brought up
from the Abha for a costume, hairdo and funny moustache
fitting. I pass one crotchety old bloke on the stairs who has
been made up as brown as a berry, with a ludicrous little white
twirly tache and goatee beard, so that he looks like nothing so
much as a crazy professor out of Hergé's *Adventures of Tintin*,
and I sympathise silently with him. Until, that is, I pass Pina and
Nicole, and realise that they haven't started working on him yet,
at which point I begin to sympathise silently with them instead.

There is a whole coachload of extras running around Sahajanand, and they are getting everywhere, like an infestation. There was a huge queue at breakfast, and you could hardly turn round without bumping into a new and unfamiliar face.

I discover later that two of these chaps walked into Jon's bedroom while he was still asleep in bed. One of them perched alongside him and began to play his guitar, which woke him up, naturally enough, and the other opened the door out on to his balcony and told him to get them some coffee. Seriously unnerving. I am looking forward to getting to know these fellows better . . .

I have had some experience of extras back home, and they can be a curious breed.

Once, during a break in filming a scene set at a large black-tie dinner at the Savoy, I passed a load of smartly dressed extras hanging around in the lobby on my way to the toilet. One of them was languidly holding forth to about a dozen others as I moved within earshot, and he was saying:

'Of course, I'll be using this dinner suit again tomorrow, because I'm up at Pinewood doing a casino scene in the new Bond . . .'

I went about my business, and when I came back through the same lobby a couple of minutes later the group had broken up and every single one of them was on his or her mobile phone haranguing their agent:

'There's a casino scene . . .'

'. . . Bond movie . . .'

'. . . Pinewood tomorrow . . .'

'. . . why aren't I . . .'

'. . . well make the call . . .'

'. . . that's your job, isn't it . . .'

'. . . or am I *very* much mistaken . . .'

I love the idea that all those extras had mobile phones. Always available. Ready to drop everything and leave at a moment's notice to go and stand in the background some-where else.

On another occasion I did a day as an extra on a comedy sketch show. I did it as a favour for the producer, who was a good mate. He needed someone to be involved in a couple of simple visual gags and didn't want to be bothered with all the faffing about that a career extra would inevitably put him through. This meant me spending the entire day with the other extras, though, and midway through the afternoon he passed through the little cafeteria area we were all waiting in and stopped for a brief chat. After he had gone a couple of these extras came over and sat with me.

'It's all right,' one of them said. 'I'm your witness.'

'Eh?' I said.

'We all saw it,' another one said.

'I'm sorry, I don't know what you're talking about,' I said.

The first chap took out a little booklet and thumbed through it, knowing exactly what he was looking for.

'Here,' he said, pointing at a line, and reading it out at the same time: 'Spoken to individually by producer, five pounds.'

'We all saw it,' the second chap said again.

Suddenly every experience I had ever had of working with extras made sense. They were obtuse and uncooperative on purpose, trying to provoke the producer or director into addressing them personally, at which point they could slap in an invoice for an extra fiver. And if I could trick my old mate into sitting with me at mealtimes I could make an absolute bloody fortune.

14 FEBRUARY

Early start, the bus leaving Sahajanand at 6 a.m. As countless celebrities have said on countless chat shows: 'I'm sure making movies must seem ever so glamorous, but the harsh reality is getting up at the crack of dawn and hours and hours of bloody hard work to create the magic you see on your big screens . . .'

We trundle out the forty-five minutes into the desert, but this time when we get to the concrete production buildings and the practice cricket pitch we carry on for another ten minutes or so, heading for the proper cricket pitch for the first time. I am very keen to get a look at this, the Victorian-style pavilion in the middle of nowhere, the playing area blasted flat with dynamite.

The bus pulls up by some large tents that have been pitched around the corner from the location, and this is where breakfast is served. Like most of my compatriots I politely decline the opportunity to start the day with a curry, and stand in line for a go at the one box of cornflakes.

The location, when we get to have our first look, is not a disappointment. Not at all. There is a flat arena, completely grassless of course, with the cracked brown look of a dried-up riverbed. A couple of the setting lads are rolling the single playing strip – which is similarly baked mud, flat and hard – with a heavy hand roller, and a neat little wooden fence marks out a boundary.

Nature has provided a grandstand at one end, a small rocky mountain covered in perfect vantage points for spectators. At the opposite end is the pavilion, a smart white building with a green roof, and a Union Jack fluttering in the desert breeze. Two tiny and incongruous little lawns have been laid in front of the pavilion steps, and to one side there is a large black scoreboard.

Away on the horizon the sun is rising, illuminating the miles of empty desert stretching away in every direction from this strange, perfect, isolated little shrine to cricket.

I find myself smiling, not only at the thought of filming a cricket movie here, but also at the prospect of playing a proper serious match against the Indians in such a perfect setting.

The wonderful, luxurious pavilion turns out to be mostly a

front, as the production offices and the costume and hair/make-up departments are camped inside, along with some poky little changing rooms. Our changing facilities extend to a nail each banged into the wall in a corridor at the back by the toilets, but nothing is going to dampen my enthusiasm at being given a whole cricket ground to play with.

When it comes to dishing out the cricketers' costumes, there is again a lucky-bag approach, but this time the range of possibilities is not so great and I manage to find something not too embarrassingly small for my fat belly.

The old-style cricket boots have been 'specially made by the finest cobblers in India'. That's as may be, but they're not sports shoes by any stretch of the imagination – they have completely smooth leather soles, and raised wooden heels. If you want sporting footwear doing properly, you see, you don't want to be using craftsmen, with skills passed down from generation to generation. You want to be using Indonesian children who are paid fourpence every six weeks to slap them together from a kit. I reckon we'll be lucky if no one comes a cropper just walking in these items, let alone going through a full-pace delivery stride.

Pads, gloves and bats have been made up to match some photos of cricketers from the turn of the century, and they give a really authentic period look. The gloves, in particular, are nothing like modern batting gloves. They consist of four padded fingers and a long leather strap with a thumbguard on the end. You wind the strap around your wrist and your thumb holds it in place. I wonder how recent an invention the whole batting glove is – I'm pretty sure I've seen film of Bradman in the thirties with his hands in contraptions like these.

As soon as we are ready, of course, all the Brits trot out to chuck a ball around. I am the last to join in, because it takes the longest to get me all Yardleyed up, what with the whiskers and the moustache and the glue.

The scene we are filming today is a practice match which the British players are playing among themselves, while Bhuvan and some of the Indian team watch to try and pick up the game's finer points.

Bhuvan's arch enemy Captain Russell is batting, and the idea is that he will dispatch the bowling to all parts. This is the first time I have seen many of the Brits play, and quite apart from wondering whether they'll be any good in the film, I'm eager to work out the strength or otherwise of the team for the real match that's coming up.

In both regards Captain Russell is something of a worry. Somewhere along the line Paul has blithely ticked the 'yes' box next to the question 'can you play cricket?', and somehow no follow-up questions have been asked. Only he and Alex are completely unknown quantities since they were not involved in the audition game at Paddington last autumn.

Paul, like many an actor before him, seems to be using 'the method', and is assuming totally and confidently the character of a man who can bat. Unfortunately there's a little more to batting than that, and after connecting with one or two lucky swipes to leg, he comes badly unstuck when Ashutosh wants the ball hit on the offside.

Ray (Willis) is bowling, and Paul cheerfully wafts air shot after air shot, saying: 'Hold on, I think I'm getting the hang of this.' After a while, though, clearly afraid he will run out of film, Ashutosh changes tack, and gets Ray to run in and mime his bowling action, while Paul lobs the ball up to himself and then tries to whack it out to the boundary. How convincing this will look, I can't really imagine.

Throughout this sequence, good old Yardley is standing at the other end, giving his captain admiring looks, which tests my meagre acting abilities to the limit.

After a while we move on to the next shot, and happily for me Yardley is facing the bowling. I hungrily eye the cover boundary, but Ashutosh comes over to tell me

I have to dab the ball down and be called through for a suicidal single. By the time we get this shot in the can I have been run out thirteen times – almost half a season's worth for an accomplished follower of Sir Geoffrey like myself.

There is no written line of dialogue here, but I am encouraged to improvise a bellow of disapproval as Captain Russell charges towards me. Of the many variations I try I am particularly pleased with:

'Get back you incontinent fool!'

Especially as he is my superior officer.

Smith (Ben) gets to play a shot next, and is served up some short stuff outside off stump to show off his square cut. Ashutosh wants to get something just so in the background, though, and Smith is required to cut the ball finer and finer until at last he realises that the shot we need is a deliberate late cut between the keeper and first slip. This proves virtually impossible until the bowling is moved, out of shot, through about ninety degrees.

Finally we come to a shot which Ashutosh has charmingly titled: 'Yardley does a stylish shot'. He asks me to suggest the bowler, and I opt for Harrison (Neil), partly because it's always easier to look good if the bowling is quick, and partly because I want to see if he's any good, with the big match against the Indians in mind.

Harrison runs in and gives me a tidy ball on my legs which I flick off my pads down to the boundary. I rather enjoy this, naturally, and am disappointed to find that we've got that one in the can straight away. It dawns on me that the only way to get a nice long innings in film cricket is to play as badly as possible.

The camera angle changes, and we go for a new shot: 'Yardley hits the ball in the direction of Willis'. Willis is at cover point, and I fancy my chances of having a bit of a bat while hitting the ball not quite at him. Harrison runs in, and second ball I accidentally whack the ball within a whisker of

Willis's right knee to the cover boundary, and that's the end of my batting for today.

This has gone well, in the context of my professional career as an actor, because we've made up some time that we lost earlier while Captain Russell swished and wafted the breeze. As a cricketer, however, I'm more than a little fed up, because of effectively being dismissed from the wicket for hitting two boundaries, whereas if I'd been bowled or caught or stumped or lbw I'd still be out there. Hey ho . . .

One good thing, though. Neil looks a pretty decent bowler, able to put the ball more or less where I asked him to, and quite nippy too. He'll be opening our bowling in the big one, I should think.

15 FEBRUARY
Up even earlier today, but just used in the background. During the long lulls in the filming, Jon introduces us to a dice game called Zilch, and we spend hours playing this and drinking free Coca-Cola in the big tent that has been erected behind the pavilion. I've got a book, but it's too hot and too noisy to read, and flies keep landing on the pages.

From time to time we grab a bat and a ball and set up an impromptu game of cricket, but we never manage to play for too long before one of the setting lads runs over to rescue his precious props. This seems more than a tad overprotective of items which are, after all, specifically designed for the very thing we are using them for, but still . . .

Had a chat with Neil. He is very serious about his acting career, and he has been spending some of his free time recently trying to find a professional portrait photographer in Bhuj to get some publicity photographs done of himself with a beard.

I discuss cricket with him, and he tells me that last summer he was troubled by a pelvic problem which inhibited his bowling. He couldn't work out what was causing it, but it doesn't seem too bad just now, so he is hopeful of being able to bowl to his full potential both in the film and in our match. I little think, as I listen to him talking about his injury, that I will be able to make a diagnosis myself, but pretty soon the solution to his problem becomes clear.

Neil is the only one of us who absolutely must be back in the UK by a certain date – March 27 – in order to start work on his next job. He is returning to a job he has done once before, which is appearing as Barney the Dinosaur in a touring stage production. Evidently this tour is going to last months and months, and will go all over the world apart from America. When I ask why not America, Harrison mutters with more than a hint of bitterness:

'Oh, American Barney has the States sewn up.'

So Neil is like Euro-Barney. The Barney show consists of a number of singalong songs, performed by Barney and a group of other brightly coloured baby dinosaurs. The other cast members are all midgets, it appears, and Barney's costume is the only one that requires a grown man to operate it. Neil shows us roughly what he has to do inside the costume.

The huge Barney head sits more or less on top of Neil's head, and as well as dancing and operating Barney's arms, Neil has to open and shut Barney's mouth. The jaw is weighted, so that it opens when Neil leans backwards from the waist, and shuts when he leans forwards again. Even the simplest 'Yup!' from Barney means that inside the purple suit poor old Neil is throwing his torso backwards and forwards.

The suit weighs a ton, and Neil has to make Barney mime to a backing track throughout the whole show, so he is constantly heaving himself around as the huge purple dinosaur yuks 'Superliduperli!'

'And you've no idea why you might have a pelvic problem?'

'Nope. It's a complete mystery . . .'

I don't think I could bring myself to do a job like that. (Well, I don't know. What are the hours . . . ?)

Jon remembers his son having a Barney the Dinosaur bubble toy, and that bubbles came out of its mouth when you blew its tail. Neil is able to confirm that the same is pretty much true of Euro-Barney himself.

Later, while I was waiting for the telephone to be free, I chatted with Mahesh and Omar Sharif. Mahesh introduced me to a game called *carom*, which is like a cross between Subbuteo and snooker, while Omar bemoaned his lack of Valentine's Day success. Evidently each of the three girls 'in his eyes' had got wind of the other two and had stood him up.

16 FEBRUARY

The scene we were filming today was called: 'The bet is set'. Basically Captain Russell and Bhuvan eyeball each other, with all the Brits and Indians backing them up on either side. Russell challenges the villagers to a game of cricket, and Bhuvan accepts on their behalf, much to the dismay and agitation of the others. This involves a lot of Hindi dialogue for Paul, and a lot of standing around in Alexei Sayle uniforms and false whiskers in the burning hot sun for the rest of us.

In the evening Aamir summons us to a get-together on the roof of Sahajanand Tower. He and Apu want to prepare us for the big day that is coming up next week, when we will be filming in front of ten thousand extras, at least one of which will be an elephant, and we will be making it rain, apparently. Sounds like fun, and lots of work for Apu, who grins apprehensively.

Aamir talks very well, seriously and enthusiastically. He is very keen to get the detail exactly right, and this is one of the reasons he wanted to produce the film himself, so that he could pay attention to this. He has asked for all the British team's caps to be changed, apparently, to match the old pictures more closely, and is concerned that we should have cloth tie-ups for our trousers rather than belts, and wants to know what we think.

I find this approach very encouraging. Sport is notoriously difficult to portray on film, and part of the reason for this is that viewers pick up on any small detail that is out of place, and this undermines the whole house of cards.

One small point that I hadn't picked up is that the Indian dialogue is not exactly in Hindi. Some of it is, that is to say the exchanges between the Indians and the Brits are, but when the villagers are talking among themselves they are speaking in Awadhi, an arcane and regionally specific dialect close to Hindi. A bit like for us watching a film about Geordies, perhaps, or Scots.

Earlier we had watched from the roof as Aamir returned from the location. As usual there was a large crowd of well-wishers outside, all of whom wanted to touch him, and he shook hands and waved and chatted before disappearing into the building. He is very good natured about this, but you can see that he couldn't possibly go out anywhere on his own anywhere in India. Watching him now, relaxed, bantering away with us, animatedly discussing the movie, it is clear that we are seeing him at his best, comfortable within the confines of a film unit.

The conversation moves on to the subject of the cricket match between the Brits and the Indian cast and crew. Aamir is suggesting a twenty-five-over match, as any longer will mean playing in the hottest part of the day, and the date of February 27th, a week on Sunday.

A tacit assumption has emerged that I will captain the England team, which suits me fine. This comes partly from my having stepped in to organise the audition match back in London, and partly from the fact that four of my team are here, but whatever the reason, I am happy to take it on.

We end up discussing the arrangements for the match in an odd parody of the 'bet is set' scene we were filming earlier on, with Aamir and me facing each other, Apu backing him up, and all the Brits arranged menacingly behind me.

Everyone is seriously up for the game, and although Aamir makes a few self-deprecating remarks about their being the underdogs, these strike me as merely the opening skirmishes in the psychological war, and I reckon he thinks that as long as he's got Apu on his side he will win. We shall see . . .

17 FEBRUARY

Before filming today some of us climb the mountain on the boundary and survey the surrounding area. The sun is just coming up, and the *Star Trek* village is casting long shadows about a mile away. Apart from that, and the cricket pavilion down below, there is barren rocky desert as far as the eye can see in every direction.

Today we film the Brits disdainfully leaving the villagers in despair at the end of the 'bet is set' scene. Howard and I are placed in a horse-drawn buggy at the front of the convoy, and we are required to sneer at the hapless locals as we pull away. Our horse, however, has other ideas. It is a snorting, frothing, spitting black demon, clearly unimpressed by the idea of pulling anything, let alone two pale specimens from the mother country. As soon as we get into the buggy it starts bucking and kicking, dragging us off round the boundary in clouds of dust. Before too long its hooves have smashed through the boarding at the driver's feet, and he, poor chap, takes a nasty blow on the shin before the beast is finally grabbed and placated.

Howard and I are withdrawn from the scene, much to our relief, and the driver is taken away to be fixed up. He is clearly out of contention for the big game, if he was up for selection, and it occurrs to me in a flash that it could just as easily have been my shin, or Howard's shin . . . They couldn't want to win *that* badly, could they . . . ?

18 FEBRUARY

At one point we are all sitting around, vaguely discussing the Pakistan situation, which is still simmering away. Suddenly two fighters rip across the sky overhead, and once they are out of sight we hear a huge air-shattering, ground-shaking boom. Not a sonic boom, either – more like a ground explosion. Some sort of exercise, presumably . . . ? I bloody hope so, anyway.

Yardley has not yet been called upon to demonstrate his fast bowling, and I still haven't managed to get any practice in. At one point this afternoon, when they were filming on the boundary somewhere, I marked out a run-up and lurched towards the wicket, but the setting guys immediately came running out and told me not to run on the wicket. This is annoying, since the ground is not firm enough to practise on anywhere else, and I begin to wonder what setting are up to. They won't let us use the bats, they won't let me practise my run-up. Could it be they don't want us to get our eyes in until after the big game a week Sunday . . . ? Hmmm . . . (scratches chin thoughtfully . . .)

I'm starting to notice that every conversation I have with an Indian features, at some point or other, a little wobble of the head from side to side, like conversational punctuation. Surely the international language of mime can provide no more confusingly eloquent gesture than the ubiquitous Indian head wobble. Perhaps the Gallic shrug might have its enthusiasts, but the range of expressions that it can convey non-verbally are all usually unhelpful or downright annoying. The head wobble, out here, ranges from a single slight cocking of the head, like a deer hearing a twig break, to a full-on side-to-side vacillation, and, what's more, it is infectious.

It can be used to express almost anything. So far, I am pretty certain I have seen the head wobble mean the following things:

I'm sorry, I don't understand you.

I do understand you but I am pretending not to.

I understand why you are becoming frustrated with me, and I sympathise.

I have made a mistake, I admit it, please leave me alone.

That's right.

That's absolutely right.

You think you are right but I know you are wrong. I'm just not going to say anything.

You are a very amusing fellow.

You clearly imagine that you are a very amusing fellow.

No, I haven't yet done the thing you asked me to do, and I'm sorry.

No, I haven't yet done the thing you asked me to do, and I'm not going to do it either.

Yes, I know where that is.

Yes, I agree the price you suggest.

Yes, I know I agreed the price earlier, but now the price is different, and there's nothing I can do.

The whole thing is out of my hands.

I know, Amin does go on a bit, but what can you do?

Yes, it's free, go ahead and use it.

Thank you, it's very kind of you to say so.

You're welcome.

You're very welcome.

You have my utter contempt, you pale white tea-drinking buffoon.

I wonder whether it might be possible to get two Indian actors to conduct an entire conversation where the two of them just wobble heads at each other, and they each understand perfectly what the other is getting at.

19 FEBRUARY

Yardley is clearly being set up to look a prize booby. North is batting, and Yardley barks to Willis, the bowler:

'Bowl it on the leg side.'

Whereupon North dispatches the ball over square leg for six.

Ray has been suffering quite badly, bent double on the bog all last night, apparently, and halfway through the morning they sent him back to town. He is in the mood for taking any medicine of any kind he can get his hands on. Priya, one of Apu's assistants, is medically trained, and unofficially a kind of unit doctor, so she bunged him some Lomotil. He went to a doctor in town as well, who prescribed him something else with a syringe attached so that he could inject it into his own backside, and he asked Priya to do this for him. I think Ray rather harbours hopes that Priya is unattached and might be on for a little off-screen courtship, but nobody looks their best face down on a bed with their pants round their ankles and a needle sticking out of their arse.

One of the slightly unsettling extras has also offered him something, which I'd think twice about taking if I were him, and as if all that was not bad enough, he's also losing a cap off one of his back teeth and is taking painkillers for that. It's a wonder he doesn't rattle as he walks.

In the early afternoon we revisit the 'bet is set' scene. As before, we are all massed behind Captain Russell as he eyeballs Bhuvan and challenges him to the cricket match.

The sun is right overhead and dazzlingly bright. Ashutosh is shooting towards the British ranks this time, and so he brings in two huge skimmers to reflect the sunlight up into our faces. These are like two huge, brilliant, blinding white sails, creaking on their ropes like the rigging of an old ship.

Because this is such a macho moment, all the Brits need to stare steadily at their Indian opposites, but the sun and the sails are so fantastically dazzling that this is almost impossible.

Captain Russell would embark on a long passage of Hindi, and as soon as he stumbled the whole pack of us behind him would double up, clutching our streaming eyes in agony.

I recall once seeing Michael Caine giving a master-class on movie acting – it was on the telly, I hasten to point out; I'd never actually go to such a thing – to a bunch of aspiring young bucks and madams who hung on his every word. He had their rapt attention, perhaps because they believed that they were only a single pearl of Cockney wisdom away from being as great, as successful and as frankly rich as Caine himself.

At one point Michael said: 'This is the single most important thing I can tell you about movie acting . . .' He paused significantly, pouring all his considerable experience and charisma into holding the pause, giving it the momentous weight it deserved. The hopefuls held their breath, and even I found myself leaning forward slightly in my armchair, wondering whether the secret of how to actually get inside a fictional character's skin, how to truly become another person, was about to be vouchsafed to me.

'Are you ready?' Caine said, and his audience trembled, one or two of them mopping drool from the corners of their mouths. Here it comes . . .

'Don't blink!' Caine suddenly blurted. 'Don't bloody blink! Did you see me then? I didn't blink that whole time. If you blink on-camera people stop believing you. Don't. Bloody. Blink!'

He's right, of course. If you've ever seen Ann Widdecombe explaining some point of Tory policy, you'll have seen her blinking so frequently, and so violently, that her eyes seem to be rolling up into her head, and I can honestly say I've never believed a single word she's said.

Even so, I'd like to see Michael Caine show us how not to blink in that 'bet is set' scene. I reckon I could still see a silhouette of Aamir, bristling with defiance, burned on to my retinas a good couple of hours after we finished shooting it.

———

In the evening Ben and cool Nakul brought some beer from somewhere and we watched England beat France at rugby.

Then upstairs to Amin's, where a slightly more subdued musical get-together was taking place. Apparently there had been some complaints about the Bhujie Nights extravaganza last week from other Sahajanand residents.

Ashutosh sang one of the songs from *Lagaan*, a lament which will come on the night before the last day of the cricket match, when the villagers have lost hope, but gradually discover a new defiant spirit and determine to go down fighting. He gave it a real performance, and one or two of the Indians were quite moved. It made me wonder whether this film is quite as insubstantial and escapist as it first seemed, and maybe our pantomime colonials are a touch on the broad side. We'll see, I suppose . . .

20 FEBRUARY

Everyone should really be preoccupied with the big technical rehearsal for the day of ten thousand extras, and then the day of ten thousand extras itself coming up this week, but actually all the talk is of the match next Sunday.

Aamir and Apu are niggling away, trying to find out my tactics. They particularly want to know who will be opening our bowling, and I am tempted to let them think that Yardley will be doing it, especially as they haven't seen me in action yet. I'm afraid, however, that when they do see me it will give their morale such a boost that it would be a counterproductive move.

Yesterday we scored a little tiny psychological point. Some of the crew were knocking a ball about – completely unmolested by the setting lads, I noticed – and Aamir joined in for a bit of batting practice. All the England lads pointedly turned and looked the other way, saying that we'd no need to see what he could do; whatever it was it wouldn't be good enough. Actually he looks pretty handy, as it happens.

We feel that, when it comes to the big match, the Indians will have the distinct advantage of familiarity with local conditions, and so we are all keen to get some practice in on our day off.

The pitch on the location out in the desert near Kunariya is, as I have said, basically rolled baked mud. While filming the first passages of cricket for the movie there in the past week, we have discovered that the proper cricket ball hardly bounces off this surface at all, and so the balls we have been using out there have been hard rubber balls with a pretend seam moulded on to them – appropriately enough, for me, since I am a pretend seam bowler.

For our actual match, however, we will be using the ball which is in widespread use in casual and street cricket in India. This is known as an MRI ball, and it looks like a deep red tennis ball. It is, though, a bit harder and heavier than a tennis ball, so that a faster bowler can give you a bit of a thump if he gets it right, but it won't be like playing with a cricket ball. The MRI ball is so common in India that if you go into a sports shop to look at cricket equipment, half the bats are for proper cricket balls, and the other half – which are as finished and logoed up as their counterparts – are exclusively for MRI use. My lads are very anxious to have a game with it among ourselves, before taking on Aamir and his team next week, and so, this afternoon, that is what we do.

Sahajanand Tower is built on the outskirts of Bhuj, and much of the land in the area is quite open. There are some houses, and a particularly noisy temple next door, but a lot of what we can see from our balconies is wasteland or empty plots, walled off and overgrown with dense thorn bushes.

A little way off there is a large, open, dusty beige – naturally – square between some quite well-to-do-looking houses. A volleyball net has been strung across the middle of it, but otherwise it is an open communal area and perfect for a knockabout game of cricket, so in the afternoon we head off over there.

Most of the players I am eyeing for selection come along –

Howard, Jon, Ben, Neil, Simon, Barry and, of course, good old 'Hardly' Yardley. Raj comes along as well, so I get a look at at least one of the opposition in action, and Andrew, one of the student extras, who is not in the movie team but can most definitely play for a place in the real team if he shows me any form. Jamie, who would have been the first to grab a bat or ball in the first week, is nowhere to be found – off somewhere with Katkin and Charlotte – and I think he's lost to the boys' gang for good now.

Andrew's ability turns into the main plus point of the afternoon, as he scores fifty and fields like a demon. I pencil him into the line-up just before he takes a good catch to get me out. Ben is a decent bowler, who gets me out with a yorker second time round. He's a bit of a flasher with the bat, though, and I get him out with a yorker myself in return, which isn't something that happens too often. Neil and Barry both acquit themselves well, and will be strong members of the team.

The players I know already from An England XI have mixed fortunes. Ray is indoors with the shits like you wouldn't believe, Jon looks in good nick, but Howard hasn't got his eye in yet and is struggling a bit. Simon – Brooksy – is very keen, but not particularly strong with bat or ball on this showing. He fields like a good 'un, though, and tells us that his nickname at home is 'The Cobra', because of the amount of fielding time he spends on his belly in the dirt.

Worryingly, however, Raj is just about the best player on the day, a big hefty swinger of the bat, and a nastily nippy right-arm-round-the-wicket bowler.

Back to Sahajanand for a televisual feast from back home. ESPN came back on yesterday, much to our relief, and so we all gear ourselves up for Leeds v Manchester United live. Howard and Jon are big Leeds fans, and I had a soft spot for them myself as a boy during the era of Peter 'Thunderboots' Lorimer and Allan 'Sniffer' Clarke. They have been top of the league until they lost to Liverpool a couple of weeks back, and need to win this to stay in touch, so the match is an exciting prospect for a load of British boys thousands of miles from their own time zone.

We all arrange to go up to Jon's apartment, and of course when we get up there ESPN has gone off again, and instead a local channel is showing a ladies' volleyball match between Kerala and Tamil Nadu. For a while we half-heartedly support whichever of these teams seems most likely to win soonest, so it will all be over and the football might come on, but gradually it dawns on us that Kerala and Tamil Nadu are playing out one of the great seesaw classics of Indian ladies' volleyball. Meanwhile, back in England, the top-of-the-table clash has already kicked off, and our optimism begins to drain away.

I go down to the production office, and badger Zaki – the guy in charge of housekeeping – into ringing the local cable company. He finds that the one bloke working there today, Sunday, has switched from ESPN to the ladies' volleyball channel because that's what he himself wants to watch alone in his office, for reasons which my imagination chooses to draw a discreet veil over. I whisper urgently to Zaki: 'Find out what will make him switch over to ESPN,' thinking that if we offer him a bribe, some baksheesh, he will let us have Leeds v Man U.

Zaki chatters away to this cable bloke – I'm imagining he is a fat bloke, careless about personal hygiene – and then covers the receiver and reports to me:

'He will only change over if people ring him up and say they want to see ESPN.'

'But that's what we *are* doing,' I cry in exasperation.

Some more chatter, then: 'He says he doesn't want to, and now he's hung up.'

There seems to be nothing for it but to wait for the volleyball to finish. Back in Jon's apartment, as the biggest football match of the season nears half-time back at Elland Road, we cheer more and more urgently for Kerala, who are a set up, but back come Tamil Nadu, and a deciding set – which would effectively wipe out the whole second half – looks ominously likely.

I go back to the production office, and get Zaki to ring the cable blob again. In my imagination this chap has definitely got food in his straggly beard, some of it two or three days old. Zaki, bless him, berates this big chuff over and over again to no avail, but whoever he is he loves his ladies' volleyball, and I get the impression that he won't be shifted even if the whole of Kutch tries to kick down his door – which may well be happening.

At the height of a spirited row – Zaki and I having decided that there is no mileage in being polite to the guy any more – Aamir comes in to the office. He is clearly amused by my sweating red-faced pop-eyed English impotence, and once he understands our situation he takes the phone. A few gentle words from the town's most celebrated guest, and the fat ladies' volleyball fan has calmed down. Then Aamir hangs up, giving me a sad little shrug and a head wobble, which I take to mean that he has been unable to do anything, sorry.

'Oh well,' I say, 'thanks anyway,' and I trudge back upstairs to report to the others in Jon's room, where . . . the football is on! It seems I have totally misunderstood the head wobble on this occasion. Normally such an eloquent gesture of apologetic powerlessness, this time it seems to have meant: 'There you are, see? Easy, no problem. Now off you go and watch your game.'

There was half an hour to go. Man U were a goal up, through Andy Cole, and that was the final result, after Lee Bowyer somehow scooped a clear chance over the bar from about a foot out.

Later I was still wound up from dealing with the cable company chap and so I went for a walk on my own into Bhuj. On the main road into town I passed a small kiosk selling cigarettes, biscuits and sweets, and I caught sight of some toffees – chocolate éclairs, actually – in a jar. I was feeling fraught and fed up so I decided to get myself some. I pointed at them and the sweet-kiosk man opened the jar, took one out, put the lid back on, put the single sweet on top of it, and languidly held up a finger to indicate one rupee.

Now I don't know how he expected to get on in the world, selling sweets one at a time, but I was used to buying these things by the quarter-pound, so I used the international language of mime to indicate that I wanted a bag, and handed him fifty rupees. That should keep me going for a while, I thought.

His eyes widened when he took in the enormity of what I was asking, and he was suddenly energised and began crashing around in his little kiosk, knocking things over in his eagerness to serve. Family members were dispatched in all directions, looking for paper bags. When none were forthcoming, sweet-kiosk man started making an elaborate little parcel out of newspaper and string, chattering happily all the while. Our transaction complete, I was obliged to have my photograph taken shaking hands with the fellow's eldest son, and while I couldn't understand exactly what was being said, I gathered that the gist of it was:

'Now, thanks to you, I will be able to send this, my eldest son, to university, where he will become a fine doctor!'

Perhaps I do eat too many sweets . . .

Barry is organising a doubles table tennis tournament, drawing the pairs out of a hat with theoretically one weak and one strong player in each. I am drawn out of the weak hat and paired with Adi, who is one of the better players, if not the best. Aamir, who is also a demon, is paired with Charlotte, who is one of the best players in the second hat, and they are the top seeds in one half of the draw, while Adi and I are the top seeds in the other. Should be fun . . .

21 FEBRUARY

Today was the technical rehearsal day for the Day of Ten Thousand Extras, which is coming up tomorrow. Ashutosh wanted to set up some bits of cricket action so that everybody knows exactly what they are supposed to be doing tomorrow when the crowds turn up. As it was only rehearsals, I had a day without sticky-itchy-glue-on-moustache misery – hurrah!

Some shots of Yardley running in to bowl with the huge crowd baying in the background were on the agenda. I did a couple of practice deliveries for Ashutosh, but he was having trouble getting the angle right, wanting the mountain behind – which will be covered with people tomorrow – and my huge great plates pounding the dirt in the foreground. He moved the line of my run-up straighter and straighter each time, and then beyond straight, until I was starting round about mid-on. I then had to pound in, arch behind the umpire's back, and deliver the ball so far past square on that I was facing cover point, effectively pushing it out sideways in an action which resembled nothing so much as a camp man telling another camp man to stop messing about. I felt sure that this must look terrible, but was assured that the magic of the cinema would make all well. I know, though, that using this crazy contorted action I only got one ball to pitch on – or indeed anywhere near – the wicket.

Another thing I had to do, in my role of chief British bully-boy, was to barge Deva, the noble Sikh, into the dirt. He bowls, I dab it for a single, and then I flatten him before he can run me out, is the idea.

Deva, though, is built like a brick shithouse. A charming, friendly bloke, he is strongly reminiscent of the late great Bernard Bresslaw in *Carry On Up the Khyber*, and I seriously doubt whether I could genuinely knock him over if he had a mind to stay on his feet, but still I gamely ran into him and he went down like David Ginola, while I hobbled off, winded, to nurse my dislocated shoulder and three or four broken ribs.

The day also afforded us the opportunity for a further warm-up for the England v India match on Sunday. Ashutosh wanted to suss out some angles, and got us to play a match while he wandered around making that oblong shape with his fingers that directors do.

Raj took charge of an Indian side, and I captained what there was of my first-choice XI. Jamie (Wesson) and Neil (Harrison) were both back in Bhuj, having been excused this rehearsal day because of having been up all night with the shits like you wouldn't believe, and so we were given stand-ins – Hardeep, the unit photographer, and Hamid, one of the crew. Alex (Flynn) was also missing, but his pal Andrew looked like taking his place in the side for the Big One in any case, so that was fine.

Any doubts I had that the Indians were taking this seriously disappeared moments before the start. Naturally Apu and Aamir were 'too busy' to play for Raj's team, but they didn't seem to have so much to do that they couldn't watch and get an idea of our form. Just as we were about to get under way, I found that Howard (Burton) and Barry (Benson) were both immediately required for 'urgent' haircuts, and in their place I was given Javed, one of the extras, and Zak, a hairdresser, who was proposing to play in platform shoes and a maroon velvet jacket with huge lapels. I bet that doesn't happen to Nasser Hussain all that often, even in the warm-up games at the start of the tour.

Raj's team, I couldn't help noticing, was positively bulging with athletic-looking stuntmen and grips. We didn't have much of a chance.

Jon and Andrew made most of the 68 runs we managed off our twelve overs. Our innings was fatally slowed down by the inept waftings of Zak, unfortunately, who teetered around on his glam-rock shoes waving his bat, looking for all the world like Marc Bolan swinging a mike stand, but with less chance of achieving a big hit. In the end I gave him out lbw just to see the back of him. Sometimes the best place for a captain to be to influence a game is in the umpire's coat.

Raj's XI got the runs with an over to spare, chiefly thanks to Nitin, the make-up man who does my moustache every morning, who walloped eighteen off one Brooks over, after clearly being caught behind first ball but not walking. That's cricket on the subcontinent for you. That's cricket on Wandsworth Common, come to think of it.

Late in the day, Kiran and Priya, two of Apu's small, slender, female assistant director's assistants, appeared in the vast army uniforms they will be wearing tomorrow in order to blend in with and manage the large crowd. They looked very funny, like small children who have dressed up in their parents' clothes.

10

The Search for Dusty

BHUVAN
There are six sticks, three this side and three that side.
Two fellows stand with planks before the sticks. One
comes running near the sticks and throws a ball. The
chap with the plank hits the ball hard with the plank and
then everyone runs helter skelter . . . It goes on all day.

(*Lagaan* – English translation)

The performance of Zak yesterday at the Polo Cricket Ground
was a landmark in my cricketing experience. Not only sartori-
ally speaking, and certainly not in terms of its sheer ineptness
– that is a commonplace. No, sharing the field with him
yesterday was the first time I have actually had a genuine
international hairstylist as a team-mate.

Ten years ago, matches between my 'An England XI' and
Arthur Smith's 'Dusty Fleming International Hairstylists XI'
proved a popular social hit, and Arthur and I began arranging
an annual 'Test series' of three or four matches every summer.
We would supplement this with other fixtures for which we
would join forces, and quickly acquired a cricket season of
sorts with all that that entails, and an annual dinner which
has become an end-of-season institution.

This always has a fancy-dress element, aping the antics
of England's cricketers on their overseas tours, when the
only item on the news on Christmas Day would be their
Christmas lunch featuring Allan Lamb and Ian Botham dressed
as pantomime women – something which stood old Beefy in
good stead for a new career once he finished playing. Our

fancy dress has a theme each year, and a prize is given to the best. One year the theme required everyone to dress in the 'most obvious and predictable fancy dress', and the prize was shared by the six people who turned up as Batman.

The dinner event always features speeches and a kind of award ceremony in which notable feats from the season are celebrated. One highly cherished prize each year goes to the fielder who takes the best catch while smoking, and it is rare that this one goes unclaimed. It was taken one year by Chris, a slip fielder whose fag was sent spiralling into the air by the arrival of a fast snick. The ball went to ground, but Chris's sprawling dive managed to rescue the cigarette before it hit the deck. Another fielder, Andy, likes to field at long on, claiming it gives him a chance to light up just in case he happens not to have a fag on the go when the batsman sends a skyer in his direction.

After the annual dinner had been going for a number of years, and the Dusty Fleming International Hairstylists XI had become an established entity, Arthur and I began to wonder idly about Dusty Fleming himself. The adverts which had so captivated Arthur had long since packed in, although I did manage to get hold of a tape of them from an ad agency, and this we showed at the next dinner to great enthusiasm. Also on the tape, as a bonus, were a couple of Dusty Fleming adverts from Brazil and Argentina – truly he is an international hairstylist.

One of these showed Dusty primping a big-haired model in slow motion, with the help of whatever positioning mousse he was advertising across South America at the time. The other showed a girl with hair like a yard of pump-water being transformed by Dusty into a glamourpuss who had to turn sideways to get her huge hairdo out of the front door. And this was extremely fortunate for her, as a sniper was waiting across the road to assassinate her, but as he is armed only with a photo of her with disappointing flat hair he fails to recognise her and doesn't pull the trigger. The advert ends before we find out whether he then shoots Dusty Fleming as he leaves the house with his magic bag of haircare products, but never mind. Both ads had the key feature – the freeze-frame with caption and breathy voice-over saying, this time:

'*Dusty Fleming, cabeleireiro internacional.*'

Exciting though these were (you probably had to be there), we still had plenty of unanswered questions about Dusty Fleming. Was Dusty Fleming his real name? Was he a real international hairstylist, or was he merely a character, an actor pretending to be an international hairstylist? If he was a genuine international hairstylist working in the glamorous film industry, then surely he was American and lived in the States, but if he was an actor pretending to be an American international hairstylist, then maybe he was based in London, and could be persuaded to make a personal appearance at one of our dinners. And in that case, did he play cricket?

I decided, being unemployed and having too much time on my hands, to embark on a Search For Dusty, in the hope of getting him to come and give away a prize or two. I didn't think it would be too hard to track him down. I was mistaken.

First of all I tried the company that made the products that Dusty advertised. I was transferred from switchboard to assistant marketing manager to brand supervisor to switchboard again. I described the Dusty ads over and over again, and nobody could remember a thing about them. It seemed that everyone in charge of the particular sprays and mousses that Dusty favoured had moved on in the years since our international hairstylist dominated the airwaves, and they might now be in the soaps department, or working with shaving foam, or have left the company altogether. Finally someone recalled the name of the ad agency that they used back in the late eighties, and I decided to try there.

The ad agency were not much more use, however. I eventually found one person who vaguely remembered the ads I was talking about – and they weren't just Honest John in front of his car showroom shouting about his bargains, remember, they were huge productions that must have cost an absolute fortune – but no one involved in the making of them was still at the agency, and all their records had been destroyed in a fire, and then a flood.

The New York office of this agency was also unable to help, even though I asked my contact there to check through a directory of industry specialists as if she were trying to decide which international hairstylist to book. International hairstylist was not, it appeared, such an exclusive tag. In fact, most high streets have someone claiming to be an international hairstylist with nothing more than the occasional trip to Torremolinos to justify the soubriquet.

A Perry Mason, say, or a John Steed would have been deeply suspicious of the way in which all information about Dusty seemed to have been oh so conveniently 'lost', and of the fact that anyone who might have been able to help seemed to have 'left the company'. They'd undoubtedly have got their younger, more active sidekicks to break into these organisations late at night to rifle through various filing cabinets and discover an international hair-related conspiracy, or possibly Dusty's corpse hanging up in a closet, a set of curling tongs dangling from his lifeless fingers.

Arthur and I had a different approach. The trail went cold and so we simply gave up. We told everyone in our respective teams that there would be a special VIP guest at the dinner, and then booked a Dusty Fleming lookalike and passed him off as the real thing. The chap we used was a street entertainer, and he had a great night. We gave him a big build-up, and then he made his entrance to a huge standing ovation, which was only increased by the fact that he was on a unicycle. He affected a mid-Atlantic drawl, and swanned around in a big flowery shirt, judging the award for 'best international hairstyle' as if to the manner born. We bunged him a few quid and would certainly have had him back the next year, except we lost the bit of paper with his phone number on.

A good number of the Dustys squad believed that we had actually tracked down the real Dusty Fleming, even though our unicycling look-alike bore only the faintest resemblance to the great man (being a human male with two arms and legs), and so the Search For Dusty seemed to have been brought to a satisfactory conclusion.

A couple of years later, however, I found myself in Los Angeles, watching a pilot being made of an American version of a sitcom I had written. I was there ostensibly to observe how the Americans did things, but really to troll around Hollywood for a few days pretending to be a player. It was in the back of my mind to try and see if anyone had heard of Dusty Fleming while I was out there – after all, if he worked in the movies, where else would he be? – so I mentioned my quest to one of the studio executives supervising the pilot. He looked blankly at me for a moment or two, and then a switch clicked in his head and he assumed that I was trying to pitch something to him. And he liked it, baby!

'Yeah, I can see it now! He's not just a hairstylist, he's an *international* hairstylist! He has his hairdryer in a little swivelling holster on his hip! He's ready, at a moment's notice, to drop everything and fly anywhere in the world . . . to do hair! It's kooky, it's camp – but not *too* camp . . . I like it! Hell, I *love* it! It's *Austin Powers* meets . . . I don't know . . . *Shampoo*!'

The guy was clearly off his head, so, pausing only to sign a $500,000 development deal, I left him to his reverie. (Not really.)

Austin Powers, as it happens, is the brainchild of an An England XI alumnus, Mike Myers. Mike was brought up in this country, and had always fancied a go at cricket, even though his first sporting love is street hockey. I ran into him when he was in London promoting *Wayne's World*, and signed him up for a debut. He turned up in a stretch limousine with black windows and a rather surly chauffeur who sat on a bench by himself a bit farther round the boundary from all of us. Mike had a good eye, and bashed a couple of boundaries before running himself out, and then he took a wicket in the first over he had ever bowled. This conformed perfectly with an immutable law of cricket at our level – that if someone comes on to bowl saying: 'I've genuinely never ever done this before in my whole life . . .', they will, as sure as eggs is eggs, take a wicket. Usually mine.

During breaks in the filming of the sitcom pilot – which didn't get made into a series, by the way – I took the opportunity to ask anyone I could whether they had heard of Dusty Fleming, the international hairstylist. I asked production assistants, make-up artists, other hairstylists, drivers, secretaries and catering people. I scoured industry directories and trade magazines for production crew details without a hint of a lead. I even looked in the Los Angeles telephone directory – a forlorn hope in the town that invented the ex-directory number. I was coming to the conclusion that Dusty Fleming was most likely a fictional entity when, towards the end of my stay, I was having dinner with an old friend. I explained about my thwarted efforts to locate Dusty, expecting the kind of baffled amusement I had been getting from everyone else, when he startled me by saying:

'Dusty Fleming? I know exactly where he is. I drive past his salon every day.'

So much information all at one go. Dusty is real, he has a salon, and it's here . . . I came out of a momentary daze to see my friend jabbing his finger triumphantly at the *Beverly Hills* phone book – 'there you are!'

The next morning I drove down the sunlit boulevards of Beverly Hills hoping to meet the man that Arthur had named a cricket team after some eight years before. I took Mark, the producer of the British version of my sitcom, with me in case I needed someone to take a photo. In exchange I had to take one of him in a Newcastle United shirt emerging shiftily from the public toilet in which George Michael had recently been arrested for public indecency.

We cruised past the chic boutiques and elegant eateries. If Dusty had a salon in this neighbourhood then clearly the people I had been asking about him were simply not rich enough to have heard of him. Suddenly, on a corner, we spotted a discreet little sign in black lettering on a marble-type wall, reading simply: 'Dusty Fleming'. What more needed to be said? Well, 'international hairstylist', I would have thought, but clearly that was felt to be superfluous here in his home-town. The sign was so discreet, in fact, that my friend must have been stuck in traffic at this junction for some considerable time to have noticed the place at all.

I parked and we went into the salon. Potted palms screened the interior from the street, and it was shady and smart inside – at least, as smart as a place can be with pieces of human hair all over the floor. I asked the smiling receptionist whether it might be possible to speak with Dusty Fleming, realising as I did so that I actually had no expectation that he would be on the premises at all. He was, after all, an international hairstylist – he could be anywhere, and was at least as likely to be in Brazil or Berlin as in Beverly Hills. It was, therefore, a stunning surprise when she smiled and said:

'Certainly. That's him right there. Dusty . . . ?'

I turned, and less than six feet away, teasing the hair of a middle-aged Californian matron, was Dusty himself. A little older, the hair a little greyer, but it was unmistakably the same chap who had wrought the big-hair miracle on the girl on the beach being chased by the black helicopter – 'Dusty, you've done it again . . . !'

As Dusty came over, eyebrows raised in polite enquiry, a pair of scissors in hand, I became oppressed by the sheer stupidity of what I was doing there, and broke out in a cold sweat. What he must have thought, poor chap. A strange sweating Englishman turns up in his salon, burbling about cricket – what is cricket, exactly? – telling him that a team which plays a sport he doesn't understand on the other side of the world have decided to name themselves after him because of an advertising campaign he did eight years before.

'This is a gag, isn't it?' he said, more than once, and I got the impression that he was checking Mark out for concealed cameras in case this was some Beadle-type stunt. He came outside with us and had his photo taken next to his sign, and gave us some bottles of Dusty Fleming shampoo – presumably now he has his own brand he doesn't advertise anyone else's. He couldn't chat for very long – there was a lady inside suspended in mid-tease – but I promised to send him a team photo, and he said to call him any time.

Dusty could hardly have been more obliging and friendly. I just walked in off the street, after all, and I could have been a nutjob or a stalker. He'd have been perfectly justified in saying that he was too busy to speak to me, and having me booted out of his shop, but he didn't. I could have learned something from his relaxed attitude. Perhaps if I had I would have let those lads on the beach at Mandvi watch me having a crap.

Later in the year, the ice broken, I called Dusty to invite him over to our annual dinner for the fêting he so richly deserved. He couldn't make it, but he did record some messages into my answer machine which I was then able to relay to the assembled mob. One of these messages was the answer to a quiz which I ran on the night, requiring those Dustys present to guess: 'Who is the most famous person whose hair Dusty Fleming has styled?'

Dusty, it turns out, is the most fantastic name-dropper, and he hummed and hawed for quite a long while over the respective degrees of fame enjoyed by the likes of Claudia Schiffer,

Jane Fonda and his old pal Nick Nolte before narrowing down to a shortlist of two. Both of the pre-Clinton First Ladies – Barbara Bush and Nancy Reagan – used to fly Dusty across the continent to the White House to do their hair at a moment's notice, and so it seems that my friendly studio exec's *Austin Powers* fantasy wasn't too far wide of the mark. I don't think Dusty has a holster for his hairdryer, though.

The best name-drop I have ever heard tripped from Dusty's lips as follows:

DUSTY:
I was cutting the hair of a countryman of yours the other day. Do you know Richie?

ME:
Richie . . . ?

DUSTY:
Oh, you probably know him as Ringo.

There is still a dent in the floor from where that one landed.

There may even be a new runner in the 'Dusty's most famous client' stakes. Recently I was out in Los Angeles again, ostensibly to watch another pilot being made of my sitcom but really to stock up on Dusty Fleming shampoos and conditioners, and went out for a charming dinner with Dusty and his wife Pamela. They had recently been to Rome, and proudly showed me an album of photos of their audience with the Pope. The pictures show Dusty in earnest discussion with the elderly pontiff about a charity that he is involved with, and in one of the shots you can see that Dusty's eyes have flicked to the top of John Paul II's head. The sparse white thatch there is looking woefully unattended, and Dusty is clearly thinking: 'I could really do something with that . . .'

Appropriately enough, years of playing both for and against the team that bears his name have given me many an opportunity for some shameless old name-dropping of my own. I have been caught by Eddie Shoestring and by Jonathan Creek. I have been trapped lbw by Ian Hislop and have bowled Paul Merton. I have smacked Dirty Den's bowling into a small forest and then, sadly, straight into the hands of square leg, and been run out by a bloke off *Emmerdale*.

I have been both caught and bowled by Ainsley Harriott, the enormous and exuberant television chef. He is also an enormous and exuberant fast bowler, whose deliveries are as often as not as wide as his smile. His late-nineties fame has led to appearances on *Test Match Special*, where he has made a habit of referring to Arthur's team as 'The Dusty Springfields', in a touchingly inappropriate tribute to the late be-beehived singer. Sometimes whoever has made the tea can be seen watching Ainsley anxiously, fearing some expert critique, but he always wolfs down his scoff like a good 'un, presumably relieved not to have had to make it himself from a carrier bag full of crap brought in by a member of the public.

All of which sets me up nicely to begin my international cricket career against the Indian star who is Bollywood's number one (although the bloke who cleans our toilets reckons he's a number two, and he should know).

II

A Crowd of Ten Thousand

Sunlight creeps up the cricket pitch. A man pulls a roller over the wicket. Three large tents, two for the British and one for the Royals, have been erected at the pavilion end. Slowly, sounds are heard in the woods, the hills, and every route leading to the ground. Thousands of villagers start accumulating in every possible corner of the field . . .

(*Lagaan* – English translation)

22 FEBRUARY

Up at 4.30 this morning, not because filming was starting earlier than usual, but so that everyone could get to the location before the single track out into the desert became clogged up with the 175 trucks that were bringing villagers and tribesmen extras from all over Kutch.

We breakfast, dress, and stick on our various facial hair, and then go up onto the mountain to wait for the show to start. Sure enough, huge clouds of dust are just visible in the distance in the pale dawn light, and pretty soon truck after truck is climbing the last little slope up to the huge carpark – or desert, to give it its proper name. Each truck must have fifty or sixty people crammed into the back, all standing and clinging on to the side boards or each other.

Every few paces around the boundary and up the mountain, the production had provided large earthenware pots – *matkas* – full of water. These thousands of people are going to have to be outside during the whole of a baking-hot sunny day, and there can be no plastic bottles or tin cans on the set. Apparently there are also cunningly concealed pipes providing running water at various points around the boundary, but they are too cunningly concealed for me to spot them.

As the first few loads disembark, the dusty trail can be seen winding back miles into the desert, back past the *Star Trek* village, each cloud bringing fifty or sixty more people. The moment they are told where the location is, these villagers hare for it, knowing they are the first, wanting to snag the best vantage points for the day. I judge it is time to leave the mountain and its panoramic view of the region, for fear of being trampled underfoot.

A recent addition to the production team is Ronit, who is in charge of security today. He is a good-looking chap with big muscles, who likes to show them off by wearing very small T-shirts. Apparently he has a short and relatively undistinguished career as a Bollywood leading man behind him, and is now for hire as a security and crowd management consultant. Ronit's boys are all costumed up and sprinkled among the throng, who continue to pour in from the hidden truck park, and at least part of their job is to stop the mob from rushing Aamir.

As the morning wears on, and the light reaches the point at which we could start filming, the crowds are still boisterously spilling up onto the mountain and round the boundary, and the word is that many hundreds more are in the log-jam out on the single track. Aamir calls us all – the British team and the Indian team – into a tent for a meeting.

Everything has been planned in minute detail so as to save as much faffing about as possible. We are each given sheets of paper showing where everyone should be fielding to whichever bowler is in action at any given time, and a detailed shot list of what Ashutosh hopes to achieve today. There will be five film cameras in action, picking up as much action with the crowds in the background as possible.

Aamir, with his producer's hat on, starts to talk us through the shots over the excited hubbub of the crowd that have thus far arrived, with hundreds more still streaming over the horizon. The first shot will be a huge aerial long shot of the two teams walking out to the middle, with the massed crowds cheering and waving. We will emerge from the clubhouse pavilion, while Aamir and his Indians will be opposite us in the other pavilion, which is a sort of low-rent thatched bus shelter affair at the foot of the mountain.

The British team will be led out by Colonel Boyer, Captain Russell's superior officer, who is there to see fair play. Or rather, he isn't, because he doesn't fly in until tomorrow, so an extra will be standing in for him. Unfortunately, the extra who most resembles Boyer is weird George.

George is in his fifties, and although born and raised in Bangalore, he insists he is more British than any of us. He likes to refer to 'the Empire' as though it still existed, and several times already I have been called over to an odd conversation with him by somebody or other – Paul, usually, or Howard – who has then melted away, leaving me alone with him for longer than I would like (i.e., anything over about fifteen seconds).

Now, in shot number one, all that weird George, standing in for Colonel Boyer, has to do is lead us out to the middle, toss a coin, shake hands with the two captains, and lead us all off again. Simple.

Aamir moves on to shot number two. George coughs and butts in.

'Now then,' he says. 'This Colonel Boyer?'

'Yes?' says Aamir, all charm.

'What is his spirit?'

'What is his . . . ?'

'Spirit, his *spirit*.'

Aamir is flummoxed for a moment, but then he ventures that the actor who will play Boyer is quite elderly, and walks with a slight stoop. This is not precise enough by half for George, who leaps to his feet, and tries to pin down Boyer's stoop to an exact number of degrees.

'Come, I will show you,' he says, grabbing hold of Bollywood's premium box-office attraction and trying to tug him out into the open where thousands of his fans will be able to see him. Aamir manages to remain out of sight, thankfully, and watches George try out a variety of stooping walks in front of the pavilion.

After a minute or two, Aamir figures he's been polite enough for long enough, and turns to his shot sheet, sharing a raised eyebrow with the rest of us, who have spent more time with weird George than he has.

'OK, shot two . . .' he says, just as George's head reappears through the tent flap.

'Who tosses the coin?' he says, as he regains his seat. 'Does Boyer toss the coin?'

Aamir says that yes, Boyer will toss the coin.

'Who picks up the coin from the ground?' says George. 'I am a senior officer, I would not pick up the coin from the ground.'

Aamir suggests that one of the captains might perhaps . . .

'In fact,' says George, unstoppable now, 'I am an old imperialist. I would not carry a coin.'

Aamir says that perhaps on this occasion . . .

'No, that is not right,' George asserts adamantly. 'It is beneath me to carry a coin. I must have a servant, a coin wallah, to carry the coin. He must then hand me the coin so that I may toss.'

Aamir politely indicates that a servant will not be necessary, but George is off on another tack now.

'What sort of coin is it?'

'The cameras are on top of a mountain a quarter of a mile away, it doesn't matter what sort of . . .'

'What is the year of the coin? Have you made sure to get a coin from the year that is the year of the film?'

By this time the tent is almost equally divided between those who are manfully suppressing open mockery, and those who have lost the will to live. Aamir, though, is, as ever, the very soul of courtesy, and tries to make George's monumentally simple task even simpler, driving through his many objections.

'Russell is to call heads, the umpire will check and say that Russell has won the toss . . .'

'What if the coin lands tails?'

'Never mind. Shake hands with Russell and Bhuvan and wish them all the best . . .'

'I am an old imperialist. I would never shake hands with any damned native. I will incline my head slightly in his direction. Come outside I will show you . . .'

On and on he goes, raising ever more minutely detailed points, until you can almost believe the film is a movie about Colonel Boyer's stand-in, a four-hour epic, in which critics will marvel at the precision of the lead character's stoop and the intricate snobbery of his attitudes to coinage.

Finally we bash on through the rest of the shots. Ben bets me a hundred rupees that George will haul us back to a discussion of shot one before the end of the meeting, which seems hardly fair, but I get it back by betting him in return that we will have to do the shot again because of him, which is similarly easy money.

We shoot the scene mid-morning, the crowd finally subdued and in place, with Apu talking them through what is about to happen over a huge booming radio microphone, his voice bouncing off the hill and thunder-rolling over the desert sands.

On 'Action!' the crowd go crazy, cheering and shouting, and the Indian team step out from their (far) pavilion and stride manfully to the middle, like warriors to combat. At the British pavilion, however, George and his bizarre stoop are still negotiating the steps, and the cricketers are concertinaed up behind him, baulked mid-stride, our noses pressed into the shoulder blades of the man in front. Eventually George's creaking parody of an elderly officer makes it out to the middle at funeral pace, and the whole toss palaver can begin.

George, incredibly, manages to hurl the coin beyond the two lines of cricketers at the first time of asking. The umpire and the two captains mime looking at their feet, and agreeing who will bat first, but it is clear we will have to do it again. The second time George hits me on the ear with the coin. Strangely, I don't notice what denomination or year it is.

When George leads us off, the curious gait he has adopted has deteriorated to the point where it looks as though he has shat himself, and by the time I reach the pavilion I am certain my silently guffawing shoulders have ruined the end of the take. We do the whole thing again, and it is certainly uplifting to walk out onto a cricket arena with ten thousand people cheering and waving you on. This time, funnily enough, Ashutosh decides George should be waiting for us in the middle with the umpire.

The filming went more or less according to plan during the morning. Apu then tipped us the wink that he was about to call 'lunch' so we could get out of the way. With a huge grin on his face, he swaggered into the middle of the field and bellowed something – 'lunch-time', presumably – into his radio mike, and in seconds the crowd evaporated. Thousands of pairs of feet pounded back to the trucks, kicking up a right old dust storm. Fair enough, there was going to be quite a queue at the impromptu canteen, and nobody wanted to be left out.

Bakshi, the catering manager, had dealt with the biblical task – nay, double Bible portions – of feeding the ten thousand by making a huge shitload of curry and rice. No surprises there, I suppose. He attempted to speed up the delivery process by prepacking it all into little brown cardboard boxes, which unfortunately went very soggy, having been kept lukewarm for several hours, and became more or less indistinguishable from the food inside.

Now when Jesus pulled off his little stunt he was working mostly with bread and fish rather than damp cardboard boxes full of curry. Nowhere in the Bible does it say that the five thousand were actually pleased with the food Jesus provided – a load of really small fish sandwiches, presumably. If, however, they'd been as unimpressed as our ten thousand were with their lunch-in-a-box, he'd have found it a bloody sight more difficult picking up followers.

Within maybe nine minutes of Apu calling 'lunch' the whole surrounding area was littered with poor Bakshi's cardboard boxes, his curry hanging from every branch of the nearby thorn bushes. And about fifty yards from the boundary of our beautiful cricket ground, dozens upon dozens of white-dhoti-clad villagers were creating the largest impromptu toilet I've seen outside of a rock festival.

Once Apu started to get people back to their places to resume filming for the afternoon the mood had changed. Our ten thousand people were hot, they were bored, they were unpredictable. They'd come to see Aamir Khan, and it was time to stop this filming nonsense and turn the whole event into a prolonged public appearance, ideally one where each of them could hug him for as long as possible.

Time and time again a section of the crowd would surge forward, trying to reach Aamir, trampling the little boundary fence underfoot, and then brandishing bits of it overhead like trophies. Once onto the outfield, however, they would lose their nerve, and just dance about on the spot, waiting for someone to be bold enough to approach the star, and this hesitation would give Ronit's security men time to rush them, and shove them back off the field. They weren't shy about how they did this, either, whacking the miscreants across the shins with huge clubs, which if anything made them dance even more manically.

No sooner did Ronit's boys get one area under control than there would be another eruption on the other side of the ground. More overexcited locals would spill over the boundary, and more of them would get cracked across the shins before they could get too far.

Aamir rode around on his black horse, partly so everyone could see him, and partly so he could make a getaway if things got out of hand. Nobody wished him harm, of course, but the crowds were becoming unmanageable. Aamir spoke using Apu's big radio mike, hoping to calm things down a bit, and this worked for a while. The problem was the crowd wanted more and more of Aamir speaking to them, and less and less faintly boring filming to watch.

Aamir sang some of one of the hit songs from one of his recent hit movies, to rapturous acclaim, but he found that he quickly exhausted the repertoire of songs he could do unaccompanied, and his fans showed signs of becoming restless again. He rode his horse over to me and shouted above the racket they were making:

'Start a cricket match, quickly, give them something to watch!'

I bustled around, bellowing above the hubbub, organising the British team into some fielding positions. I made sure that nobody was too close to the boundary, in case they were swallowed up by a pitch invasion. Aamir announced to the increasingly frenzied mob that we were about to start a match, and Raj and Guran came out to bat to wild cheering.

It may not exactly have been cricket, but the old adrenalin was certainly pumping. I chucked a ball to Jon and he ran in to bowl.

By this time, Ashutosh had more or less given up on the carefully choreographed cricket routines he had planned for the afternoon, and was contenting himself with picking up crowd reaction shots wherever he could.

Guran, the village wild man in the film, was batting in character, which meant standing face on with the bat between his feet, roaring his head off, and shaking his huge mane of black hair. This technique is all very well in pretend cricket, in fictional film cricket, but once you start playing real cricket like that you're going to come unstuck. In my head I could hear Geoffrey Boycott:

'Now, you see, it's wrong is that, it's the wrong tech-*neek*. He doesn't want to wave his head about shouting, he wants to keep his head still. And cricket is a side-on game, not face-on like he's got it, with the wicket-keeper looking at his backside. That's French cricket, is that. And he wants a haircut, as well, while he's about it . . .'

Imaginary Geoffrey was right, of course, and Guran was bowled second ball, between his legs, and if Brian Johnston had had to commentate on it he'd have been laughing yet. The crowd howled, and I looked around at my team. Everyone was on their toes, everyone was pumped up, and even though everything about the set-up was somehow unreal – pretend pavilion, pretend pitch, an enormous and unruly crowd who hadn't really come to watch us – at the core of the moment we were playing cricket for real.

Raj was facing, and straightaway Jon got a short ball to kick up at him, which he fended off. The ball looped up and dropped six feet in front of him, where I, driven on by the excitement of playing in front of this huge audience, dived forward and caught it one handed just above the deck.

India 0 for 2, and we were momentarily in danger of tipping the crowd's mood from exuberance into ugliness, but then Aamir Khan himself came out to bat to huge excitement, and the audience settled back for an exhibition.

He gave it a full bat-twirling performance, and settled down to face Smith, who was bowling the second over from the mountain end. The crowd noise swelled behind Smith as he ran in, as though he were the away goalie about to take a goal kick. His arm came over, Aamir swished through an elegant cut shot, but the cheer died in ten thousand throats as the off stump crashed back and the hero was bowled.

At this point my team became a little sheepish. We suddenly became aware of the purpose of the exercise, which was to entertain a huge crowd of Aamir's fans in order to quell a riot, and the famous old quote of W.G. Grace sprang to everyone's mind:

'They've come to see me bat, not you bowl.'

Thinking about it, I feel sure that the strange-bearded old doctor added a withering 'sonny', or something, to his famous remark, to make the bowler feel even more insignificant and crushed. I wish he'd had the opportunity to try that one on me. I like to think I'd have replied:

'No, sir, they've come to see you taking your pads off and sitting in a deckchair on the boundary pulling yesterday's bread rolls out of your disgusting thatch, you fat old has-been.'

But you always think of the best thing to say when it's too late, don't you? Like about a hundred and thirty years too late.

Anyway, we all saw the wisdom of giving Aamir a life on this occasion, and resolved not to get him out again. Unfortunately, we couldn't help ourselves, and poor old Aamir was caught again at point and run out before the end of the over.

At this point, with India notionally 1 for 5, the cricket-match to entertain the crowd idea suddenly became a bad idea, and we moved on to the crucial last shot of the day, which would also be the climactic shot of the film.

This sequence was the huge crowd's reaction to the hit by Bhuvan that wins the match. They all have to run on to the pitch, lift Bhuvan above their shoulders and dance for joy. Then the rains will come, bringing an end to the cruel drought which has stricken Champaner, and they dance for joy even more.

It took ages for Apu and Ronit to get the crowds back behind the boundary. Knowing they were going to be allowed to charge across the field, they were like big kids wanting to be first, and kept trying to steal a yard start on their neighbours so that they would be able to see themselves leading the surge when the film came out. The result of this was that while Apu and Ronit's men with sticks and Aamir on his horse drove one section of the crowd back, the other section would be inching across, creeping forward, and the whole exercise would have to begin again, like the painting of the Forth Bridge.

The British cricketers were placed in our fielding positions, under strict instructions to run like hell for the pavilion as soon as we heard the word 'Action!'

Finally the mob, a rippling coiled mass, was persuaded to rein itself in long enough for the camera to be focused, Ashutosh checked that the huge water pipes that would provide the magical downpour from the clear blue sky were ready, and looked around one last time, because we would only get one shot at this.

Out in the middle, Yardley has just bowled the final ball and so is in the middle of the strip. Willis is at slip, and I glance across at him. Behind him the boundary is a heaving, writhing beast on a straining leash. I look down at the crowd's feet, and can see the whole line inching perceptibly forward.

Over by the camera, Ashutosh smiles. He brings the microphone to his lips and says the 'and . . .' which is the prelude to a small pause and then the call of 'Action!'

At 'and . . .', though, the dam breaks, and thousands of Indian movie fans and villagers stampede towards us. Willis comes galloping past me, and the slip position he was occupying has already disappeared under hundreds of bare and sandalled feet. I turn and head for the pavilion, and Howard – Burton, the wicket-keeper – hurtles by me, gloves and pads pumping, like Scooby Doo being chased by an evil museum curator with a false plastic face.

As we reach the pavilion, I glance back and see the huge press of people surrounding Aamir, his black shirt just visible and his bat waving in the sky, and I wonder how on earth he will get out of there alive. Then I spot him standing next to me, and realise that the poor schmuck in the middle of that lot is his stunt double, Ijaz.

Suddenly the water starts up, and in seconds the field is a mudbath, and there are rainbows everywhere you look, some of them seemingly close enough to touch. Ashutosh is smiling contentedly, and I hope he has got something he can use. Essentially we have filmed only the first and last shots of a day into which he had put such meticulous planning, with the rest of his scheme just torn up and thrown out of the window.

Still, it's not every day you get to lead your country in front of ten thousand people, take a catch, and get the opposition 1 for 5. It was real cricket, too, for a few minutes, even if the rain that eventually stopped play was pretend rain.

———

At dinner Aamir was telling us about an occasion in Hyderabad recently, when he was making a public appearance at a theatre. The manager apparently led him through the wrong door by mistake, so that instead of taking him on to the stage, the man led Aamir into the back of the packed auditorium. His fans saw him at once, of course, and surged up to him, much as they had tried to do all day today, which closed the door on Aamir's police protection. Everyone was trying to hug him, or pull him, or touch him, and he said he felt himself being inadvertently half strangled, and all the while he was surrounded by faces smiling at him. He was certain that if the police hadn't got to him as quickly as they did he could have been seriously harmed, even though no one there had anything but the greatest goodwill and admiration for him.

He told us about this scary near-miss with the same unfailing calm and good humour that he showed all day, even with infuriating George. Indian cinema fans are just like big kids, really, he said, and get excited very easily.

It's easy to see why Aamir seems so relaxed within the camaraderie of a closed film production, when you can imagine what it's like for him the moment he sets foot outside anywhere in India. Or in London, apparently. He likes to shop on Oxford Street, but is stopped every few minutes by Bollywood fans, who will more than likely then ring up a dozen others on their mobile phones to say 'He's heading for Harrods' or wherever, and before you know it he's being mobbed again. I hadn't realised he was so well known in the UK, but evidently he does sell-out shows of the songs from his movies at Wembley Arena, and when he appeared live in South Africa last year there were twenty-five thousand fans to meet him at the airport. Whew . . .

Fax from Susan, in which she says that Peter has taken to being 'either a tiger who thinks he's an otter, or an otter who *behaves* like a tiger'.

12
Someone Shows Me the Boundary

YARDLEY
I cannot take it when someone shows me the boundary.

(*Lagaan* – English translation)

23 FEBRUARY

Postscript to the Day of Ten Thousand Extras. Chatted with Apu during a slow part of the day today. He has worked in the USA a fair bit, and was hired for *Lagaan* because of his experience in working with synchronised sound.

Apu said that yesterday's was the largest crowd scene he had ever been involved with. He had previously worked with as many as three thousand extras on a scene in New York for the film *Deep Impact*. The difference, he said, was that they were all educated, and when he told them to smile they smiled. The Indian crowd yesterday were a lot more difficult to handle once they lost interest in watching the filming – which is a dull way to spend a day at the very best of times – partly at least because they were not prepared to take orders from women. This meant that Apu's little gang of female sidekicks, Reema, Kiran and Priya, who were stationed in the crowd in disguise, had a really hard time. Interestingly, this attitude to being bossed by women is also to be found among some of the crew, which must make things a little awkward.

Apu didn't reckon much to *Deep Impact*. I haven't seen it myself, but I can't really say I'm surprised. It conforms perfectly to one of my own crackpot theories about films, which is that any film with a two-word title of this type will, as eggs is eggs, be a crock of shit. Two words is the magic formula, or rather the anti-magic formula. First word an adjective, second word a noun. The noun should if possible be abstract, a concept rather than an object.

I'm tempted to say that once you start you'll think of dozens, but the uncanny fact about titles like these is that they simply refuse to stay in the memory. You've seen loads of them, I assure you, but they conjure up no mental picture of any kind. The eye glides effortlessly past the box on the video shelf, without registering at all, except that the cover will more than likely have a partially bare lady on it as well, as if to distract from or compensate for the sheer unimaginative awfulness of the title.

I think this has come about through American studio executives trying to recreate the surprise appeal – *Surprise Appeal,* that'd be a good one – of *Fatal Attraction* all those years ago. Glenn Close went on to *Jagged Edge,* Michael Douglas to *Basic Instinct,* and ever since we've been bombarded with Adjective Nouns, each more vague and less appealing than the last.

Often in an Adjective Noun it will be impossible to work out what job the main character does, unless they're some kind of policeman. It can have good people in it, but they won't be doing their best work. Arnold Schwarzenegger and his clones are enthusiastic purveyors of this subgenre: *Total Recall, True Lies, Red Scorpion, Universal Soldier* and the like. One of them should just make *Big Chests* and have done with it.

No doubt I'm being grossly unfair to a decent bunch of people doing an honest day's work, but nothing would induce me to sample the likes of *Strategic Command, Supreme Sanction, Active Stealth, Risky Business, Wise Blood* or *Final Analysis.*

One day I'm going to make a film and call it *Adjective Noun.* It will have the brother of someone famous in it and go straight to video.

Apu is not the only one who has worked with Western filmmakers, as it happens. Nakul, the cool sound man, recently made a film with Wim Wenders, no less, and his expertise with synch sound is also a valuable commodity on *Lagaan*. Some of the crew are so used to working on films that will be dubbed later, basically shooting silent films, that they chatter away loudly during shots, which is a bit of a problem. Similarly, actors used to having a director talk them through a scene while they shoot it are getting accustomed to a new way of doing things. Nakul's experiences in Europe and America have made him extremely fluent in English, and especially in swearing, at which he could give troopers the odd lesson.

Anupam, one of the senior Indian actors, was telling me that he did *Little Buddha* with Keanu Reeves, and used the money to buy a tractor, which he now hires out in his home village for 1500R a day.

Today we film Yardley and Burton's big scene. The British officers are playing their friendly match, and Burton, the grizzled wicket-keeper/batsman and occasional bicycle juggler, drives Yardley for four through the covers. He then somewhat ill-advisedly sneers: 'How was that?'

Yardley is incensed by this, and steams in again. This time he bowls a bouncer which hits Burton and flattens him all over his stumps, before crowing 'How was *that*?' in return. The fielders gather round the stricken Burton, and Yardley delivers his big line:

'I cannot take it when someone shows me the boundary!'

There are a few other coughs and farts elsewhere in the script, and I've already been called upon to improvise a few shouts in the field, but this is the only line in which I will be asked to convey any emotion of any kind. I've seen this coming, of course, and have been experimenting with an extravagantly histrionic Bollywood-style delivery, first clenching my fists in front of my face, and then sweeping my hands out to the sides to emphasise how very strongly I feel about someone showing me the boundary. It's difficult, it's only a short line, but I feel I may just be able to force a tear.

Or there's a camp scouser I've been toying with – now there's a phrase I never thought I'd read myself writing. A camp scouse accent, I mean. It makes Yardley quite a jolly character, because your scouser, of course, as he would tell you himself, has a natural sense of humour. Given that Yardley is supposed to be a dangerous fast bowler, I reckon his voice should be more menacing, and I settle for a slightly posh gruff growl, which would be perfectly suited to delivering a line like:

'So, we meet again . . . Doc . . . torrrr!'

For example.

First we filmed Howard unbuckling his cover drive in close-up, to a ball lobbed in from just behind the camera, and he looked very stylish and pleased with himself. Then the camera was pulled right back to film Yardley bowling the ball which leads up to the shot.

You read a lot about pressure in sport. The youngster on his debut, playing in front of a large crowd for the first time. The golfer with a short putt for his first major. The striker, lethal at club level, who can't buy a goal in international football. Or, about every three months or so, the freshly recalled Graeme Hick playing for his place in the Test team.

The pressure on me, as I stood at the end of my thirty-yard run-up waiting to bowl for the first time, was of a different sort. I think I've already made clear that I'm not up to much as a bowler. On the rare occasions when I do bring myself on to bowl, it is usually in the hope that a well-set batsman will be so distracted by laughing that he will make an unexpected error. As for bowling fast – well, I never do it, never have done it, and I should say in my defence here that I actually never said, never pretended for a moment, that I could do it.

I looked around. There was Howard, Johnny Player to the life, tapping his bat in his crease. There was the umpire, his hands clasped behind his back. There were the fielders, some crouching in the slips, others carefully positioned in the shot, ready to walk in with me in the traditional coaching textbook fashion as I ran up to deliver the ball. There was Anil, the cameraman, and his focus puller, ready to be whisked up into the sky on the crane to capture my every stride, and three lads, grips they're called, whose job it is to manhandle the counterweights and whisk them up there.

There was Ashutosh, watching the playback monitor, about to discover that his fearsome fast-bowling spearhead chucked like a girl. There was Apu, microphone in hand, himself a fine fast bowler, of course, checking that everything was in place for the shot. Cool Nakul, headphones on, hunched over his tape decks, and his assistant prepared to capture my footfalls with his long boom mike; Hardeep focusing his stills cameras; the setting guys who've prepared the pitch, and who are coiled to pounce on the cricket equipment as soon as the shot is taken in case we manage to grab a moment's illicit practice.

Away in the pavilion there's all the costume lads, and Pina and Nicole buffing and sprauncing someone for shots yet to come, as well as some production accountants sweltering in their tiny office along with the one miserable bloke who's in charge of the fridge full of free Coke. Any number of sparks connecting and checking cables, and other fellows running around with umbrellas, or water, or cups of a rather odd-tasting salty eggy lime drink.

Behind the hill the catering people and the various bus and Sumo drivers lurked out of sight, and scattered near the boundary a handful of extras in period costume languidly looked on, poised to shove a racy novel or a modern pair of sunglasses out of sight on the shout of 'Action!'

Maybe fifty people, all doing *their* jobs, just waiting for me to do mine.

Apu: 'Quiet everyone . . . we're going to shoot this one. And . . .'

A hush. They're shooting the rehearsal, so I don't even get a dry run.

Anil: 'Rolling . . .'
Nakul: 'Speed . . .'
Ashutosh: 'And . . . action!'

I toss the ball from hand to hand. I scrape my foot on the floor like a bull, which is going to be Yardley's trademark. I begin my run towards the wicket. Out of the corner of my eye I can see the camera rising on the crane, but I block it out, trying to concentrate, trying to do my best impression of a fast bowler's action.

I gather myself at full tilt – it feels like it's going OK – I fix Howard with a menacing glare, left arm leads through – textbook fashion – left leg stamps down, right arm swings over and down and the ball is on its way . . . well! That felt fine! In fact better than fine, it felt like a proper delivery. I got a good follow-through, got a bit of weight behind it, it might not be too bad, now if only Howard can connect with the shot I might get away with it . . .

A nanosecond later I realise that the ball is in fact hurtling head high towards the square leg umpire, who is obliged to sway judiciously out of its path. It then plops down on the sun-baked mud flat outfield and trickles away not quite to the boundary, with one of the stuntmen waddling after it.

A beat.

Ashutosh: 'And . . . cut it. Go again.'

There is an embarrassed and embarrassing silence, broken only by Nakul muttering 'Fuck me . . .' to himself. My antennae seem to be able to pick up the sound of fifty people looking at one another and raising their eyebrows silently.

I smile at everyone. 'Just loosening up,' I say. Actually this is true in more than one sense, as my churning insides decide that now is the moment to make themselves heard, and, like many a bowler on the subcontinent before me, I realise I am going to have to pay very careful attention to my follow-through. It could be a long morning . . .

In the event my bowling radar, such as it is, gradually homes in on the target. Each delivery seems to halve the amount by which the previous one had sailed by on the leg side, until the sixth ball is an almost perfect match to the juicy half-volley on off stump that I am trying for. Howard, startled, misses it altogether, naturally, and it comes within a whisker of bowling him. Remarkably, Ashutosh and Apu are satisfied that this will cut together with the earlier shot, and to my enormous relief they decide to move on. I've only bowled one over, which is much, much less than I feared I would have to, and I think perhaps they realise that I could bowl for the rest of the day without getting as close as we just did, and have come to the conclusion that life is just too short.

––––––––––

Later we had to get a close-up of Yardley's bouncer striking Burton such a fearsome blow that he topples over on to his stumps. The stuntmen, Saleem and Ijaz, took turns lobbing the rubber cricket ball at Howard, but they were both so scared of damaging him that they couldn't bring themselves to throw the ball hard enough for the blow to look convincing.

Howard is a Yorkshireman, with a Yorkshire cricket pedigree. His cricketing uncle once had to pull out of a junior match, years ago, and was replaced by his team's reserve, who was a young Brian Close.

There was a very funny cartoon of Close in *Punch* (I think) during the 1976 West Indies series, when he and John Edrich took such a battering from Andy Roberts, Michael Holding and Wayne Daniel at Old Trafford. Close is shown walking from the field of play, his craggy bald head covered with fresh bruises, and a wag from the crowd shouts: 'Bit rough out there, eh, Brian?' The second frame shows Close turning side on and grunting: 'What?', and you can see a cricket-ball-sized hole clean through his head.

The spirit of Brian Close lived on this morning in the Kutchi desert, as we were treated to the spectacle of Howard

jutting his chest out, thumping it with his fists, and shouting:

'Harder! Come on! You won't hurt me! Harder! Throw it
properly! Come on, you girl . . . !'

Even when Salaam – or maybe Ijaz – accidentally hit him
in the face, Howard egged them on still more, adhering to the
first Yorkshire rule of cricket – 'Never rub', never let 'em see
they've hurt you. Howard is still proud of the fact that he didn't
go down once, long ago, when a fast bowler hit him on the jaw
– none of us has ever had the heart to tell him that actually he
did go down, he just doesn't remember on account of having
been knocked unconscious.

Then I got to do my line – 'I can't take it when someone
shows me the boundary'. After the first run-through Ash came
over and gave me one or two helpful tips.

'About eighty per cent as gruff,' he said, and headed back
to his monitor. Then he turned, a thoughtful expression on
his face, and came back to me.

'Of course,' he said, 'Yardley is mad.'

'Mad?' I said.

'Oh yes. Quite mad.'

I had thought bad tempered, maybe, and a bit mean, but
no. Mad. I dread to think what your average Bollywood actor
would do, given the licence to play a character who is actually
mad. Guran, for example, the village oddball in this, is giving
a massive performance, eyes rolling, hair all over the shop,
arms waving about. And Bhura, the little chicken farmer, is
being played by another highly respected Bolly actor, and as
soon as the camera is rolling he whirls about chattering at the
top of his voice like a little Tasmanian devil.

I tried for a sort of understated Great British dementia, with
eighty per cent gruffness, and it seemed to go OK. The words
didn't seem to mean anything any more, but at least I got them
in the right order, and we moved on.

In the afternoon the three senior English officers arrived,

Colonel Boyer, Major Warren, and Major Cotton. All three exuded an air of veteran nonchalance, having seen it all before on shoots all over the world. They had their working-abroad wardrobe all sorted out – the battered sandals, the Eric Morecambe shorts – and Ben fastened on to them immediately, angling for pearls of theatrical wisdom.

They can teach him a thing or two, as well. David, who is Major Warren, is to be our flatmate back at Sahajanand Tower. He has very dramatic features and a great mane of grey hair, which he ties back, and he looks a bit like a cross between Christopher Lee and My Little Pony. At one point he wandered out of the pavilion in his army costume, languidly amused that no one seemed be bothered to check whether it was all right or not, and ventured:

'Well. It's not exactly *Inspector Morse*, is it . . . ?'

This makes Ben's constant name-dropping look very amateurish indeed. What David's dropped here is basically a line from his CV, disguised as a light-hearted dig at the production. A very classy piece of work. Ben, eager to learn and to better himself, monopolised the newcomers all evening like a little puppy.

24 FEBRUARY

Paul went off to buy beer using Ray's precious alcohol permit. At the off-licence at Hotel Prince the chap looked quizzically at him and said:

'You are Ray?'

'Um, yes . . . ?' Paul said, warily.

'Then who is this Paul Blackthorne?'

Paul was baffled by the man's seeming extrasensory perception, until he realised that he'd signed his own name on the form, the silly arse.

Jeremy, who is Major Cotton, rages around complaining about stuff at the top of his foghorn voice, in complete contrast to David, who is relaxed to an almost superhuman degree. During the morning we heard – well, I should think every goatherd and villager for miles around heard – him going on about a commercial director who had the temerity to ask what he had done.

'What have I done?!' Jeremy had exploded. 'What have *I* done? What have *you* bloody done?!' It turned out the poor chap had just done a commercial for tights.

'Tights! I mean to say! I bloody said to him: "What gives you the bloody right to tell me what to do, eh? Eh?"'

I shouldn't think Jeremy got that particular job.

Three days before the big England–India clash there is an injury scare for the home side. Raj, one of their best players, has injured his back. It is not clear exactly how he has done this, but there are rumours that he, Howard and Anupam were attempting some sort of acrobatic lifting trick, or possibly a human pyramid, on the roof of Sahajanand Tower.

25 FEBRUARY

Day off today.

Once the hottest part of the afternoon was over, I ventured out into Bhuj. I thought it was about time I looked at the town's main – only – tourist attraction, the two palaces of the Maharao of Kutch.

I avoided the dusty main drag into town, walking instead along a road that ran across wasteland on either side. A short way off to the left, there was a squat little temple, very ornately carved but not painted, that seemed to have been abandoned. There was no sign to say what it was, and yet it was a striking building, and I felt my camera reflex twitching. Perhaps a town that was more conscious of, or reliant on, tourism would have made more of this little place.

As I came up towards the Hamirsar Tank, the big lake or reservoir, a young man on a scooter pulled up alongside me and matched his speed to mine. He opened up with the usual conversational gambits – 'What is your name? What is your country?' – and then became quite chatty.

His name was Micky, short for – or just different from, actually – his real name, which was Manan, and he was maybe seventeen or eighteen. Micky works as an offset printer in a small print works in town, and is also, he told me, a journalist and a writer. He edits and publishes his own local magazine, which he describes as 'about Bhuj, literature, and philosophy'.

When I told him that I was going to visit the Maharao's palaces he insisted on parking his scooter and guiding me round, not because he was a tour guide on the make, but just as a hospitable gesture to a visitor to his town. He smiled a shy smile the whole time he was with me, except when he was asking his extremely polite questions. He was interested in what I was doing in Bhuj, and naturally, being a local journalist of sorts, he'd heard of the filming that was going on and was eager for snippets about Aamir and the other Indian actors, some of whom he'd heard of. Of all of them, actually, Micky was most impressed to hear that Ronit, the one-time-actor-now-security-consultant, was in town, being a fan of his brief film career.

Micky took me through the narrow streets of the old town. No need to worry about traffic here, although you could always be nudged aside by a cow sauntering indolently along in search of litter to eat. Nestling amidst the sandy beige buildings, we came across the dazzlingly decorated Swaminarayan temple, a riot of pinks, blues, greens and yellows. It belongs to the Hindu revivalist sect inspired by the guru Swaminarayan, and is home to sadhus who follow the precepts of Vedic study, vegetarianism, chastity and moderation that he laid down. Moderation, that is, in all things except the colours they use to paint the temple with.

Around the corner we found ourselves outside the huge main gates of the palace complex. These gates are extremely solid bits of business, great, thick slabs of wood with huge metal studs all over them. The dark, narrow alleys of the bazaar bustle right up to the entrance, but once through the gates you are instantly in a quiet, open courtyard.

Only a couple of the buildings in the palace complex are open to the public, the Aina Mahal, or old palace, which is now a museum, and the Prag Mahal, which is newer. The other buildings surrounding the courtyard were closed, it seems, principally because they have been allowed to fall into disrepair. Paint and plaster peels and cracks away from the high white walls, and the slatted wooden shutters across the ornately carved window arches are mostly hanging off or missing. Once upon a time it must have been quite a fancy spot, though, and indeed, inside the museum Micky showed me an old black-and-white photograph of a Maharao's parade filling this courtyard with brilliantly decorated elephants and horses, and the palace looking remarkably fine.

The Prag Mahal was built in the 1860s, and is a plain brick building with a vaguely Florentine feel, which sports the clock tower that is Bhuj's only real landmark. There are fine views of Bhuj from the top, apparently. I wouldn't know – by this time it was late afternoon and it was closed.

The Aina Mahal was still open, though, and Micky and I took off our shoes and went in. I had been led to believe, by one of the guidebooks I had read, that this old palace had some spectacular interior features. Certainly the outside is nothing to write home about, not that you could buy a postcard to write home about it on in tourist-free Bhuj for love or money.

One of these, the glorious Hall of Mirrors, a marble apartment covered from floor to ceiling in decorative glasswork, I managed to walk right through without realising what it was. The mirrors are so blackened by age that it looks like a badly tiled suburban bathroom. Similarly the much-vaunted Pleasure Pool, another chamber in which the Maharao was wont to write poetry on a little raised platform while fountains played all around him and dancers and musicians splashed at his feet, had no water in it at all, and so I had to go back and check that I had actually seen it.

What were striking, as well, were the pictures that decorated the walls. There was a twenty-metre-long scroll showing the Maharao Pragmalji celebrating a victory over the Moghuls in the 1850s, but there were also battle scenes from European campaigns, the battles of Iena and Inkerman, scenes from Sebastopol. And while many of the portraits in the picture gallery were of the Maharaos themselves – smoking hookahs, hunting, showing off various finery including pearls actually studded into the painting – there were many more of Europeans, obscure aristocrats like Bessie, Countess of Rochford, and Frederick, King of Prussia.

Clearly the royal Maharaos of Kutch had been great Europhiles, right up to the last incumbent, who died in 1991. His correspondence with Mountbatten had been copied and framed, including a letter of condolence sent to the Queen when the former Viceroy was assassinated in 1979.

At the far end of the Aina Mahal, we came to a huge set of wooden doors, inlaid with the most intricate ivory carving, and these it appears are the artist Ram Singh's masterpiece dating from the early 1700s. Framed alongside them are letters from the Maharao to the British Museum, flatly refusing to consider lending the doors for exhibition in London. Not that much of a Europhile after all, then.

Back outside, Micky led me through the bazaar, which was thriving in the early evening now that the temperature was a little more bearable. Tiny, open-fronted shops offered rolls of brightly coloured cloth, and down one side street there was a silver market, but Micky was hurrying past all this.

He was keen to show me the printing works where his magazine was printed. It was a tiny workshop, with one ancient printing press, which he insisted on demonstrating and explaining in great detail. He introduced me to his workmates, but not in English, so I don't know what he said. I'm fairly sure he told them something about *Lagaan*, however, because they all started to look at me with that shy smile that the Indians seem to use in the presence of actors.

Micky gave me a copy of his Gujarati magazine, which has something of the look of a British football fanzine. He said he wanted to interview Aamir Khan, and I said I didn't think that was likely to happen. He said he would settle for interviewing me, and I said I'd ask whether that would be all right.

Looking at Micky's magazine, with its indecipherable – to me – Gujarati hieroglyphics, it occurred to me that I could say anything I liked, and he could write anything he liked, and nobody would be any the wiser.

Back at Sahajanand, the big cricket match for Sunday has been postponed, amidst dark mutterings that Howard has nobbled Raj on purpose by tricking him into some rooftop gymnastics. The England boys, in our turn, feel that our preparations have been hampered by the setting department, who won't let us so much as hold a bat unless the camera is rolling.

26 FEBRUARY

Day off. I planned to watch some of the Test match between India and South Africa, which is heading for an exciting climax after both teams took it in turns to collapse yesterday. It could be going either way right now, but there is a power cut in the building so there's no way of knowing.

Out for a walk instead – head into Bhuj with Mister Spill-it . . .

We pass a general store – food, rice, household implements – and Howard's eye lights on a bright red bucket full of lavatory brushes. They are quite presentable, as lavatory brushes go, with shiny wooden handles, and he weighs a couple in his hand, thinking they would make a pleasingly unusual addition to his selection of juggling equipment. He picks up a third, and sends all three spiralling through the air, nodding, pleased with their balance and the visual effect.

Suddenly the storekeeper comes running out in a panic.

'What are you doing?' he cries.

'Oh, hallo,' says H brightly. 'I'd like to buy these.'

'For what are you going to use them?'

'Well, I'm going to juggle with them, see . . .'

H begins to lob the brushes in the air again, whereupon the storekeeper darts forward and gathers them to his ample tum.

'No, no, no, this is not what they are for. I cannot sell you them for this. It is not right.'

Howard is flabbergasted. 'Well . . . what does it matter what I want to use them for? All right, look, let's just say I've got three toilets . . .'

But the storekeeper has made up his mind. He juts out his bottom lip, he shakes his head, and he clutches his merchandise close to his chest. It's the brushes I feel sorry for. This was their chance to avoid their horrible destiny and make a bid for a showbiz stardom of sorts, but it wasn't to be. We move on . . .

Later: the power came back on just in time for us to see South Africa win the Test match by four wickets, with the revolting Boucher hitting the winning runs. Disappointing.

Pina had a party on the roof in the evening, and there was plenty of drink on offer. Not much beer, but numerous bottles of rum and whisky. Some of this stuff was bought in Bhuj using the handful of permits we have acquired between us, some was brought in hand luggage from Mumbai by various people who've been home for the weekend, and some was provided by Bakshi's caterers, who've brought it in from Delhi.

I drank quite a lot of rum without getting at all drunk, and then moved on to the whisky, which similarly had no effect on me. I've a feeling that not all of this stuff is what it's cracked up to be. I reckon people are being fobbed off with rum-flavoured beverage – the alcoholic equivalent of Thums Up cola.

27 FEBRUARY
Day off. This was to have been the day of the big match, and a few of us went over to the sandy square with the big volleyball net on it and had a practice game. Actually, the postponement probably suits us. We got another game in with the MRI ball, familiarising ourselves with its bounce on the dusty wicket. Ray and Howard both got a bit of time with the bat in their hands and are starting to get their respective eyes in. I was trying to gee Howard up, as his wicket-keeping has been a bit below par, and naturally he then caught me behind first ball.

We attracted a crowd of Indian boys who wanted to join in. They chattered away at one another and swarmed all over our game. It immediately became apparent that their idea of 'joining in' involved the noisiest one batting, the second-noisiest one bowling, and the middle-aged Englishmen all puffing around fielding for them and marvelling at how naturally talented they all were.

Adi, my table tennis partner, is getting very wound up about the doubles tournament, and made me practise with him this evening. He was telling me, along the way, that Bhuj is reckoned quite a wealthy town by Indian standards. Gujarat is a wealthy state, in fact, thanks to its production of wool and cotton, and Ahmadabad, where Adi's family lives, is nicknamed the 'Manchester of India' – I presume from this that it rains all the time and people from all over India support its football team.

Bhuj entrepreneurs own property all over the place, including large sections of Mumbai, and one of the reasons why there are so few beggars in the town is that the locals are notoriously tight fisted and money conscious.

Spoke to John at dinner, the third of the senior Brits who arrived the other day, who is Colonel Boyer. He has

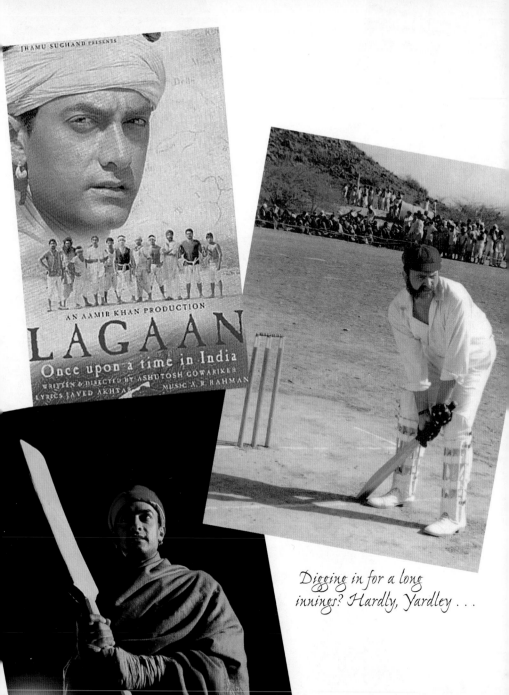

Digging in for a long innings? Hardly, Yardley . . .

He-e-ere's Bhuvan . . .

Bhuj

Main street: rush hour.

Even the sliced bread here is charming.

Jamie tries roadside batmaker's equipment for size.

Bhuj's cinema, showing A. Khan in Mela.

Mr Spill-it with bike, not bent (yet).

Tuc-tuc on Station Road.

Local kids show their enthusiasm for Howard's act.

(above) Three Bhuj landmarks: AinaMahal, PragMahal, and Bhajanand Tower.

(below) Location, location, location . . . Vijay Vilas palace, the pavilion at the PCG, and Champaner, the Star Trek village.

Gappy helps me aboard my co-star.

The picture I took of Howard taking a picture of Paul taking a picture of an elephant taking a dump.

Hooray, hooray, it's Holi, Holi day . . .

Another victim of the Yardley beamer bites the dust.

Ben models the full English kit –
cane pads, wraparound gloves, small
sneery moustache . . .

. . . and sling.

Simon and Barry have
been playing cricket long
enough not to get caught
out by a shower, even in
the middle of a desert.

Three blokes
with Cokes –
Ash, Aamir
and Anil.

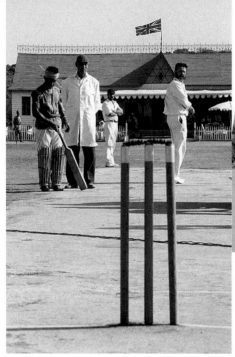

Some of the ten thousand
extras waiting patiently . . .

Yardley prepares to bowl
again, unperturbed by
the fact that there is no
batsman, and that the
non-striker and umpire
are standing halfway
down the track.

. . . celebratin
Yardley fails to cut off
boundary . . .

. . . and mobbing Aamir
stunt double, while the m
himself watches from on
horseback.

Shots from the Big
Match at the PCG.

Twister stops play.

Danger man: Apu.

e: Brooksy scoring.

Jamie and Jon after their whirlwind
partnership.

Jon celebrates, Grand Prix-
style, at the end of the Big
Match.

(top) The England and India teams in front of the PCG pavilion after the Big Match.

(right) Needs no introduction. He comes with his own caption.

Dusty Fleming
International Hairst

(bottom) The British XI from Lagaan. Back row: Benson, Flynn, Wesson, North, Yardley, Russell (Capt). Front row: Harrison, Brooks, Willis, Burton, Smith. Note authentic nineteenth-century moulded plastic chairs.

arrived with a little project, having developed an interest in a clergyman called Gray, who was resident in Bhuj from 1826 to 1830. John stumbled upon a reference to him quite by accident while researching for another production altogether, one about Earl Grey, of the unpleasant perfumed tea fame. He has been reading letters in the British Library which date back to a time when there was a British presence here in Bhuj, in a cantonment outside the town.

From the roof of Sahajanand Tower you can get a good view of where this cantonment was once located. There is a hill outside the town, with a small fort on top, and a fortified wall running along a ridge and partly circling Bhuj. The fort looks like it might be worth a trip. You'd certainly get a fine view of Kutch from up there, but for that very reason visitors are denied access to the place. The military are very jumpy, being so close to Pakistan, and panoramic photography is forbidden here, although how such a ban could be enforced is difficult to imagine. I'd certainly taken loads of pictures across Bhuj from the roof of our building before hearing that it wasn't allowed.

John had discovered how the British had established a foothold in Kutch in the early part of the last century – or the last but one, depending on how you count them. It was a time when Kutch was ruled by a Maharao who was barking mad, and the British helped him fight off an uprising by local tribesmen, who quite reasonably wanted someone sane to take over, and then unseated him and established a regency over his ten-year-old successor. Another glorious chapter in British military history.

A couple of rumours are flying around. One is that *Lagaan* is the most expensive Bollywood feature ever made. Another concerns the script. Ashutosh and Aamir have locked themselves away for the last couple of days, and apparently the word is that the two-innings cricket match in the film is becoming a one-innings game.

28 FEBRUARY

In to the location today but not used and sent home again early. A new date has been set for the proper match – next Monday, 6 March. We played some more cricket on the volleyball pitch when we got back, and I hit some big shots, feeling in good nick. Bring them on . . .

The majors have been conspicuously absent from the Sahajanand dining room over the past couple of days, and we have now found out why. I am heartily fed up with the food now, after four and a bit weeks here, and would love to just have some chips or a pizza or something instead of the dodgy-looking mutton and chicken that Bakshi's boys are always serving up.

David and Jeremy lost patience much more quickly than the rest of us, and headed out into the town to sample the local restaurants. The range is very small indeed, actually, as Bhuj is just not set up for tourists at all. The Hotel Prince, Bhuj's top establishment, has a restaurant/dining room, but reports have not been great from there, and other than that there is hardly anything open in the evening at all. The majors, however, have stumbled across a café not far away, on one of the roads out of town to the South, and they have rather smugly adopted the place and have christened it 'The Ivy'.

29 FEBRUARY

The hottest day so far. The British cricketers had to stand around in the desert in these thick woollen maroon cricket blazers, and we were fortunate that nobody passed out.

Paul is getting a bit anxious, given that much of the filming over the next few days is going to be of him, Captain Russell, scoring a big century. He confided in me today that when he'd been auditioned, back in London, Ashutosh and Aamir had asked him whether he could play cricket, and he'd airily said: 'Of course, everyone knows how to play cricket.'

At lunch-time today we grabbed a bat and ball and I started

giving him a bit of coaching. He's not much of a player, really, but we may need him when it comes to playing the real match, given our limited options, and so it was good to see him start to middle a few as we warmed up. I got his bat coming through reasonably straight by suggesting he started with it at the top of his backlift, and reminding him every ball to lead with his elbow. After about half an hour he was starting to look the part, and his apprehension was making way for a little self-belief. And then Aamir came over.

'No, no, no,' he said, 'don't stand like that, don't hold the bat up there. Look, here, give it to me . . .'

In half a minute he'd completely dismantled Paul's embryonic technique and his confidence and the lad was back at square one. Maybe even square nought.

I suppose it's fanciful to suppose that Aamir might be so keen to win our cricket match that he'd be prepared to undermine one of my team in this way, to the possible detriment of the film we're all supposed to be working on. Or is it . . . ?

And is it equally fanciful to suppose that Apu might be trying to pay us back for 'nobbling' Raj – as they see it – when he took over the bowling himself during the filming of a scene today in which Smith was opening the batting for the British team, and struck him a painful blow on the foot which had him hobbling for the rest of the day?

13
The Big Rewrite

Wesson scrutinises the home-made pads – 'godhadees' –
and gloves.

WESSON
Look at these works of art!

(*Lagaan* – English translation)

29 FEBRUARY (STILL)

Back in Bhuj a craft festival has begun, coinciding with the full moon of Shivaratri. It is known as Rann Utsav, or the desert festival, and lots of local craftsmen have set up stalls on the Jubli cricket ground down the road. I wandered down there late in the afternoon, and it was the first time I'd seen the place, night or day, without a cricket match taking place on it.

Many of the stalls that had appeared overnight were displaying the leather embroidery that is seen everywhere, particularly framing wall mirrors. The leather items all have a pale beige colour, which comes from a process in which the hide is soaked in water, lime and latex in earthen pots underground. This seems a lot of trouble to go to when everything else here has become beige just by being outdoors for a little while. The motifs are carved into the leather in repeating patterns – fish, diamonds, peacock feathers – and embroidered with brightly coloured threads. I bought a mirror, and the old chap who had fashioned it got very excited about the idea of selling me some of his special embroidered shoes, until he caught sight of my enormous plates of meat. He muttered something to his companion, which I gathered was something along the lines of:

'It would take me and my nine sons several months to make even one shoe for such a huge slab-footed giant.' Something like that.

Other stalls were showing off some very intricate embroidered cloth, items ranging from small hats to enormous wall hangings with great bold designs which someone must have been embroidering since the last Rann Utsav.

These Kutchi craftsmen may be very skilled in the old ways, but they are some of the most inept salesmen I have come across on my travels anywhere in the world. I would wander up to a stall, and pause to look at, say, a gaudy little camel, made from prettily embroidered cloth padded until it was quite solid, with a dopey little face and tassels everywhere, and I'd be thinking: 'Maybe Peter and Johnny would like one of these as a present . . .'

Suddenly the artist would leap to his feet, grab something else, and shove it in between my face and the thing I'm actually considering buying, shouting: 'Elephant! Elephant!' at the top of his voice. The crucial and baffling point – and the reason why they all really need to go on some sort of motivational sales weekend, perhaps in Loughborough or Dorking, to have the basics of the whole selling game spelled out to them – being that the elephant, or whatever else they were pushing, was invariably a cheaper item than the one I was casually looking at in the first place.

Some friends of mine got married eight years ago today, so this is their second wedding anniversary.

I MARCH
We are well into filming the cricket sequences now, but the British opening pair of Burton and Smith have not been separated until today. For the rest of us this has meant hours of sitting round watching Howard and Ben batting. Their partnership comes to an abrupt end today, however, in dramatic circumstances.

Smith has to hit the ball to square leg, set off for a run, be sent back by Burton, and get run out by the wicket-keeper, Ishwar, who is keeping in some delightful home-made wicket-keeping gloves that look like two brightly coloured tea cosies and pads – 'godhadees' – which resemble the backs of a pair of cane chairs.

Ash shouts 'Action!', Smith duly tips the ball round the corner, sets off, gets sent back, and dives full length in a despairing attempt to make his ground. The crowd of about a thousand – who are clustered together in the background pretending to be part of a much larger crowd, now that we don't have the ten thousand any more, thank goodness – make a hell of a racket, and Ishwar and his team-mates go absolutely mental, in an extravagant display of celebrating in which each of them seems to be trying to outdo the next man.

Everyone is making so much noise that no one notices that poor old Ben is screaming in agony. He has dislocated his left shoulder, jarring the bat on the ground as he runs it into the crease, and knocking his arm out of the joint backwards.

This take seems to be going on for ever, no one has shouted 'Cut!', and through a cloud of pain Ben realises that it must be a good take, and moreover that he will not be able to do it again, so he rolls all his weight on to his shoulder and pops the arm bone back into the socket. He then picks himself up, hauls himself out of the shot, and collapses in a heap on the ground, which is when everyone else realises that something is wrong.

Later Ben sits in the shade in front of the pavilion with his left arm in a sling, and a huge beaming grin on his face. I can't quite work this out at first, but it dawns on me that after weeks of name-dropping away like a champion, trying to establish the smallest possible number of degrees of separation between himself and anyone who comes up in conversation, hungrily hoovering up everyone else's theatrical anecdotes, he now has an authentic 'What an old trouper' theatrical anecdote of his own.

Sitting here, with everyone making a fuss of him, he can probably see many ways of working this incident into future conversations – anything about sporting injuries, for example, a hugely common topic among men of our age and only likely to get more common the older we get, or anything about mishaps during filming or onstage. He will be able to smile a brave smile, and wheel out his own bona fide theatrical anecdote, one moreover beginning with the exotic phrase: 'When I was filming out in India . . .'

From the grin on his face it seems that this is almost worth the pain – he'll be able to dine out on this one indefinitely. He could start right away if only there was anywhere in Bhuj to dine out.

Which of course there is.

There's 'The Ivy', the little café so proudly patronised by its discoverers, the Majors Cotton and Warren. This evening some more of us finally reach the end of our tether with the Sahajanand catering, and take ourselves off there, to find the senior Brits holding court on the pavement outside the establishment at one of the white-moulded plastic tables arranged there, which are, of course, the internationally acknowledged indicators of high-class cuisine.

The attraction of the menu here is that it includes things – not many, but one or two – that are not served with rice and are not some sort of curry. I try a pizza and a plate of chips, and it is a welcome break from what I've been eating for the last four weeks. Where the unit caterers like to spice everything very powerfully, so that often my throat feels raw and burnt, the chef here at 'The Ivy' seems to like to douse everything in ordinary table pepper. So I have a peppery pizza with a side order of peppery chips, an acquired taste which I don't think I shall be acquiring. Still, it makes a change.

On the way back we pass the craft fair, and the whole of Bhuj seems to be crammed into the Jubli. We look in for a nose around, and Paul's attention is caught by a photographic exhibition. He himself has exhibited his own photos back home, and has half a plan to show the photos he is taking here when we get home. He has brought at least seventy rolls of film and a number of cameras with him, and has been spotted taking pictures of an elephant having a crap, so he must be an artist. Howard, who took a picture of Paul taking a picture of an elephant having a crap, and I, who took a picture of Howard taking a picture of Paul taking a picture of an elephant having a crap, are merely humorists.

The pictures on show at the Jubli are mostly black-and-white prints of Kutchi buildings, the sort of thing which a proper photographer like Paul will look at and say things like: 'Wow! Just look at his use of light, and the fantastic way the cloud counterpoints the façade in the composition . . .' while I shrug gormlessly and say things like: 'Oh yeah . . . ?' and 'Look, a camel'.

Paul causes quite a stir by being so much taller than everyone else. He must be six foot two or three, I suppose, but to the locals he is practically a circus attraction. One of them plucks up the courage to ask:

'Where do you get your height from?'

And there's no answer to that, really, without a short treatise on the basics of genetics. A little later on Paul and I are looking at one of the stalls which is displaying some huge embroidered bedspreads, when the crowd suddenly becomes a little claustrophobic, and I look round to see if there is a quieter area to head for. The main press of people, oddly, is just around Paul, who is pottering around blithely oblivious to the commotion, and I see that what they've done is this. Someone has gone to find the current holder of the title 'tallest man in town', and they are trying to sneak him up back to back with Paul, without Paul knowing, to see who is the taller (Paul is).

2 MARCH

Today, during a break in the filming, Aamir had a couple of visitors who were treated like royalty. It turned out they actually were like royalty, if not royalty exactly. At the weekend there will be some filming at the Prag Mahal in town, which is serving as the British headquarters, and this is owned by the family of the former Maharao of Kutch. The heir no longer has the title, but he has the palaces, and he and his brother had condescended to pay the production a visit at our desert location.

These two portly middle-aged chaps arrived in the middle of the afternoon. They didn't look particularly regal, at first sight. They were wearing, not ancient traditional Kutchi finery, but ghastly, garish, loud chequered jackets and cream-coloured golfing slacks which rode up their legs to reveal vast expanses of calf and paisley sockage. Both had huge grins on their faces and big cameras slung around their necks, and they looked like nothing so much as a pair of lost American tourists.

'Say, buddy, can you tell me the way to the Tarj May-hal?'

The Indian stars were reverently introduced to these smiley gentlemen – they weren't interested in meeting any of us, apparently – and afternoon tea was served out there in the middle of the desert, on proper fine china with little cucumber sandwiches with the crusts cut off, under two enormous Coca-Cola umbrellas.

Even from a distance, we could tell that Aamir was treating these gentlemen with the utmost charm and politeness, but as we made our way to the bus to go back into town he flashed us a glance which eloquently said: 'Man, I wish I was going with you . . .'

Later, at Sahajanand Tower, I was making my way across the landing to the stairs when the lift doors flew open, and there was Jeremy, steaming with rage and frustration.

'This fucking lift!' he shouted. 'I've been trying to make it go down for ten minutes! I've been up to the fucking roof twice!'

He punched the buttons – all the buttons, by the look of it – and the doors slammed shut again. As I walked down the stairs I could hear him arriving at the roof again.

'Oh, for fuck's sake!'

3 MARCH

The match has been postponed again to give Ben a chance to recover. He reckons he'll be able to bowl again in a couple of weeks, as it wasn't his bowling arm that he damaged, but whether he'll be able to bat or not remains to be seen. If he can't, this will be a big blow for our chances, as he has looked one of our better batsmen.

Apu was taunting us today, saying that we are running scared. This seems a bit rich, since I basically only have eleven players to choose from, whereas they postponed the game when Raj was injured and they have something like 150 people eager to take his place. In fact we heard a rumour that Aamir has actually picked his team and Raj isn't even in it. Apu seems a bit cheesed off, since Adi has also been left out while Sanjay and Lakha – whom he doesn't rate too highly – are in.

Meanwhile, at work, we've been filming the cricket sequences for several days now, and it is becoming clear that if we're not careful we are going to run out of time.

Ashutosh and Aamir have been closeted away in secret again, and there are rumours that the script is being heftily rewritten. The four-day, two-innings clash may be reduced to a one-innings contest, which would take place over three fictional days. Personally, I am a little sad to see the back of the two-innings match – it's one for the purist, perhaps – but there's no denying that the reduction will make dramatic and practical sense. And while the five-day Test match is still very popular and revered here in India, one-day cricket is king.

There has been some speculation among the British cricketers about what the rewrite might mean. Captain Russell, Smith and Burton already have runs in the bank, as it were, but maybe Ashutosh and Aamir will make changes that accommodate what they've seen of our prowess so far. Surely Flynn is going to be out for a duck, for a start off. Just thinking of the time they've already spent trying to nudge the non-playing Captain Russell up to a decent score – if Flynn has to get into double figures we could still be here at Christmas.

I am secretly concerned that Yardley's bowling has not been impressive, and he may find that one of the others – Harrison, say, or North – has been considered a better bet to deliver that crucial dramatic last over . . .

4 MARCH

Today the shoot was split in two. Unit one went to the Prag Mahal, while unit two came back to the cricket ground to spend the day picking up some general action shots.

The production had negotiated with the heir to the Maharao of Kutch to film both inside the palace and outside it in the courtyard – some atmospheric shots of characters arriving on horseback, and the Indian cricket team being marched through under arrest on their way to jail. When they got there this morning it turned out that the courtyard didn't actually belong to the heir to the Maharao of Kutch, even though he'd given permission for the production to film there. It belonged to his brother, and this fellow was utterly unshakable in his determination not to allow filming to take place on his property. This meant that no filming could take place inside the palace either, because the plan was to set up all the equipment in the courtyard, and this was now forbidden.

At first it seemed that the brothers had a volatile relationship, and had fallen out after a row about which of them had been treated most deferentially on their visit to the set a couple of days ago. As the day wore on, however, and diplomatic efforts were still coming to nothing, the suspicion grew that they had been impressed by the scale of the production, and cooked up this whole situation in order to screw more money from us. By the end of the day it was in the hands of various lawyers, and we all have a day off tomorrow.

Aamir directed the second unit, which had a much more productive day. Aamir has been in films all his life, and turned out to be a very fast and effective director, confident of exactly what he wants to get and able to explain things clearly and quickly.

Mostly it was action shots of the British team fielding, which positively rattled into the can. Aamir sweet-talked a crowd of around a thousand adoring fans into co-operating by promising to sing for them at the end of the day, which he did.

Lakshmi, the elephant, was sweltering on the boundary with all her finery and Puran Singh's howdah on her back, and one of the bits of business we shot today involved the cricket ball being hit for four and coming to rest between her feet. Yardley – the mug – then has to crawl around under the beast trying to retrieve the cherry, to as much humorous effect as he can muster.

I was assured that the creature was completely docile, but several hundredweight of elephant flesh falling on you by accident is still going to hurt, and moreover I was crawling around where she couldn't see me – much as, oh, I don't know, a predator might do just before trying to kill her, for example.

The cameras rolled, and Aamir threw the ball at the elephant. Well, the hot sun, the paraphernalia, someone hurling a hard wooden ball at you for no readily understandable reason . . . that's got to be annoying, hasn't it? And then a pasty white figure with ludicrous sideburns comes galloping over and starts fiddling about by your undercarriage – I mean, you'd be pissed off, wouldn't you?

Down beneath the elephant my hand closed on the ball. There was a snort from the end of the trunk, which was waving in my face and seemed to be trying to work out what I was up to down there. The beast shifted its not inconsiderable weight overhead, making a noise like a small earthquake, and grunted what sounded to me like really quite an angry grunt. I scrambled the hell out of there.

Fortunately, Yardley scooting out from under like a startled rat was exactly what the script called for, so that was that. The elephant man – that is to say the man in charge of the elephant, not John Merrick – came over and said: 'See? She is very good, very gentle . . .' Hmm . . .

Just then, Goli wandered over to have his photograph taken with the elephant in all her finery. He stood alongside her huge head, and patted her in a familiar fashion.

Well, she'd had too much, and suddenly swung her great trunk and smacked poor Goli a fearsome thump, which sent him flying bodily through the air. He landed on his arse in a cloud of dust about ten feet away with a surprised look on his face.

Lakshmi, meanwhile, was eyeing the rest of us, as if to say: 'Yeah? You want to make something of it? Come on, then, I'll take the lot of you . . .'

It was a religious day today – Shivkati, I think it's called – which meant no meat. No change for me – I've been a de facto vegetarian for days now, not fancying the suspicious-looking mutton or the 'hen necks', which have been the meat option.

In any case, those of us who went to 'The Ivy' last night have been feeling decidedly iffy today. I blame the icecream. Ray was again violently ill, and didn't even make it to the shoot. He was taken to the hospital in Bhuj and injected in the arse twice and then again in the arm – presumably the last of those was a clerical error of some kind. He then spent the evening on an intravenous drip, and the time has come to rechristen that café, I reckon. 'The I.V.' it is, then, from now on.

If these lads are anything to go by, and I think they probably are, Bollywood film-makers have an entertainingly cavalier attitude towards continuity. The maharaj in *Lagaan,* Puran Singh, is being played by the venerable Bolly actor K. Kharbanda, veteran of many dozens of epics over the years. He is so much in demand that he has lost count of how many films he is currently working on, and is the only player in the movie to boast a personal assistant, a lean young chap in a leather jacket who trots around fetching him cups of water.

Lagaan only has the use of him for a couple of days – he's kind of like a Bolly Brando – but the story requires him to watch the entire cricket match, which is taking five weeks to shoot. He has a stand-in, but the positioning of this chap has been erratic to say the least. Mostly they stick him behind a pillar, in the worst kind of restricted-view seat imaginable, so no one can tell he's a stand-in, but they can't do that with the genuine Kharbanda, of course. The result will be that Puran Singh will appear to bounce around the front of the pavilion like Zebedee out of *The Magic Roundabout.* Whenever we see new evidence that this has occurred, the Brits have taken to singing a little football-type chant among ourselves:

'He's here, he's there, he's every fucking where, Puran Singh, Puran Singh . . .'

The prime continuity moment, the one which I'm going to be looking out for, and maybe writing a letter under an assumed name to Indian *Points of View* about, concerns a shot of Captain Russell hitting a crucial show-off six during the practice match which the Brits play among themselves. This big hit was covered from three different angles. In the first Smith is the non-striking batsman, in the second he is fielding at first slip, and in the third he is leading the applause in the pavilion. Corking.

Some fun and games with the umpires, Umpire Roy and

Umpire Noel, today. Umpire Roy, a splendid chap who sailed in minesweepers during the war, looks every inch the first-class umpire until he actually has to signal something. Then we find that his grasp of the appropriate gestures is shaky, to say the least.

Wesson (Jamie) was batting. He hit a four; Roy gave four byes. Wesson hit a six; Roy gave him out. Wesson was out; Roy snapped into a rather alarming Nazi salute. Not his fault, entirely, of course, but with this sort of preparation it's hardly surprising that rumours are starting to circulate about the filming falling behind schedule . . .

The big rewrite is in. The British team get away to a very healthy start, with runs for all the top five. Captain Russell gets 128, for heaven's sake, and Smith, Burton, Brooks and Wesson all contribute.

Then there is a big collapse. North, Flynn, Benson, Harrison, Willis and Yardley manage just one scoring shot between them, a six by Harrison. Flynn bags a first-ball duck, which is fair enough. So does North, though, which seems a shame, since he has been in tremendous form with the bat out here. And so does Yardley.

I am desperately disappointed by this, and am beginning to feel I have been brought out here under false pretences. I showed in the match at Paddington last September that I could bat and couldn't really bowl. Now here I am on the other side of the world for ten weeks, ostensibly as a cricketer, and I'm going to face one ball and I'm not going to be allowed to hit it.

At least Yardley's role as the main strike weapon has not been diminished – if anything it has increased slightly – which won't help their chances of speeding up the filming any more than Captain Russell's century will. Hey ho . . .

Chatting to Benson on the bus – he is terribly fed up. Actors sign up to 'play as cast', I suppose, and if they find their part is altered from what they were expecting then that is part of the territory. Benson, though, isn't an actor, really (although he's doing perfectly well), he's a cricketer and a lifelong enthusiast of the great game. He has been enticed out to India by the prospect of appearing in a film about cricket, and now he has discovered that he has come all this way to be out for a duck

5 MARCH

All greatly amused by Brooks's impression of Major Cotton yesterday at the Prag Mahal. The two zany brothers backed down in the face of threatened litigators from Bombay, and so filming took place at the nineteenth-century palace which was being used as the British Army's headquarters. A day had been lost, though, and so scenes were being cut or relocated as they went along. In the midst of this panic, Cotton throws a classic thespy tantrum at the state of the toilet:

'It's just a hole in the ground, lovey, covered in shit. This is absolutely unacceptable . . .'

Despite the fact that everyone is really up against it to get two days' work done in one day, he insists on being driven back to his apartment on the other side of Bhuj, 'and if they lose an hour's filming because I want a crap, lovey, then that's their lookout'.

This morning a few of us joined a group of our Indian friends in Lakha's room for a gathering which was billed as a prayer meeting but which turned out to be another right old singsong. The reason for the event was to celebrate the birthday of Shiva, which they were doing in a very idiosyncratic way. The group mainly consisted of those members of the Indian cricket team who I think of as perhaps somewhat less anglicised than those like Raj, Adi and Aamir himself, with whom I have probably been spending more time – Lakha, Bhura, Ishwar, Akhilendra, Anupam, Mr Gupta and Gopal.

In the absence of any formal religious artefacts, they had constructed a shrine of their own with a cluster of little items.

A bag of soil represented mortality, and the rest they described as 'things that make us happy' – a bottle of rum, a joint, some sweets, and the ace of spades, which signified both that Shiva is the one god, and that playing cards makes them happy.

Bhura, the little Tasmanian Devil, played the squeeze-box while everyone sang, and the atmosphere was very friendly and inclusive. I thought to myself that if I was ever going to get religion, then one that glorified a bottle of rum, a joint, sweets and games of cards would certainly be one that I would consider very carefully.

Downstairs to the dining room for a meeting with Aamir, who had his producer hat on. He was preparing the ground for us to extend our stay, since the cricket match is taking so long to film.

The only one of us who is desperate to get back is Harrison, who is going straight into another job. In fact he will be joining the international touring company of the Barney the Dinosaur show a couple of days late as it is, and he is concerned that any further delay might cost him the gig.

Aamir is so apologetic and likeable, though, that even those of us who are cheesed off at our parts having been reduced to a first-ball duck, like myself, Flynn, Benson and North, can find it in our hearts to oblige him. He butters us up, in any case, with a lengthy discussion of the proper match, in which nobody is yet destined to be out first ball. It should now be at the end of the shoot at the Polo Cricket Ground, on March 19.

Aamir suggests that we should maybe start at 7 a.m., so as to avoid playing during the hottest part of the day. I suppose we have been getting to the location every day before seven, so it won't hurt to do the same on our day off. I look around at my team, and see shrugs and steely-eyed determination. They are all thinking the same thing as me: 'It doesn't matter what time we start – just bring it on . . .'

As the meeting breaks up I ask Aamir if it will be all right if

I do an interview with young Micky for his Gujarati cultural fanzine, and he says:

'OK, but don't say that the film is about cricket – that is our big surprise.'

That will be tricky, since I've already told Micky that the film is about cricket. Hmm . . .

This afternoon *Ghulam*, one of Aamir's recent films, was on the box. Howard and I gave it a try for a while, and caught sight of Goli and Amin as a biker and a boxer respectively. There was no getting away from the fact that it was pretty exciting stuff, as one dramatic stunt piled on top of another. At one point two gangs of bikers seemed to be engaged in a deadly game of chicken, which involved Aamir galloping along a railway track pursued by a train, jumping clear at the last possible second. We also saw the proper performance of his hit song, 'Aati Kya Khandala', which he has sung unaccompanied several times on the shoot, usually at the request of a large crowd of extras.

Although, like *Mela*, the film I saw back in England, it is in Hindi, *Ghulam* is much easier to follow. It is also very, very long. I have also been able to get the gist of a Hindi soap opera – *Quite a Lot Further EastEnders*, I think it's called. At first I put this down to the International Language of Soap, the compendium of looks, camera angles, musical stings and facial expressions that let you know what is going on almost as much as the dialogue. Then I noticed that every so often a character would drop in a complete phrase in English.

Two women were having a row, clearly about a man they were both interested in, and the scene went something like this:

FIRST WOMAN (glamorous, dark hair, business suit):
Yada yada yada yada under no circumstances!

SECOND WOMAN (slim, casual, more relaxed):
Yada yada yada yada yada. Yada yada difficult

situation. Yada yada some sort of compromise yada
yada . . .

FIRST WOMAN (agitated):
Yada yada yada absolutely unacceptable!

SECOND WOMAN (shrugs):
Yada yada knows what he wants yada yada not
getting it at home yada yada yada . . .

FIRST WOMAN (steaming):
Yada yada! Yada yada hearing from my solicitors
yada yada! (*Leaves*)

More cricket practice on the volleyball square. Ray hit me a
painful blow with a full toss, which caught me right on the
diaphragm, and later, whenever I tried to eat or drink, I got
the hiccups. Bizarre.

Micky, the young writer/printer who showed me around the
Aina Mahal a week or two ago, came to Sahajanand Tower
to get his interview with me for his Gujarati magazine this
evening. Fortunately for me and for him he had also bumped
into Ben wandering around Bhuj, and so he was getting us
both at once.

Over the years, both Ben and I have done our share of
press interviews. Indeed, Ben, during a spell as a regular on
the prime-time drama *Soldier, Soldier*, was a celebrity guest
on a short-lived and unmourned chat show hosted by Jerry
Hall, of all people. This means that every now and again a
clip of Ben looking on politely while Jerry flounders around
gorgeously trying to remember things like his name, and her
own name, and what the hell day it is, turns up on other shows
with names like *TV Hell 6* and *More TV Nightmares*, shows
whose viewing figures are artificially boosted by numbers of
curious and quickly disappointed fans of cross-dressing.

Micky joined us at a table in the dining room, and got out
his pad and a pencil. He smiled at me, then he smiled at Ben,

then he smiled at me again. I smiled back, in what I hope was an encouraging manner, and Micky looked down at his pristine blank pad. He looked up at both of us, smiled again, and said:

'I don't know what to ask you.'

Well, I said, how do you usually start when you interview someone?

'I've never interviewed anybody before.'

So how, I asked, do you get stuff for your magazine, which is all about what's happening in Bhuj, Kutchi culture and philosophy?

'I make it all up.'

He was a nice lad, Micky, although slightly disconcerting company. It was clear that he was very very shy of us, but to his credit he hadn't let that get in the way of arranging an interview. In the end Ben and I asked each other a few questions in the style of those that we had been fielding for years, and hoped that the lad would be able to make an article out of that. It would be in Gujarati, in any case, so even if we were really badly misquoted we would hardly know or care.

Micky was yet another example of how awestruck the Indians are by their movie folk. Ben and I barely qualify, and yet the poor chap – a journalist, remember – could hardly pluck up the courage to speak to us. Imagine Micky meeting Aamir – he might lapse into full-blown smiling catatonia.

Paul's birthday, and the production wheeled out two huge birthday cakes, which seemed a little excessive until it became clear that one of them was for cutting up and handing round and the other was for shoving his face into. Later there was a small celebration at Jon's apartment, with rum-flavoured beverage and Coke all round . . .

14

A Long Slog

COLONEL BOYER
What on earth do you think you're here for? To
play games?

(*Lagaan* – English translation)

9 MARCH

A few days later. The filming has taken a real turn for the worse for those of us on the British team. The Polo Cricket Ground – the PCG, as it is called – has the pavilion at one end, where the British supporters will sit to watch the match. At the other end is a rudimentary thatched shack, which serves as the Indian team's pavilion, and the mountain, which is nature's grandstand. Up to now, all the filming has been from the pavilion end, and has consequently needed Indian villagers and supporters as the backdrop.

This week, however, Ashutosh has started to film towards the pavilion, and those British players not out in the middle batting have all been required to sit out in the sun for nine hours a day, clapping and cheering every run. It has made us realise how cushy we've had it so far, as it is now impossible to slink off and play Jon's dice game, Zilch, or read a book, or catch flies, or sit on the veranda of the pavilion gazing off towards Pakistan, occasionally jotting down thoughts in this diary.

No, now we have to sit in the same position for hours of tedium, punctuated every few minutes by Kiran and Priya yelling at us to bung our sunglasses out of sight and little umbrella wallahs whisking away our shade, because these

Lagaan Englishmen, like the ones in the Noël Coward song, sit 'out in the noonday sun'.

Mulchand, the gaffer, who helps Anil set up the lighting for each shot, has a reputation for having an uncanny knack of predicting the weather by monitoring cloud movements. I think I could acquire this reputation myself pretty quickly. There aren't any clouds, and I'm predicting it will be bloody hot all day. Every day.

Howard has now been batting for something like six days for the twenty-seven runs the script has awarded him, which is slow going even by the standards of his great Yorkshire heroes. I think even Sir Geoffrey might have got to his half-century by now.

One of the extras, Stephen, keeps complaining that cricket is dull, and when a single-innings match is taking five whole weeks in front of your eyes it's difficult to put up much of an argument. I was interested to discover that he is a screenwriter who came out from England to try his luck pitching ideas in Bollywood. He has some achingly familiar stories of studio executives not reading his stuff, and directors not knowing what they are talking about, and the same basic banging of head against brick wall tales that writers everywhere swap bitterly whenever they congregate.

After a miserable night, poor old Ray was whisked off to the hospital in town, where he had nine separate injections to combat his fever, his diarrhoea, and dehydration. Meanwhile, out at the PCG, the filming reached a point at which Willis was required to make an appearance to deliver perhaps his most eye-catching, screen-filling moment of the whole film. Ray was lying on a hospital bed with various drips plugged into his arm, and a unit driver by his side, when the call came through on the shortwave radio that he was needed at once. He struggled out to the car, with doctors taping up the various sockets for his drips, came out to the set, did his scene, and then went straight back to hospital to be plugged in again. What an old-fashioned trouper.

Watching Ray gingerly trotting in to bowl was strongly reminiscent of the old apocryphal story about Alf Gover, who was once playing for England in India, and felt an imminent onset of the shits like you wouldn't believe as he ran in to deliver. Realising there was no time to lose, he simply carried on running, past the umpire, past both bewildered batsmen, straight on towards the pavilion toilet. His captain, Douglas Jardine, followed him and was sympathetic.

'Take your time, Gover,' he said, 'but could we have the ball back . . . ?'

The table tennis tournament has proceeded in its stately fashion. Aamir and Charlotte are in the quarter-finals in one half of the draw, while Adi and I progressed in the other half by knocking out Jon and Ronit (the muscle-bound former actor turned security man). Next we meet Ben and Ishwar.

The schedule has been reorganised, and so Jeremy is heading back to London for a few days. He kindly asks whether any of the long-term inmates want him to bring anything back with him when he returns. The only thing I can think of is a newspaper with the league tables in it, but before I can suggest it the assembled bunch of British actors are tripping over themselves.

'Oooh yes! Peppermint tea! I'd die for some peppermint tea!'

'Oooh! Camomile, how about some camomile?!'

'Fruit teas!'

'Oooh yes! What sort?'

'Any! Any lovely fruity teas . . . !'

This reminds me why, whenever someone asks me what I do, I never say I'm an actor. I always say 'self-employed' . . .

The child star, Tipu, has fallen out with me for the moment, and signalled the fact that he is no longer talking to me with a little playground ritual. This involves linking little fingers with me – much as Laurel and Hardy do when they have accidentally said the same thing – and then suddenly pulling away and shouting the word which lets me know that communication between us is to cease. Unfortunately, this magic word is 'Kunti!', and my hysterical laughter only makes him sulk more than ever.

I'm still not particularly enjoying the food, with its three daily doses of rice, roti, dall, and something else to take the skin off the inside of your throat. Time and again I've asked Bakshi to let us have a gentler, European option, but to no avail, and the only alternative to the canteen at Sahajanand – a trip to the I.V. – is no longer particularly appealing. Even the two majors seem to be giving it a wide berth lately.

This evening came down to dinner and – glory be – there was pasta for once. I filled a plate, took a mouthful, gasped, and headed for the water. Pasta shells in a jalapeno pepper sauce, that was Bakshi's idea of something a little milder. Not to put too fine a point on it – it was hot as old fuck.

India lost the Test match, despite 102 from the increasingly unpopular Mohammed Azharuddin. Nicky Boje, the spinner, was man of the match, after taking eight wickets and scoring 85 as night-watchman. It is India's first home series defeat for thirteen years, and there is a deal of doom and gloom.

The suffix 'ji' is added to the name of someone you are addressing or referring to as a mark of serious respect. Maybe one day the South African spinner will be addressed as Bojeji. I wonder whether Indians might ever find a horse so remarkable and worthy of respect that they would refer to it as a geegeeji. Or perhaps a particularly venerable and fine window-cleaning mop might be a squeegeeji? Just a thought . . .

10 MARCH
One of the most depressing things I've ever had to do. I know it's daft to feel this way about it, but hearing Apu announce:

'OK, listen up, everyone. The next shot is Yardley gets clean bowled for nought. First ball . . .'

I felt like a prizefighter who's been told that he has to go down in the second round. Apu really enjoyed it as well. It made me wonder how much say he and Aamir had in the fictional batting order, and deciding who gets the runs. They both have the real match in mind, I'm sure about that. Ashutosh wouldn't compromise his film for the sake of our cricket match, but Aamir knew that, after the big rewrite, some of us were going to spend plenty of time in the middle, getting our eyes in, and some of us were going to be twiddling our thumbs.

I'm looking at my batting line-up, and four of my best bats are barely batting at all in the film – that's myself, North, Benson and Harrison – while two of my weakest lads – Captain Russell and Brooks – are scoring all the runs. Coincidence . . . ?

When you're on tour you sometimes have to pick players who haven't had the chance to shine in the build-up games – it's just the same as that. Nothing to worry about . . .

So I'm wearing my vintage pads and gloves, about to head out into the middle to face my one ball, looking round for a bat, thinking I might as well not even take one out there, I'm not going to get to use it . . . when I catch sight of a bright yellow parasol leaning against a chair, and take that instead.

As Yardley strides out to meet his nemesis, all the Brits in the pavilion can see right away that I have this flouncy yellow item in my hand, and I can hear some distant giggling going on, but the crew are so intent on their various jobs that none of them notices. I begin to wonder how far I can go . . . I've got to my position, I take guard with the parasol, I scratch out a mark on the crease with it, twirl it a few times, look around the imaginary field placings . . . and all the while the camera is being focused on me, the shot is being framed . . . Finally everything is ready, and Apu calls for attention:

'OK, places everybody, we're going to shoot this one, nice and quiet, and . . . that's an interesting bat you have there, Yardley . . .'

He played cricket for India under-19s. You'd have thought he might have spotted it a little earlier.

I watch Flynn (Alex) and Benson (Barry) facing their own solitary deliveries today as well. Flynn's task is not too taxing. He is required only to miss the ball and be stumped by Ishwar and his fancy gloves. However, the first time he tried this he swished the bat and made a lovely contact with the ball, middling it firmly through mid-off. For a moment or two I wondered if there might not be room for him in the team after all. There was a good swing of the bat, nice timing . . . is it possible that he has been hiding his light under a proverbial bushel? Then I noticed he wasn't wearing his glasses.

Apu lost patience with Flynn right away – quite unfairly, since he'd only failed to miss the ball once. He grabbed the bat and swung it around a few times to demonstrate, but as he is a left-hander and Flynn is not, this only served to confuse the lad.

The two stuntmen who take it in turns to try to deliver the ball have their own private agenda. Saleem is a fairly quick bowler, who has already slung down some deliveries on Yardley's behalf, and no doubt will do so again. Ijaz, his mate, has a range of bowling to offer – off-spin, leg spin, medium pace – all of extremely variable accuracy.

Of course, they want to do their jobs well, and make the filming go quickly and smoothly. But Saleem and Ijaz also want to top each other, and furthermore they are both angling for a place in Aamir's team.

So now, when all that is required is a straight ball outside off stump for Flynn to miss so that Ishwar can stump him, we are treated to a demonstration of outrageously competitive bowling. The cameras roll, and Ijaz whips down a vicious off-spinner, which jags in from outside off and thumps into

Flynn's pads. Ijaz leaps into the air, just managing to contain his appeal for the lbw, and he looks around for Aamir imploringly, his body language screaming: 'Did you see that? Did you see what I can do?'

Aamir stands impassively – of course, for the purposes of the shot it is utterly useless – and Apu, irritated, calls 'Cut!' Ijaz sends down another – this time a spitting leg break which Flynn wouldn't be able to hit with a bat the size of a suitcase – and slaps his hands to his head in frustration as it runs away behind Ishwar, the keeper.

Apu grabs the ball, and takes over lobbing it down until the shot is in the can, but Ijaz feels he has made his point, and from the boundary we can see him miming the huge amount of turn he has extracted from the flat dusty surface to Saleem.

When it is Benson's turn to get himself out, Saleem has grabbed the ball. He won't be in shot, and in fact could stand still and throw the ball at Benson, but while the camera is being reset, and the crew are grabbing drinks or moving equipment, Saleem is secretly pacing out his run-up, and preparing to give it his best shot.

Barry is a key member of my team, and I have been impressed with his form so far on the trip. He is frustrated and fed up that he will barely be required to show what he can do for the film. Now he is asked to cut the ball in the air to backward point, where the cameras are ready to film the catch being taken.

Obviously Barry needs a short ball outside off stump to have any chance of effecting this shot, but Saleem is after catching the eye of the Indian selectors. He thunders in and sends a quick ball arrowing towards Barry's toes. There's no way Barry can cut this to backward point, so he leans over and whips it wristily, with a minimum of effort, to the boundary in front of the pavilion, which erupts in cheers and applause.

Saleem's arms have shot up and his mouth has made an 'O'

of disappointment as though he had almost got through, but if anyone has made a point it is Barry.

———

We are by no means the first English actors to work in a Bollywood feature, although we are perhaps the largest bunch to do so in a single film. Each of us has heard tales about film financing being distinctly dodgy out here, and horror stories about friends of friends of friends who came out to do a movie in India and ended up never being paid. The financial reputation of the Indian film industry, in a word, is flaky.

This evening we have a meeting, a council of war, in which the atmosphere is quite militant. There has been a dispute over the amount of the per diem payments – the actor's life-blood away from home – and the punctuality of their arrival. Most of us recall being told that this would be 250R a day, and it appears to be 150R a day, with any laundry fees being deducted at source. It's not really a very big deal – the difference between about three quid and about two quid, and it's not as if there's that much to spend it on – but we wouldn't be able to call ourselves actors if we couldn't get worked up over something like this. Some of the lads are also concerned that none of the promised fees have yet arrived in bank accounts back home, although when I check this I find that I have certainly been paid everything I am expecting so far myself.

By the end of this council of war we have resolved to take a very tough stand with Aamir in a clear-the-air summit meeting tomorrow, and as if to emphasise our no-surrender policy we allow Hassan, one of the production team who looks uncannily like a young Sammy Davis Junior, to overhear us bandying about the word 'Strike!'

11 MARCH
I have just returned to the apartment from our worker/boss

confrontation on the roof with Aamir. We caved in utterly on everything. He was so genial, and effortlessly deflected our concerns on to Reena, his co-producer and wife, who is arriving tomorrow.

He says the money will all be sorted out very soon, and it is impossible not to believe him. Aamir seems to have none of the difficulties faced by footballers like Kenny Dalglish, to pick an example, when they try to be the boss while remaining one of the lads, and he obviously knows that, however steamed up we appear to be getting, all we really want to talk about is the cricket match.

Our head of steam dissipates comically into pitiful minutiae. Alex suddenly and unilaterally demands itemised laundry receipts – an absolutely laughable idea which would require more paperwork than the rest of the production put together. Neil complains that although he has been rinsing out his own smalls in a bucket and drying them on his balcony, in order to save himself something like fourteen pence a week, the laundry wallah has been coming into his room and taking all the clothes he has just cleaned, dried, and neatly folded himself and washed them all over again, and charged him for the pleasure. As I listen to our one-out-all-out rebellion dissolving into a discussion of Harrison's over-clean pants, I am almost ashamed to be a socialist.

Today it was 37 degrees in the desert, and Yardley was brought on to bowl. I had to bowl a bouncer at Lakha, which was very difficult. The rubber fake cricket ball we are using on the flat baked-mud wicket bounces a little more than a cricket ball, but even so it is hard to get it above stump high. Saleem and Apu had no better luck when they tried, so that shot will have to be cheated. The other thing I had to do was hit Raj/Ismail a painful blow on the foot. Miraculously my first attempt with the cameras rolling arrowed in menacingly at Ismail's bare foot, whereupon he suddenly chickened out and leaped out of the way. The ball ripped the leg stump out of the dirt, which looked impressive but was, of course, completely useless.

12 MARCH

This is the former day off we are working to oblige Aamir. Apu's frustration with everyone's inability to do things as well as he can do them has spread from the cricket into other areas of the shoot. Today we shoot a bit of dialogue at a drinks break in the fictional match. A splendidly beturbanned waiter brings out a silver tray with a crystal pitcher of fruit juice and eleven glasses on it. He can manage this well enough with two hands, but when he tries to balance the tray on one hand and actually pour drinks with the other this, not surprisingly, proves beyond him. Frankly I'd be quite impressed if David Copperfield managed to do it – the magician, not the third one off of *Three of a Kind*. Apu, however, strides forward, intent on showing this hapless chap where he is going wrong.

'Give it to me . . . Here, like this!' he bellows furiously, balancing the heavily laden tray on one huge paw, where it teeters precariously for a split second before crashing to the deck. The jug of fruit juice empties down the front of the waiter's gleaming white uniform, centring unfortunately on his groin region so that he looks like a martyr to incontinence.

Amidst much poorly stifled mirth, Ashutosh wanders over and says:

'It's OK, we got it the first time.'

———————

37 degrees again today, and getting very windy. Every now and then the dust gets whipped up into little tornadoes that swirl across the pitch, gathering up stray bits of litter, plastic cups, and so on, which are then deposited as the twister breaks up when it reaches the start of the scrubby thorn bushes at the perimeter. One of these twisters, larger than usual, swept right through the unit this afternoon, turning the large

red-and-black Coca-Cola umbrellas inside out and depositing them over the boundary. Pages of script flew round and round, with light plastic deckchairs chasing each other, and anything that wasn't weighed down took off into the air.

Luckily it wasn't quite strong enough to actually pick up any people or damage the larger and more expensive bits of equipment, but it was a disaster for the paperwork, as Sanjay's fielding charts rearranged themselves around the playing arena.

During a break in filming, cool Nakul brought out a frisbee, and quickly persuaded a couple of the technicians to have a game with him. After about thirty seconds, though, a gust whipped the thing away from them and it was last seen heading for the Pakistani border, where it will either be shot down or eaten by bomb-crazed wild pigs.

On the subject of Pakistan, there is new tension in the air at the moment because of the imminent state visit to India of President Clinton. The new(ish) Pakistani regime is losing face because Clinton is not going there as well, and they are portraying this as a deliberate snub. In addition, their former leader, Nawaz Sharif, unseated last October, is currently on trial in Karachi, and his defence lawyer has just been assassinated. The worry here in India is that Pakistan may provoke a new conflict to deflect attention from their domestic troubles, and to try and persuade Arkansas Billy to stay at home.

As a result, the skies above this little piece of Kutchi desert, selected for this synch-sound shoot because of its perfect quietness, have been buzzing with fighters from the nearby airbase, either on exercises or border patrols. Sound recording has also been disrupted by birdsong recently, and Apu has managed to put a stop to this, rather tactlessly in the current political climate, by exploding two huge bombs in the undergrowth. We thought the shelling had begun . . .

I have been toying with the idea of slipping away for a

few days – if a gap in the schedule presents itself – to take a look at the old Taj Mahal in Agra, but apparently all the big national tourist attractions have been closed for weeks now so that they can be cleaned for the Clintons. I suppose I should find out when they are opening to the public again – it's a long way to go just to send home postcards reading: 'Went to Taj Mahal. Shut.'

India have gone 2–0 up in the one-day series against the Boers, thanks to a century by Saurav Ganguly. A sizeable cluster of people listened to him making his way through the nineties, not particularly nervously, on a transistor radio. When he reached the hundred with a four, the commentator said:

'Ganguly strokes that away, it'll be a boundary, and that brings up his hundred. That four was brought to you by MaQintosh, the original and best Scotch whisky . . .'

Fantastic. The radio station have done a sponsorship deal whereby individual incidents within a match, which, let's face it, may or may not happen, can be parcelled up, priced and sold. They've said to MaQintosh: 'OK, if anyone reaches a century with a four, that's yours for however much it is. We are also offering a deal on any left-handed slip catches, batsmen getting off the mark with a six, and anyone getting run out while trying to rearrange their protective box which has slipped down inside their trouser leg . . .'

If this were to catch on in England, some things would happen so often that sponsoring them would become prohibitively expensive. Only someone like IBM could afford a deal for every dot ball in a Michael Atherton innings, for example, or every time Mark Stumprakrash lost his off peg to a straight ball, or every time Graeme Hick was ever so slightly disappointing. Still, look out, Jack Bannister. It's coming . . .

A small digression: MaQintosh Scotch whisky has an extraordinary ad running on the television here. A businessman returns home from a busy day, and walks through his house removing items of clothing and draping them about the place. He reaches the bathroom just about naked, and steps straight into a full steaming bubble bath, settling down, eyes closing, and the camera closes in on his hand, with which he seems to be holding an imaginary flagpole, for all the world like he is about to crack one off.

There is a clink of ice cubes and a glass of MaQintosh slides into his grasp, and we pull back to see that a gorgeous model is there with him, ready to attend to his every need. So far so sexist (what's wrong with being sexy . . . ?), but I'm still thinking back to when he discards his nylon shirt, draping it over a small table lamp. I'm sure I've seen this exact thing happen in a seventies public information film, and every time I see this ad I'm expecting the room behind to crackle suddenly into flames, and Patrick Allen's voice to bark: 'Fire! It only takes a second!'

Saurav Ganguly is married to a dancer, Dona, and there has been some serious talk of the two of them starring in a film together. Strangely this isn't being greeted with the same derision as you'd expect if, say, David Beckham announced he was releasing a single with Posh. And he wouldn't be the first cricketer to go Bollywood. Sandeep Patil, the scourge of England in the early eighties, managed to reinvent himself as a leather-clad pelvis-thrusting musical star, and Sunil Gavaskar has also given it a go. Sachin Tendulkar and Kapil Dev were rumoured to be involved with *Lagaan*, too, but nothing seems to be coming of that.

13 MARCH

The psychological war is hotting up now, with only six days to go to the game. *The* game.

I was dismayed to hear, today, that Ben rates himself as only fifty-fifty to play, because of his shoulder injury. When I cornered him about this, however, he said:

'Oh that's only what I'm telling Aamir. I'll be fine.'

Phew.

The opposition camp is split over team selection, with Aamir, the captain, and Apu, the senior player, at loggerheads. Aamir was persisting in his decision to favour Lakha over both Raj and Adi, much to Apu's disgruntlement. Apu has settled this matter in his own inimitable style this afternoon, however.

Lakha is the traitor in the film who betrays the Indian villagers' cause to Captain Russell. During the match he repents and has the chance to redeem himself in the field by taking a brilliant catch. This shot was being filmed this afternoon.

Lakha stands ready in the covers, the cameras roll. Apu has grabbed the ball from the stunt guys and he hurls it at Lakha for him to make the catch. Somehow he has managed to throw it so hard that he has broken Lakha's hand, ruling him out of the match, the table tennis tournament, and the rest of the day's filming.

If I were Sanjay, another member of the Indian team whom Apu doesn't approve of, I'd be watching my step . . .

From the start there has been a rumour that Sachin Tendulkar is going to visit the set – indeed, there was some talk of him actually appearing in *Lagaan*, perhaps as a villager who doesn't quite have what it takes to make the Champaner team, which would be quite a good gag. He and Aamir are great mates – despite the fact that Sachin is a Pepsi man, appearing with Shah Rukh Khan in their ads, while our Khan is committed to the real thing. Now it seems that the best chance of this happening will be at the weekend, when the India team have completed a one-day international in Vadodara – not desperately near, but nearer than anywhere else they are playing.

'Wouldn't it be great,' Aamir is now musing, 'if Sachin were here for *our* match . . . ?'

That really would be the ringer of all time, no doubt about

it. Once, a few years ago, Arthur let me know that the Dusty Fleming International Hairstylists had recruited Imran Khan, and An England XI approached the next Test match with a certain amount of trepidation, in fear partly of facing that infamous and startling late in-swing, partly of serious physical pain. Come the day, though, and it turned out that Arthur had acquired the services of *an* Imran Khan – a small and affable young Asian lawyer – and not *the* Imran Khan. He was out for a duck on his only appearance, and so is forever rooted to the foot of our all-time averages, a pleasing curiosity.

Tendulkar, though, that would be a real test of my captaincy. I gave it some thought, and the best plan I could come up with was to bring myself on to bowl and hope that the great man had some sort of hysterical seizure. A long shot, I know.

Neil's lucky streak continues. After being butted by a cow, gashing his back on the volleyball post, and having his fresh laundry rewashed, this morning he fell asleep leaning on the window of the bus, and the whole pane fell out and smashed on the road.

Micky turned up at Sahajanand Tower with a copy of his Gujarati magazine, in which he proudly showed me the article he'd written about me and Ben. It was all in Gujarati, of course, and I got him to circle my name, at least, but it could be an elaborate prank, for all I know, or the article could say I am a child molester. Apparently Micky has also interviewed 'Lucky' Harrison, but his piece won't appear until after we've gone home, naturally.

14 MARCH

Spent the day at the *Star Trek* village of Champaner. We were filming the Brits shipping out, defeated, at the very end of the picture. I was sitting on the front of a buggy about halfway back in the wagon train, which meant that I spent most of the day watching a camel's arse. This camel seemed able to piss and shit constantly, more or less all day, and there was a grim fascination in watching it bat its own testicles dry with its tail. A few feet closer to home, the horses pulling the buggy were inspired, and kept up a torrent of piss and shit of their own. These animals simply must have been eating for a month.

Occasionally we were allowed to take refuge from the 39 degree heat in one of the mud huts, which are nice and cool, and basically made from cow shit and straw in the traditional fashion. The thatched roofs are riddled with woodworm, and sawdust trickles down on our heads the whole time – woodworm shit, in fact. So, to sum up, today was shit, shit, shit, and more shit. With extra shit and a side order of shit.

15 MARCH

I am sitting in the pavilion with my feet up watching Aamir/ Bhuvan bat. The bowler is not in shot. It is Yardley. This means that the much quicker and much more accurate Saleem, the stunt co-ordinator, is standing in for me, while I lean back languidly and watch him strutting his stuff. Or rather, my stuff. I feel like calling out:

'I say, bowler wallah? Knock this johnny over for me, would you, there's a good chap . . .'

Saleem is playing for his place in the Indian side. His first ball beats Aamir all ends up and takes out the off stump. Saleem is very pleased with himself, and Aamir does actually look quite impressed, but check the score book, Saleem old son, and I think you'll find it says: 'b. Yardley'.

I could get used to this – I wonder if Saleem fancies coming back to England and standing in for me next season. It would do wonders for my bowling average, that's for sure.

Aamir is directing at the moment, because Ashutosh has gone to the hospital in town to visit poor old Bhura, the Tasmanian devil, who has been taken ill during the night. It is not clear what is wrong, but, depending on what rumour you listen to, he has had either a heart attack, a heart episode, or a stroke. The important thing is he is expected to be fine in a few days.

So Aamir is directing himself, which has led to an interesting interpretation of Ashutosh's shot list. Bhuvan, Aamir's character, is down to play a defensive shot or two, and in Aamir's book a defensive shot is merely one that doesn't go for four or six.

'There are no dot balls!' he cries when asked about this, defensively slashing the ball over slip for three to third man, or – slipping into ultra-defensive mode – lofting through mid-wicket for a couple more.

―――――――

Last night, returning to Bhuj from the *Star Trek* village, I sat next to Barry on the bus. Of all of us, he and Alex are the ones who don't really think of themselves as actors. Alex is a student, working here with a view to funding the backpacking trip around India that he is embarking on with Rob and Andrew as soon as we are done. Barry is here as a cricketer, and since the rewrite he finds himself without any cricket in the film, which is a great disappointment to him, and he's been pretty fed up. He's a lovely jolly bloke, excellent company, and he's been hiding it well, but I think he's regretting making the trip at all.

I sympathise, finding myself in a somewhat similar boat, but at least Yardley gets to do plenty of showy bowling. This morning I grabbed a quiet word with Ashutosh, and asked if it mightn't be possible for Benson to score a few runs on-camera. He had, after all, been cast for his cricket ability, and his excellent lugubrious look, and it seemed a waste not to take advantage of these things. Ashutosh frowned, and I wondered if I'd put my foot in it, but what the hell.

Later, though, Barry was summoned to the middle and asked

to hit a four on the leg side and a big straight six. He knocked them off in a handful of takes, was clearly enjoying himself, and afterwards he had a bit more of a spring in his step. Ashutosh was delighted and came trotting over to me to say:

'He has an excellent wintage look. Excellent!'

The time seemed right for my next big suggestion – that Yardley should be involved in a huge last-wicket stand. I turned to Ashutosh, but he'd gone.

The table tennis tournament reached the semi-final stage this evening. In the first game Adi and I played Ray and Satya, and it was a thriller. Adi and Satya are both demon spinners of the ball with nasty unplayable serves, while Ray and I are both plonkers of the ball over the net and happy to try and keep the ball in play, so we were evenly matched. Adi and I won 3–2 in the end, having been 2–1 down. In the other semi Aamir and Charlotte, the favourites, beat Nakul and Jon – standing in for Lakha because of his broken hand – by three games to none. Aamir's serve is the wickedest of the lot, and I reckon that makes us the underdogs for the final. I wonder what support we'll be able to muster, playing against the boss.

16 MARCH
Another day in the desert picking up cricket shots, this time of the Indian team batting. Late in the day, Amin – who is playing Bagha the mute in the oddest bit of casting against type, since he is simply the most talkative chap I have ever met – has the bat in his hand. He is not much of a cricketer, but the script calls for a big straight six.

Amin tries some practice swipes, which look OK. He taps the ground where he wants the ball, and Saleem steps up to throw the ball from just off-camera for him to hit. Of course, Saleem can't get the ball in the right place, and Amin has five or six air shots. Apu then shoves Saleem out of the way and grabs the ball himself. He proceeds to throw it even worse than Saleem has done, and Amin still cannot lay bat on ball. Apu is all impatience, and Amin's confidence is draining away. Another huge heave misses the ball, but sends the bat flying away over mid-wicket. Apu stomps over to fetch it and shoves Amin aside.

'Like this!' he growls, helpfully, and heaves the ball over long off. 'See? That's how you do it!'

Well, those of us watching think, that's bound to work. They stop the camera while Amin has another practice, and of course he begins to make contact with the ball, but as soon as they switch the camera back on he's back to swishing clean air.

Ashutosh realises that the basic problem is with the way Saleem and Apu are throwing the ball, and comes over to try himself. His first throw is pretty much in the slot, but Amin smashes wildly, hits the ground, and the blade snaps off and hurtles towards the director's head. Ashutosh retreats behind the camera again, and Aamir takes over. Amin absolutely idolises Aamir, and gradually responds to his gentle coaxing. With a new bat in his hands, he relaxes, and edges a couple, and then, glory be, he smacks one out of the middle of the bat straight back over the camera.

There is a huge cheer, and wild hooting and back-slapping all round, as take thirty-four looks like being a beauty. They check it back, and someone spots that Benson, at slip, has his sunglasses on. Ha ha ha ha ha!

On the way back to Bhuj from the location I had fallen asleep on the bus, taking care not to lean on the window. I was woken by a sudden commotion outside. The bus had stopped by the airport and was surrounded by armed military police, who were involved in a heated exchange with our driver.

It flashed through my mind that none of us had been allowed to see a paper yesterday morning, and when I finally did see the *Times of India* there was a huge headline about Pakistan pointing all its nuclear weapons at India and threatening to blow up Bill Clinton. Presumably this was kept from us in case we all kacked ourselves, piled into tuc-tucs and headed for the airport.

So what was going on? Had it really all kicked off? Were we to be forbidden from working so close to the Pakistani border? Was the road past the airport – a military base, remember – being closed to non-essential traffic? It turned out that the bus-driver had been stopped on some bogus pretext to do with 'bus tax', because all these soldiers wanted to get Aamir Khan's autograph.

17 MARCH

A very ragged day. We have been filming cricket for a fortnight now without a day off, and everybody is exhausted and dying for a rest, so Aamir proposes yet another postponement of the cricket match. I agree, and we settle on the 26th. This is the last possible day we can play, as Neil is due to leave on the 27th to meet up with his mates on the Euro-Barney tour, which he is fretfully anxious to do. Later I discover that Apu hurt an arm – his own for a change – while berating poor old Amin the other day, and wouldn't have been able to play tomorrow, but he should be fit for next week. Aha . . .

This latest postponement does have an effect on the Indian side's options, though, as a number of the cast are heading for Bombay tomorrow. *Lagaan* is being filmed in an unusual way for a Bollywood film, in that the cast and crew have been asked to commit to filming it all in one six-month shoot. So many films are being made all the time out here – around nine hundred every year – that arranging a schedule so that the cast's availabilities all coincide for such a lengthy engagement is virtually impossible. The norm is for movies to be shot piecemeal, picking around various cast members' other commitments, and it's not uncommon for a Bollywood epic to take three or four years to shoot. Equally it is not uncommon for a Bollywood film actor to be working on four, five, six – more, even – films at any one time.

Such is the prestige of *Lagaan* and its star/producer that a large cast has been persuaded to set aside other projects, but we have now reached a point at which Aamir had promised that the cricket section would be all over and done with, and so several key players – including Raj – have been allowed to take on a couple of weeks' work on other movies. We must finish the fictional cricket match, and play the real one, without them.

15
Holi and the I.V.

BHUVAN

Here you are, memsahib. You must be hungry.

Elizabeth takes the roll and eats it. She likes the taste,
but suddenly starts shaking her hand.

ELIZABETH

(*Gasps*) Oh! Hot! *Water . . . !*

(*Lagaan* – English translation)

18 MARCH

After a few weeks now of rice, dall, roti, mutton, hen necks, etc
etc etc three times a day, we are heartily throat-seared and fed
up. Howard's girlfriend has tried to cheer him up by sending
him a huge colour photograph of a full English breakfast,
which he has stuck on the wall of his room. Sometimes, of
an evening, we sit and gaze at it, drooling slightly.

The number of brave souls prepared to pay the price of
eating in 'The I.V.' – drips in the arms, injections up the arse,
days spent clinging helplessly to the rim of the bog – has
dwindled away to nought, and so Rachel gamely volunteered
to speak to Bakshi about the food on everyone's behalf. Today
she proudly announced to great enthusiasm all round that her
negotiations had borne fruit, and that dinner tonight would
be chicken casserole and mashed potato. This turned out to
be true, but sadly Bakshi had only cooked it for her. The rest
of us were on the usual diet of rice, dall, roti, mutton, hen
necks . . .

Unable to sleep, because water is dripping loudly on to the

outside of the air-conditioning unit, the inside of which is right next to my bed.

Tracked down the source of the dripping water, and it is coming from the apartment two floors above. Aamir's apartment.

19 MARCH

Sunday. Our first day off for a fortnight, and the temperature was up around 45 degrees outside, so I didn't venture outside until almost dusk. Howard and Brooks borrowed some bikes and cycled to the nearby village of Bhujeri, returning almost visibly thinner a couple of hours later with some spangly embroidered souvenirs.

This evening was the table tennis tournament final. A large crowd of cast and crew gathered to watch, and Aamir – very hyped up and competitive – opened with a psychological ploy, insisting on 'international rules', as he called it. This meant Adi and I both having to change our white T-shirts so that the ball would be clearly visible. It was only after I had gone up five floors to do this that I remembered that the balls we would be using were bright orange.

I was surprised to find that the mood of the room was mostly in our favour. When I remarked on this to Adi, he just shrugged and said: 'We are popular guys.'

The match itself was close. I could barely return Aamir's serve, let alone win any points on it, but Adi was in his element, and we won the first two sets. Aamir and Charlotte took the third, but we took the fourth and the match.

Aamir was very gracious afterwards, and said he would have his revenge on the cricket field next week – we'll have to see about that . . .

Apu was delighted, partly because Adi is his cousin, and partly because he secretly enjoyed seeing Aamir not having things all his own way. He hosted a small celebration in his apartment, at which he showed me the 'publicity' for the

cricket match next week. Every day a call sheet is issued
to every member of the company, outlining what work is
scheduled for the next day, and when Apu has a special
announcement of any kind to make, he attaches another
page to the call sheets. For the announcement of the match
he has got one of the crew, an amateur cartoonist, to do a little
poster spoof. A trophy gleams in the centre, and either side of
it he has drawn two heads glowering at each other like boxers
at a weigh-in – Aamir's (handsome, chiselled, determined)
on the left and mine on the right, in full moustache and
sideburn regalia, my eyes narrowed to mean-looking slits.
The enemy.

It does make the contest seem very personal between the
two of us, and consequently the table tennis tournament feels
like the opening skirmish. I've contrived to win that, largely
because of Adi – but will I win the war . . . ?

20 MARCH

Yesterday evening, before the table tennis final, I went out into
Bhuj on my own. Ordinarily the town is pretty quiet at dusk,
but yesterday the place was buzzing with frankly mystifying
activity. Every hundred yards or so it seemed a group of
children was building a huge mud pie. They were doing this
by watering the ground, and then scooping and shaping the
mud – I say mud; really I would estimate an unusually high
donkey crap and fag-end content – into round patties like
large mud beefburgers, which they then piled carefully on to
growing mounds.

I shrugged, puzzled, and carried on into town. When I
returned a little while later the mounds of muddy quarter-
pounders were finished, each about five feet high, and they had
been decorated. Coloured powder paint, all the colours you
could think of, had been sprinkled over these little mountains,
and in a circle around them on the ground.

Next to one of these hillocks a small girl, plastered from

head to toe in mud and paint, was surveying her handiwork proudly. I pointed and asked her:

'What is this for?'

'Holi!' she grinned.

'Ho-li!' I grinned back, thinking: Fair enough, she doesn't speak English, and I carried on back to Sahajanand.

Today in the desert the temperatures reached 45 degrees. We were filming reaction shots of the spectators in the pavilion, and the heat drained all our enthusiasm. Not that we had a deal of that anyway. Every now and again Apu would shout to us what we were supposed to be applauding: 'Captain Russell hits a cover drive for four!'

I found I could corpse Brooks, who was nearby, by having Yardley bellow over-the-top remarks extolling Russell as the finest batsman of his generation.

'The man's seeing it like the proverbial football!' was one, I remember, and the sheer irony of it all finally wore down Brooks's professional self-control. That kept me amused for about a minute and a half, anyway ...

As the light faded at the end of a long hot dull day at the cutting edge of Bollywood cinema, I could sense a growing feeling of anticipation and excitement in the crew, and when a wrap for the day was called everyone suddenly started galloping around like schoolkids on the last day of term.

'What's going on?' I shouted at a couple of previously quite sensible sound technicians.

'Holi!' they yelled, and galloped off to an open space just beyond the boundary where a large group of crew members was gathering.

The hosepipes that were used to make the fake rainstorm on the Day of the Ten Thousand Extras were hauled out, and within seconds everyone and everything in the vicinity was drenched. Figures slipped and sprawled in the mud, others scooped up handfuls of filth and hurled them at their mates.

Holi, it appears, is a day where everyone has licence to muck about, and get as wet and as dirty as they can. The mounds I saw yesterday, being created by, among others, a small girl who knew perfectly well what I was asking her, were piles of ammunition for a huge mud fight, which was presumably happening even now on the streets of Bhuj.

Oh well, when in Rome, I suppose . . . I wandered over to watch the mayhem, given maybe a moment's pause by the thought that much of the mud that was being so energetically slung around came from more or less exactly where the elephant had been standing for the past fortnight. A sopping figure, more mud than man, emerged from the mêlée in front of me – Ashutosh, our director.

'Now then,' I said to him, 'I'm new to all this, what exactly do I . . . ?' Whereupon he pinned my arms while someone else turned the hose on me, and then mud and old elephant crap flew at me from all directions.

'Ah,' I said. 'I see.'

The team bus, full of half-naked soaking mud creatures, eventually made its way back to Sahajanand Tower, where we were assaulted afresh by those who had not been involved in the filming today, who showered us with handfuls of brightly coloured powder paint. All very childish, of course, but fun.

This evening – appropriately enough, since we are working on 'the Bollywood Titanic' – the Hollywood *Titanic* was on the movie channel.

21 MARCH

It's bad enough to be up at six in the morning, and sitting having two small rodents glued to the side of my face as the sun rises, but Paul has discovered a new layer to the torture. He has taken to sitting in the chair next to me reading out loud passages from *Winnie-the-Pooh*, every now and then stopping to exclaim:

'I love these stories. They're fantastic!'

I have to be careful not to grimace or wince too much, or

my face fuzz will go on wonky and Sherry (my moustache wrangler) will have to go back to the beginning of the whole process. Pina and Nicole love this, though, and coo encouragingly whenever he whips out his slim volume. If I ever find it lying around there will be a small and mysterious fire, let me assure you of that . . .

---

45 degrees again, and tempers are fraying. Today we did a small scene where the whole British cantonment community was posing for a photograph with its cricket team. George, Colonel Boyer's one-time stand-in, was again making a nuisance of himself, and Apu suddenly decided that we needed a shot of someone watching from the top of the mountain. George was dispatched to be the lone watcher, and once he had scaled the rocky hill Apu waved him back down again. George eventually made it back to the pavilion, puffing and sweating, where Apu told him that there had been a hair in the gate – the classic heart-sinking reason for doing a perfectly good shot again – and George set off to climb the mountain again.

Five times Apu sent George up and down, in the middle of a 45 degree desert afternoon, and at no time was a camera pointed anywhere near the mountain. On the last occasion the tall extra presented himself, dusty, sweaty, weary and subdued, Apu hissed at him:

'Now don't fuck with me again, got it?'

George got it.

Another character who has got under Apu's skin is Guran, the wild man of Champaner, whose fake facial hair is even more extravagant than mine. He has been refusing to wear his great itchy mess of a beard until the last minute in this hot weather – and I sympathise, I must say. This has, however, meant delaying the filming on a number of occasions because he is not ready, and Apu finally snapped. He hauled the beardless Guran out of the pavilion and made him do his scene sitting behind a bush with his hands over his face.

Guran is quite an oddball. Another time, recently, filming of a scene featuring the whole Indian team had to be aborted over and over again because Nakul, the sound man, kept picking up a strange buzzing noise. The buzzing stopped when the camera stopped rolling, and technicians clambered all over the equipment looking for a fault. Eventually the noise turned out to be coming from Guran, who was unilaterally improvising being bothered by a bee, and making the sound effect himself.

—————

At mealtimes one of the catering lads, a sunny-faced boy called Sutenand, always leaps up as I approach, ready to lift the metal lids off anything I fancy. He is so sharp, and so keen to anticipate my wishes, that I have taken to dummying him, heading for the rice and then suddenly veering off to something else as soon as he whips off the cover. This simple slapstick routine has not varied for weeks now, and yet still has the kid in tucks every time. I went through a phase of feeling guilty for taking the mickey out of him, but now I think he would be upset if I didn't do it. Today he was giggling even more than ever, and suddenly blurted out:

'You're fantastic!'

Now suddenly I am oppressed by the fear that it is he who has been taking the piss out of me for the last seven weeks . . .

22 MARCH
Filming in the evening today, so had the morning off. I went into Bhuj and wandered around in the bazaar next to the the Aina Mahal, after first taking some photographs of the fading, peeling Gormenghastian splendour of the old palace's crumbling façade.

The bazaar is made up of narrow alleys, with cramped little open-fronted shops facing each other across eight feet of cobblestoned path. A typical store is about as wide as a large garden shed, with rolls of brightly coloured material lurking in the gloom behind the shopkeeper, sitting cross-legged on his front step watching the world go by.

There is none of the yammering for attention and hard-selling haggling that is commonplace in more tourist-oriented areas of the world, and when I ask to have a look at one particular startling green-and-gold sari which I am eyeing as a present for my wife, one tradesman creaks grumbling to his feet as though I have asked him a particularly onerous personal favour, eventually proffering his wares with a surly indifference which is so nearly British that I feel almost homesick.

Up a side street is the silver bazaar, where all the tiny shops are displaying locally crafted silver jewellery. None of the various bracelets, necklaces, bangles and anklets is labelled with a particular price, and so when one object – a nicely wrought little neck bauble – catches my eye, I ask how much it costs. The silver merchant slowly leans forward and gathers the necklace into his palm, and then deposits it into one bowl of an ancient set of scales.

I am surprised by this for a moment. Is the craftsmanship to count for nothing? Are all these items, whether beautifully carved out by an unsung local genius or thrown together in ten minutes by the village idiot, to be sold by weight? It dawns on me, though, as the fellow takes his time, dawdling his little weights on and off the scales, that he is really weighing me up, trying to decide just how large he dares to make the price he is about to draw from thin air. Just how fat is the fat duck he is preparing to pluck?

Interestingly, given that I am a rather scruffy and unshaven individual, he reaches the conclusion that I am fabulously wealthy, and finally quotes a price that is so high it makes me laugh out loud. I'm sure he would have been happy to haggle, but I don't really like haggling myself. On the rare occasions I do venture to try it I like to ensure that both parties are in the same ball park, and this lad and I weren't in the same county. I am getting close to agreeing to buy a cricket bat after one long-term haggle. Every time I come into town I nip into the tiny sports shop, pick up a big, heavy bat called 'The Tusker', which has a picture of a rhino on it, and haggle the bloke down another couple of hundred rupees before leaving it for another few days.

Down in the market you can now buy photographs and blown-up colour photocopies of shots from the filming. Pictures of Aamir are being snapped up, and the production are becoming anxious that security is being breached. Ashutosh and Aamir are particularly keen that the outside world should not find out that the story of the film centres around a cricket match, and when photos clearly show the Khan involved in a suspiciously cricket-like game they naturally become fretful. No one has seen any photographers on the set, though, and Ronit and his enormous bouncers would be enough to deter all but the most determined paparazzo. I suppose it is possible that someone from Bolly *Hello! – Namaste!* – is up the mountain with a telephoto lens, but the pictures in question all seem to be taken from right among us, right in the middle of the action.

The answer to this conundrum emerges when I catch sight of a little guy on a street corner in the old part of town. He has a little crowd of kids around him, and he is flicking through a handful of photos for them. After a moment money changes hands, and one of the kids gallops off with her prize. As I walk past I crane my neck to see the pictures for myself, and bugger me if I don't recognise one of them. It is a shot of some of the Indian team with the crowd in the background, and the reason it is so familiar is that I took it myself.

Some of us have been using a local shop to get photos developed while we are out here. It is run by a rather miserable chap, who makes you take your shoes off before you go in, and who has contrived to allocate me a different new surname every time I've taken a film in. Clearly this fellow is behind the on-location photo racket, and without leaving the shoeless comfort of his own premises – he's developing our films, and running off an extra set for his own private black-market uses, the cunning swine.

Out to the location in the afternoon, and in the evening we film a short scene in front of the pavilion. The British cricketers are lounging around the night before the match begins, discussing Captain Russell's tactics – which, interestingly enough, are to score loads of runs and then bowl the Indians out for very few. I wonder whether I should use those tactics when we play the real game next Sunday . . . ?

Yardley kicks this little interlude off with one of his few actual scripted lines of dialogue:

'So, sir. What is our plan for the match tomorrow?'

Whereupon Russell unveils his Brearleyesque master plan to me, Burton and Puran Singh the maharaj, sitting around a table. When we block this scene, before dinner, there are four chairs (one each). After dinner, when we come back to actually film it, there are only three. Russell and Burton clock this first, and bag theirs with childish glee, leaving me in an unseemly elbow-to-elbow scramble with the venerable Bollywood veteran K. Kharbanda for the third. When the music stops, I am the one left standing.

I look around, but the chair is not just misplaced, it has gone completely. Now this is not a problem, of course. There are literally dozens of people scurrying around the set making tiny adjustments to the scenery and props. All I need to do is point out that a chair has gone missing, and one will appear in seconds. Oddly, though, at this moment I become the invisible man. This has happened to me before, I should say, usually when I'm trying to get served in a pub. I can suddenly find myself surrounded by a force field of anti-charisma, which is able to curve a barmaid's attention right round me and my proffered fiver towards a bloke who has just walked in and who wants eight pints of Guinness.

This is the first time this phenomenon – which has baffled some of our finest minds (well, mine anyway) – has shown itself to operate in a professional situation, though. A couple of the lads from setting come past.

'Excuse me, we need another chair . . . excuse . . . ?'

Apu scuttles by.

'Hey, Apu? We're a chair short here . . . Apu . . . ?'

Ashutosh comes over and turns one of the extras in the background through about ten degrees, and then stands back to look at the (insignificant) effect of the (tiny) change he has made. I have the first line of the scene, and if I'm not sitting down then my head will have disappeared off the top of the frame, but can I make him hear me? Can I knackers. Perhaps they want my head to be out of shot? Perhaps they have become as tired of Yardley's silly moustache as I have myself.

'Please! Somebody! A chair has gone missing from here! Please? Anyone . . . ?!'

Some sniggering begins from those who are unaffected by the anti-charisma field – i.e. those who have no idea where the chair has gone and no way of finding one – but then Apu shouts:

'Places, everybody, let's shoot one! Full power!'

Well then, I think. I'll simply have to *show* you that there should be a chair here. The camera rolls, and I crouch down between Russell and Puran Singh, sitting on an invisible mime chair. Russell and Burton are giggling – Puran Singh is in a world of his own, and may be asleep.

'Action!'

The camera tracks towards us. Yardley, perching absurdly in a half-sitting half-crouch, says:

'So, sir. What is our plan for the . . . yaaargh!'

And topples over backwards out of sight behind the table.

As I hit the floor I'm thinking: Well, I think I've made my point. Then I roll backwards into the shins of a poor unfortunate passing waiter, making him spill a tray-load of glasses of pretend red wine down the front of his pristine white uniform, and I've not only made my point, I've made one hell of a mess as well.

'Cut!'

Now this piece of old-fashioned slapstick is, I have to admit, only a half-hit. Those Brits who've seen the whole thing are properly amused. The crew, Apu and the setting guys, however, come running over, frankly baffled. They think that my chair has exploded, and can't understand what I've done with all the pieces. Such is the power of the anti-charisma field. There's a decent *X Files* episode in there somewhere, if you ask me . . .

Interesting, and an honour, to do a scene with the great K. Kharbanda. Kharbanda has done so many films where the dialogue is added in post-production that he barely actually vocalises his lines at all. I'm sitting next to him, and I can't hear a blind word he's growling. Ashutosh comes over and tries to coax him into upping the volume a bit. Kharbanda nods, barely perceptibly, and we go again. The second take is exactly the same, but such is the reverence in which the great man is held that we move on, and it seems that one character, at least, will be dubbed on in post in the traditional Bollywood fashion.

23 MARCH

Talking to Hassan Kutty, the clapperboard guy, although actually I shouldn't call him that. He is quite a popular figure for photographs on account of his eerie likeness to a young Sammy Davis Junior, and I am daily tempted to ask him about the Rat Pack years. He has aspirations to become a first assistant director, or even a director, and won't be snapped with his trademark clapperboard in case a picture of him should fall into the wrong hands and undermine his chances of advancement – showbiz paranoia of a high order. Anyway, with his surname he should become an editor.

Hassan is a good source of minutiae about the film, and he reckons that the cricket sequence in *Lagaan* contains 650 set-ups, will use 40,000 feet of film, and will last 38 minutes on screen. You'd think they could have found room for me to score one run. One miserable run . . .

Like any Bollywood epic, *Lagaan* will feature several musical numbers. These are being composed by the distinguished Indian composer A.R. Rahman, who has been in the news recently both here and at home because he is collaborating with his UK equivalent, Sir Andrew Lloyd Webber, on a bi-continental musical project called *Bombay Dreams*.

We have already heard Ashutosh rendering one of the songs unaccompanied, at one of the musical get-togethers that have punctuated our stay, and now two more numbers have arrived in demo form, which Apu played over the speakers to the desert at large and the assembled company at the end of filming one day.

One is a romantic love song, which comes at the most complicated point in the film's love triangle, when Gauri, the village girl, and Elizabeth, Captain Russell's sister, are both clearly in love with good old Bhuvan, and it is not clear who he will favour. A.R. Rahman's song interweaves an Indian theme and a Western theme, as the two girls express themselves in their own language and musical tradition, and the effect is oddly reminiscent of *I Know Him So Well*, which – interestingly, given Rahman's Lloyd Webber connection – is the work of Tim Rice. And Bjorn and Benny out of Abba.

The second is a driving, rhythmic piece, in which the Hindi lyrics chatter by at great pace. Trying to get into this song, and maybe even sing along, Howard and I find ourselves substituting the phrase: 'Gobbledy-gobbledy-gobbledygook'.

Which seems to fit pretty well, and I hasten to add at this point that no disrespect is intended, and we rather like the song. We do, really.

CUT TO: THIS EVENING, SAHAJANAND TOWER, INT.

Back at Sahajanand Tower we get an urgent summons to the seventh floor, and Howard and I dutifully trot upstairs. There Aamir introduces us to A.R. Rahman himself, who has dropped in for a personal appearance. He seems like quite a shy, sensitive, man, younger than Lloyd Webber and with shoulder-length dark hair. Aamir, I notice, is being extremely deferential, and even seems a little star struck. After all, in a film industry where music is an integral part of almost every film, Rahman is absolutely the most prestigious music man around, and Aamir is clearly delighted and grateful to have him on board, and careful to treat him with the utmost respect and courtesy.

The atmosphere is so heavy with awe that as I am presented to the great man I feel a strong urge to bow, as though he were royalty. In a way he is – Bollywood royalty. Howard, though, feels no such compunction when he bounds into the room half a minute behind me. Aamir guides him over to the shy genius, and says:

'Howard, this is A.R. Rahman.'

'Great, great, hello, hi, how are you?' says Howard, pumping the little composer's hand. 'Now tell me, what do you do?'

Aamir flinches, and a slight frown darkens Rahman's brow. 'Howard, this is the gentleman who has written the music for our film.'

Howard's face brightens, and, still clutching Rahman by the hand, he looks him straight in the eye, winks, and sings:

'Gobbledy-gobbledy-gobbledygook!' Really quite loud.

Rahman's face is a picture. A half-smile frozen in place, his eyes wide with horror, he seems unable or unwilling to withdraw his hand, for fear of provoking more brutal criticism from this ebullient and overpowering Englishman.

Howard, trying to explain, decides to go again: 'Gobbledy-gobbledy-gobbledygook!'

Rahman gasps, and throws his free hand up to protect himself, Aamir steps between them, and I hustle Howard through to the next room, where he mutters:

'Huh! He doesn't even recognise his own tune . . .'

16
The Art of Captaincy

CAPT. RUSSELL
I'm going to announce the batting order now.

(*Lagaan* – English translation)

Six days to go now before the Big Match, and, unusually for me, I am feeling at a loose end.

Ordinarily the days, and hours, and minutes leading up to a match are filled with telephoning potential players in an attempt to scratch together a team, but out here there's not so much for me to do. My team has more or less picked itself, so I have no selection dilemmas. The opposition is arranging a coach to take everyone to the game so I don't have to work out who is getting a lift with who. We are the away team, so I don't have to do the tea. I don't have to book a pitch, as the opposition have built one specially in the middle of the desert. I don't even have to nip out to a sports shop and buy a ball.

With all this organising energy in my system and nowhere for it to go, I have the time to contemplate the whole business of captaining a cricket team.

It is very important for the married cricket captain to have an understanding wife. Susan and I were married six years ago and began our life together with a brilliant honeymoon in Barbados. Alec Stewart made a century in each innings, Angus Fraser took eight wickets, and we won on the fifth afternoon.

The team that I captain back home, An England XI, is made up of amiable part-timers, blokes who enjoy playing the game but who can't be arsed to go through all the rigmarole of joining a proper club and 'taking it seriously'. At this level, players' wives and partners can have a crucial say in the make-up of the side. At least four or five times a week I will speak to a prospective player on the phone, and hear:

'Yeah, yeah, I'd love to play, yeah. Let me just check with [insert partner's name here] . . . [PAUSE] . . . um, apparently my wife's father is having a golf barbecue thing all day, and I've . . . well, I've got to go . . . Sorry . . .'

Of course, I'm never a hundred per cent sure that the poor wife or partner isn't merely being used as an excuse by someone who doesn't really fancy it. Although why the someone couldn't just say he doesn't fancy it, I don't know. On one fondly remembered occasion, I gave a late call up to an occasional fast bowler, who said:

'We-ell, I'd like to, but I don't think Jane would be very happy if I . . .'

Then in the background I could clearly hear her interrupting, with:

'Don't bring me into it! I'd be glad to see the back of you, you silly bastard . . . !'

Followed by a sheepish:

'OK, then. Where are we playing . . . ?'

Far more frequently I speak to the wife or girlfriend of a potential player when she answers the phone, and half-hear her say as she passes the phone over:

'It's Chris England – you're not playing.'

One significant development in recent years which has transformed the business of getting a team together is the spread of the mobile phone. I don't have one myself, but the fact that so many other people do simplifies matters enormously.

I hate to leave answer-machine messages for people about cricket matches. If you do this the chances are you will end up with more players than you need. Consequently a hierarchy has emerged whereby I will favour those who are contactable by mobile phone, because then there's a much greater chance that I will be able to speak to my potential cricketer directly. Although of course sometimes you will find an answer machine on a mobile phone, which I can never understand. What is the point of being contactable wherever you are twenty-four hours a day, seven days a week, if you're not going to answer the bloody thing when it rings?

The great thing about a mobile phone, for the dilettante cricket captain, is that the period of trying to assemble a team for a match can extend even past the start time of the match itself. In this modern digital age you can be walking out to field while still trying to ascertain what part of the ring road your opening bowler is lost on.

It has become commonplace, now, for Arthur and me to go out to the wicket for the toss at the start of an England XI/Dusty Fleming International Hairstylists Test match and just stand in the middle of the field bellowing into these contraptions at our eleventh, tenth or even ninth men, who haven't got out of bed yet, or who have missed a train at Clapham Junction and there isn't another one for forty-five minutes.

They are annoying things, though, mobile phones, and I have enjoyed the few weeks' respite this trip to India has provided. The relief of being able to walk down the street without being bombarded with the noise pollution of people bellowing: 'I'm just walking down the street . . . What . . . ?! I can't hear you, can you hear me . . . ?' is one thing I'll miss when I get home, that's for sure.

At our level, being a good captain is at least as much about having the ability to cajole people into giving up half a Sunday as it is about motivation, skill or tactics. This means that I often find myself pitted against the type of captain I fear becoming above all others – the passenger captain. He is alarmingly common in the cricketing circles in which I move, and his approach has too many similarities to my own for me to sleep easy at nights.

He is the captain who organises a team, and puts himself through all the torture that entails, because he knows he wouldn't ever get a game otherwise. Typically he will begin his career by forging a side from a bunch of old college mates or work colleagues, fixing up the odd friendly here and there. Soon he will move on to building up a fixture list of more frightening proportions, until the team threatens to take over the entire summer.

He makes all the telephone calls, he makes all the teas. He frets all week about some dilettante who doesn't let him know whether he can actually play until the morning of the match. When the dilettante does finally withdraw, usually because otherwise he'll only see his girlfriend for six days in the week, the passenger captain knocks himself out ringing everyone he knows trying to get an eleventh man. He turns up at the pub at lunch-time, twitching and sweating, having just persuaded someone who lived across the corridor from him at university fifteen years ago and whom he hasn't seen since to turn out for his team.

He then spends a will-sapping three-quarters of an hour trying to hurry his team out of the pub to actually start the game. He goes out to do the toss with the opposing captain, which he loses, and then scuttles off to pad up, because nobody else wants to open the batting. Instead of having a couple of balls lobbed at him to get his eye in, he trots around trying to get someone to do the scoring, begging others to put down the Sunday paper and do a couple of overs' umpiring.

Some years ago we played against an archetypal passenger captain. It happened that the team I had managed to put together for the occasion had only one decent bowler, and he hadn't appeared by the time the match got under way. As it turned out he had left my painstakingly detailed directions to the ground by the phone and then gone to another completely different ground on the other side of London that he once vaguely remembered playing on. I thus was forced to open the bowling with someone who hadn't bowled in years, and wasn't really sure he could remember how to do it.

The umpires came out, followed by their openers. One, relaxed, swinging his arms, grinning, made his way to the non-striker's end with his pal the umpire. The other, the passenger captain, was wound tight as a coiled spring. His kit gleamed whiter than white. Brand-new pads and gloves, an expensive, new, freshly linseeded and as yet unmarked bat, and, amazingly given my bowling attack, a bright spanking white helmet with a grille.

Grub, my makeshift opening bowler, shuffled in to begin the innings. As he brought his arm over, the ball slipped from his grasp a split second too soon and looped gently twenty feet up into the sky. As it arced slowly down the pitch some giggling broke out in the field, but nothing disturbed the awesomely tense concentration of the passenger captain. He kept his eye on the ball all the way, brand-new bat paused at the top of his backlift, just telling himself to wait, wait, wait and see if he would need to play the ball.

At the last instant, he seemed to realise that if he continued to keep his eye on the ball, the ball was actually going to smack him right in the eye. Perhaps not trusting his new grille, he ducked. The ball dropped over and behind his crouching form and, descending almost vertically now, landed perfectly on the top of middle stump, dislodging a single apologetic bail.

As I watched the passenger captain trudge disconsolately back to the pavilion to spend the rest of the innings either scoring or umpiring while his team-mates read the paper, what could I think, except: 'There but for the grace of God . . .'

The tragedy of the passenger captain is that he is the captain, and yet he is a passenger. He almost certainly cannot bowl or bat to save his life, and he finds it impossible to hide himself in the field.

I have, on a couple of occasions, nurtured the innings of an opposing passenger captain, not out of pity or fellow feeling, but because if you cut off the edged single down to third man he could bat for several hours without reaching double figures, thus demolishing his own beloved team's chances of making a competitive total.

I know that I exhibit passenger captain tendencies myself. On one occasion I constructed a scoreboard, which we still use today, out of an old collapsible picnic table. I introduced it to the predictable derision the amateur sportsman reserves for 'the one who takes it too seriously', and decided that I should open the batting, thus having the honour, such as it was, of being the first to register something with my new and painstakingly hand-painted white-on-black hardboard numbers.

The first change the new scoreboard had to record was me running out my opening partner, Andy, at the non-striker's end – he was ever so slightly delayed in setting off for an easy single by carefully handing his half-smoked cigarette to the umpire, as I remember – off the first ball. Then, off the second ball, I was clean bowled, off stump, for nought. And thus the gods of cricket punish us for taking the whole thing too seriously.

I look at the passenger captain and think, 'Poor sod'. But he probably looks at me and thinks exactly the same.

Sooner or later the passenger captain's team will begin a process of change. It may take decades before this starts, or just a couple of seasons. He will find himself becoming impatient with his old college mates and their inability to carry him. Perhaps goaded by their open mockery of his own shortcomings, he will drop them one by one, replacing them with his baby-sitter's brother-in-law, who once played for Berkshire, or the Australian barman at his local. The barman will occasionally have to miss a shift to play, but the passenger captain will happily recompense him for his lost earnings, and will thus take his first step down a slippery slope. Before long he is advertising for new blood in *The Cricketer* magazine, and acquiring mercenaries who he pays 'expenses'. By this time his old chums are playing more and more infrequently, pleading children and pressures of work, and muttering behind his back about how 'the atmosphere has really changed'.

In the final phase of the metamorphosis of his team, the passenger captain is steam-rollering sides who used to look forward to playing him. He is surrounded now by ten super-fit young athletes, all at least fifteen years younger than him, mostly originating in the southern hemisphere. Some of them are not sure of his name. The passenger captain stalks the field with bright, staring eyes, basking in the efficiency of his cricket machine. His team has become known for the nastiness of its sledging, and its willingness to bowl beamers at number-eleven batsmen. Opposition captains are not returning his calls about the fixture for next summer.

The passenger captain is still banging out his noughts and his three-overs-noughts-for-twenty-fives, but his new generation of team-mates are now muttering behind his back about whether he is worth his place in the side. They are talking about dumping him, and maybe joining a league . . .

Many a passenger captain will fancy that he is a Mike Brearley, worth his place in the side for his tactical acumen alone, but the patron saint of the passenger captain is actually Johnny Abrahams. Brearley, never forget, was first brought into the Test team as a specialist batsman during Tony Greig's captaincy. Abrahams once led Lancashire to a one-day trophy final win at Lord's in the mid-eighties. He scored nought, took no catches, and didn't bowl, but he marshalled his troops so well that he was made man of the match for his captaincy. My hero.

Of course, Johnny Abrahams didn't have to deal with what I have to deal with. My team once conceded five runs when the ball struck the portable television set on which mid-off was watching the Sweden v. Saudi Arabia match in the 1994 World Cup. And then there's Tony, whom I have come to think of as the anti-captain. He is an absolutely hyperactive fielder, who can't remain in one fielding position for longer than one ball. Countless times over the years we've played together I've seen an opposition player tumble into a guilefully laid trap, hoicking the ball into the air towards my pinpoint-positioned fieldsman. Tony's got that! I've stupidly thought to myself, nanoseconds before the ball plonks, uncaught, into about an acre of untended outfield.

Tony, you see, will reposition himself according to his own theory of fielding, which is that the batsman, any batsman, is bound to try and hit any ball in exactly the same place as he hit the one before it. Sometimes this will mean Tony unilaterally moving from fine leg to mid-off, say, or perhaps from the square-leg boundary to third slip, without any consultation or approval from me. Tony will do this even if it means moving to stand directly alongside a team-mate already fielding in that position. This team-mate will be looking at Tony with either a quizzical or a long-suffering expression on his face, depending on how long he has been playing for my team. It really is infuriating, and if only Tony wasn't able to bowl really fast and hit the ball miles it might be enough to get him dropped. His own book, *The Art of Anti-Captaincy*, will be a useful companion to the famous Brearley tome, if he ever gets it together to write it.

17
The Big-Match Build-up

BHUVAN
But remember . . . for the Whities, it's just a game. But for
us, it is our life . . . !

(*Lagaan* – English translation)

23 MARCH
As the match approaches the psychological warfare intensifies.
I hesitate to think that Aamir might be prepared to use his
position as producer of the film – and thus our employer – to
increase his chances of beating us in a cricket contest, but I
can't help noticing that the shooting schedule for Thursday,
Friday and Saturday will see all the Brits in the field for three
solid days. The temperature is consistently getting up around
forty-five degrees, and we are unlikely to be at our best on
Sunday after that little lot.

The artificiality of film-making is a given, of course. After
all, the magic of film is (hopefully) going to transform me into
a fast bowler. The oddest touch of all, though, for my money, is
the artificial sweat. I am toiling away in forty-five degree desert
heat, galloping into the wicket and hurling the ball with all the
effort I can muster, and yet I am not working up a sweat. That
is, I must be, but the heat is so dry that sweat is evaporating
as soon as it appears, with the result that, on-camera, I don't
look as if I'm working hard at all. This means that I, and all
the fielders who are in shot, and the batsman too, have to be
sprayed just before the camera rolls with beads of artificial
sweat, made out of a sort of glycerine solution, as far as I can
gather, which doesn't disappear quite so quickly.

Now, in the story, we are playing a cricket match in a desert, a land stricken by drought and baking heat. The fact is that when we recreate those exact circumstances in a real baking-hot desert nobody is visibly sweating, the perspiration is actually burning straight off us. For the purposes of the film, however, we have to be seen to sweat – it is cinema language for effort. It is no great hardship – the spray itself is actually cool and quite refreshing, which ludicrously makes us sweat real sweat even less.

The call sheet this evening features a cartoon of the two teams for the match on Sunday, arranged either side of a gleaming trophy. The blurb reads:

'As the days come close, the pressure mounts.
Can Aamir's team overcome this hurdle?
Or will the England team succumb under pressure?'

I can't help noticing that both those alternatives involve us losing.

The cartoons are basic, but quite nicely done, and some of us have appropriate speech bubbles coming from our mouths, which helps us to identify which is meant to be which of us. I am drawn in my Yardley moustache, with a speech bubble saying 'If we lose the game I will shave'. Captain Russell has a trademark camera hanging from his neck, and is depicted saying something long-winded and in Hindi, 'Shady' Benson is saying 'At least I can put my shades on for this one', while Jamie is muttering 'I wanna sleep . . .'

On the Indian side, little cartoon Aamir is declaiming: 'We will thrash them all the way to London,' while a sinister cartoon Apu lurks at the back in his shades, saying: 'Full power, guys!' – something of a catch-phrase of his.

The Indians have yet to disclose their actual line-up, and so we are pleased to see that the cartoonist, at least, is under the impression that some of the actors from the fictional village team will make the side, including wild man Guran, blacksmith Arjan and Bagha, who aren't much cop, and the little boy, Tipu. The cartoonist has clearly got the measure of old Guran, as his speech bubble reads: 'I will run fast like camel and get kiss on lips!'

It is not clear, though, whether this is the side that will face us on Sunday, or simply the easiest ones to draw . . .

As I look around my team I am starting to have one or two fitness concerns. Jamie has been a slight worry, not because he has been ill, particularly, or injured, but because he simply hasn't played as much cricket as the rest of us. Since his fiancée, Katkin, arrived, Jamie hasn't really come out to play with the boys. He has had his fair share of gastric turmoil, as well, although I can't help noticing that the days when he has been too ill to make it to the set have tended to coincide with days when Katkin is not working. Still, I have hardly seen him in action, and his form is something of a grey area for me, his captain, with only a couple of days to go. At the end of play today, as the setting sun turns the face of the mountain orange and Apu wraps the shoot for the day, my team grab the bat and the ball for a bit of a practice. I get hold of the ball – not the MRI ball that we will be using for the match, but the hard, heavy rubber ball that we use for the filming – and lob it to Jamie to make sure that he has a bowl.

Jamie lollops in and whips his arm over, mucking about, trying to bowl quick. Still, even though he's not really bowling as he will on Sunday, he's getting an impressive amount of bounce from the deadest imaginable track. He moves one away, and Howard, batting, is beaten all ends up. This is very encouraging. Jamie trundles in again, and this time moves a quick one in at Howard. It beats the inside edge and whacks Howard right in the nuts.

Now Howard is not a man to go unprotected, under normal circumstances. Since he got a nasty blow on the jaw some years ago, necessitating some complicated surgery which you must get him to tell you about some time, he always wears a helmet, even in the most casual knockabout game. Usually he is similarly committed to the concept of the protective box, but on this occasion – after all, we were only messing about, and if he'd trotted into the pavilion to get his abdominal protector he'd have missed the chance of getting hold of the bat – he's playing commando.

Howard doubles over, and, as with any group of men when something like this happens to a comrade, we piss ourselves. After a moment or two, however, it becomes clear that he isn't going to just brush this one off, and he is carried, still bent double and moaning piteously, over to the pavilion.

Later, back at Sahajanand, the swelling and bruising kick in, and as his room-mate I am rather more privy to Howard's discomfort than I would like.

'Here,' he says, dropping his shorts, 'I think I should go to the hospital. What do you reckon?'

It is as if he were wearing an aubergine-coloured posing pouch. A horrid, semi-transparent, aubergine-coloured posing pouch, through which the outlines of his genitalia are clearly visible.

As his captain, I feel it is my responsibility to reassure him, put his mind at rest.

'Christ almighty!' I shout, covering my eyes. 'Go to the hospital now, quick, before it all drops off!'

He must be a serious doubt for Sunday now.

Ray's love affair with curry has taken another serious blow, as he succumbed in the night to another bout of vomiting and shits like you wouldn't believe. I've a feeling they'll patch things up when he gets back to England, and proper curries like he's used to, but for the time being he is pretty poorly, and hardly likely to be a hundred per cent on Sunday.

Then there's Ben, still recovering from his dislocated shoulder, and Neil with his long-standing pelvic injury. Both say they will be able to bowl, but there's got to be a chance that one or other of them may break down, perhaps even during the match itself.

Late in the evening Howard returns from exhibiting his blackened genitals to the doctor, whose advice was to 'keep them elewated'. He takes them up on to the roof.

24 MARCH

Aamir has been angling for a preview of my tactics. He has been asking who will open the bowling for us on Sunday. I don't see any harm in letting him know that Harrison will be my main strike bowler, opening from the North end. Or maybe I'll use North from the North end, and Harrison from the South end, which we could rename the Harrison end . . .

During a break in the shooting a few of us are sitting around in the pavilion, discussing our plans for Sunday, when Aamir wanders over.

'Great news!' he suddenly says to Harrison.

'Really?' says Harrison, surprised to be picked out. 'What is it?'

'We've managed to move your flight home to Sunday morning. You'll be able to join your tour a day early.'

And having dropped his bombshell he strolls away again. England will be without Barney the Dinosaur.

In retrospect I should have told Aamir that George the weird upstaging extra was opening our bowling. I'd have liked to have seen that pain in the backside bumped on to the first available plane out of here.

So I am left with a selection dilemma after all. I can bring in Flynn, but he'd really just be making up the numbers, and anyway he was a little put out that he wasn't in the team in the first place so has made other plans for his day off on Sunday.

Only one of the extras has shown the slightest inclination to play any cricket, and that's Andrew, who's already in the side.

There is another option – I could 'turn' one of the Indians. There is a fair bit of dissension in the Indian ranks about Aamir's team selection. Several people who have not disgraced themselves in the matches they have played feel that they should be playing, but have missed the cut. Nakul approaches me to offer his services, and then Goli seeks me out for a private word, saying that it is his dearest wish to see the Indian team fail, since they have not seen fit to include him.

I decide to ask Adi first, to see if we can bring some of our table tennis trophy-winning magic to the cricket field. In my mind's eye I can already see him sending a wristy topspin smash to the cover boundary. Adi, an avid Beatles fan, says:

'It will be an honour to represent the nation of Paul McCartney.'

In the afternoon Ben is bowling. He is showing no ill effects from his recently dislocated shoulder, although it is more likely to trouble him when he is batting. I try a bit of Brearleyesque captaincy psychology, getting to the very heart of what makes him tick to bring the best out of him. I offer him 100R if he can hit the stumps. Within a few minutes I am 200R down. Ben slips one through the guard of Arjan the blacksmith, who, in this form, is not going to make the team for Sunday. He then strikes a valuable psychological blow by bowling Aamir himself, who is still pursuing his 'no dot balls' policy.

A little later it is Yardley's turn, and Ben shows his contempt for poor old 'Hardly''s bowling by offering me the princely sum of 500R if I can hit the stumps. The way I have been bowling he could offer me money to land it on the strip and be reasonably sure of holding on to his cash. He doesn't seem to have a much higher opinion of Howard's wicket-keeping, as he offers me 1,000R for a caught-behind.

These may not seem like huge amounts, but Ben has taken pride in the fact that he has only spent about twenty quid in the eight weeks we have been here, and I could put a real dent in his finances. On the face of it, though, it doesn't seem particularly likely.

However, cricket is a funny old game. The shot list called for Aamir's character, Bhuvan, to pull Yardley for four. I was doing reasonably well at serving up the requisite dross when all of a sudden he played all across the line at one and I cleaned up off stump.

Frankly I did him for pace (he was expecting considerably more of it).

Late afternoon a rumour crackles round the unit like wildfire. Apu is not going to play! I am convinced that this is some bullshit mind game, and laugh it off. Only yesterday Apu was bragging about how many runs he was going to take off Jamie's bowling, and he has been riding us all mercilessly for weeks. I can't believe he won't want to rub our noses in the Kutchi dirt.

Later, though, I speak to Apu, and apparently it's true. He has been invited to play for his old public school in a huge showpiece game in Delhi, a prestigious affair which sounds like the equivalent of the Varsity match, perhaps, at home. The game is a floodlit day/night contest at Feroz Shah Kotla, the Test ground, and it is being televised live on the Sony channel.

Apu is disappointed to have to miss our game, but thrilled to be asked to turn out in this Delhi fixture. His school old boys' team features a former Test player or two, including Navjot Sidhu, the terrifying Sikh opener who once killed a man with a single punch in a bar brawl. The opposition – which is, it seems, the alma mater of our friends Nakul and Adi – can boast an international of their own in Arun Lal.

Now, we are due to finish filming at the Polo Cricket Ground on Saturday, although Monday has been set aside as a spillover day. Aamir has said that Apu can leave a couple of hours early on Saturday provided the filming is almost done, leaving the first AD duties to his assistant Reema, who has already proved more than capable.

This will give Apu the chance, having missed the only flight out of Bhuj in the morning, to drive to Ahmadabad – which will take hours and hours – catch the overnight train to Delhi, and arrive at the stadium with very little time to spare and having had next to no sleep. In short, ideal preparation for playing a big match in front of a nationwide live television audience.

Apu has carefully worked out this transportation miracle, but even he has to admit that there is no way he could get back for Monday morning if the filming overruns.

Aamir has decided on Apu's replacement in the Indian team. It is Adi.

———

We hauled our dusty, exhausted carcasses back to Sahajanand, thinking only of shower and sleep, to find a bright-eyed, bushy-tailed new arrival. Terry is the choreographer, and if you introduced a character like this into a fiction you'd be accused of stooping to the lowest form of stereotyping. He pranced camply around in tight luminous green cycle shorts, proclaiming that he would make dancers of us all despite our two left feet – without, I may say, bothering to ascertain whether any of us, in fact, had two left feet. I found myself fascinated by this conundrum: did Terry become a choreographer because he was naturally rather camp, or did he become rather camp as a result of his career in choreography?

There was a dance rehearsal on the roof, for the ball scene that is coming up next week. Mercifully for my blistered feet it was made clear to us that this was optional. I opted out.

25 MARCH
We filmed Yardley's 'end' of the climactic last over today. Bhuvan/Aamir smiting the winning blow – his 'end' of the

scene – is already in the can from days, or it may be weeks, ago. It is one of the peculiarities of single-camera filming, this dislocation of the two halves of the same event, and this is by no means an extreme example. William Gaunt told me once that during the filming of an episode of *The Champions*, the sixties adventure series about a trio endowed with unusual powers after a plane crash in Tibet, his regular character was involved in a scene with that particular week's guest star. The guest's 'end' of the scene was shot, but there was no time to move the camera round to shoot William that day, and he ended up doing his 'end' to thin air some nine months later.

The last ball of the film is going to be a supremely tense moment, and Ashutosh's idea is to switch backwards and forwards from Bhuvan's sweat-streaked face to Yardley running in to bowl – in super-slow motion. They will be shooting my run-up at forty-eight frames a second, so although the temptation to do a slow-motion running mime for them, cheeks puffed out like Geoff Hurst, is strong, this particular party piece will not be required today.

This idea of Ashutosh's is a fine and dramatic one on paper, but I have to say I fear for him and his project at this moment. Only the other day I saw a super-slow-motion sequence on television from a one-day international in which Pakistan were playing. The bowler under scrutiny was Shoaib Akhtar, the 'Rawalpindi Express', a lithe young whippet of an athlete without a spare ounce anywhere on his finely tuned frame. His bowling action is a perfect whirling whiplash, an ever so slightly suspect double-jointed slingshot of lethal efficiency, one of the most impressive sights in top-class cricket, and yet I have to say that, examined in slow motion, he looked like shit. His taut, almost skeletal face developed unexpected acres of rippling jowl, his eyes bulged and stared, and his whole body seemed to rattle and shake on the very brink of falling apart at any moment.

And this is possibly the finest physical specimen that world cricket has to offer. What on earth am I going to look like pounding across the Kutchi desert in super-slow motion? A fourteen-stone, face-sliding, moustache-flapping, eye-popping, gut-wobbling, love-handle-rippling, steaming, sweating, gasping, bright pink wreck, that's what – Indian cinemagoers are going to be hurling up their popcorn and fleeing for the exits in their droves.

In the middle of the afternoon, we reach the point at which Apu will really have to leave if he is to get to Ahmadabad in time to catch the overnight train to Delhi. He is getting more and more agitated, chivvying people along, but it seems inevitable now that there will be some filming left over until Monday. The question now is whether the production will let him have the time off to make the trip. We hold our collective breath, as depriving the opposition of their most dangerous man – as we have been deprived of ours, don't forget – would be a considerable advantage to us.

Apu goes into a huddle with Aamir and Ashutosh and a brief discussion takes place. We can't see any reason why Reema could not stand in for Apu on Monday, and are expecting to see the Indians' star player running towards one of the unit cars at any minute. When he does emerge, however, Apu is subdued, and he shuffles back to the wicket and calls people into position for the next shot.

I go over to him. 'Don't you have to get going?' I ask.

Apu shrugs. 'They're not letting me go,' he says.

So Aamir will have his big gun after all, while mine – Barney the Dinosaur – will be somewhere over Turkey eating complimentary nuts.

At the end of Saturday we get the call sheet for Monday, which has the team sheets on it for the game. As we suspected, there is no place in the side for crazy Guran, big Arjan, Bagha or Tipu the little boy.

This is how the Indians line up:

Aamir Khan – the Khan himself. Appears to be a fine player both with bat and ball. He took a hat-trick for the Champaner XI against the crew to win that game in the last over, but it has to be said that no one has been inadvertently bowled or caught out more often during the filming, not even Paul.

Apoorva – the mighty Apu, former Indian under-19 star, still seething with frustration at being deprived of his trip to play in a televised match in Delhi, threatens to channel all his considerable energies into grinding us into the desert dust.

Saleem – the stunt co-ordinator, and Yardley's fast-bowling stunt double. Could be dangerous, although some of his work during the filming of the cricket sequences has been almost as wild and inaccurate as Yardley himself.

Ijaz – the stunt co-ordinator's little sidekick. Has seemed frustrated by the lack of martial-arts action in this movie, and he will demonstrate his proficiency at throwing himself to the ground in feigned agony at the drop of a hat. Not especially useful in a game of cricket, although he must have a chance of making it big in the Spanish Primera Liga.

Sanjay – not entirely sure what his role is in the production. He is officially described, I think, as a director's assistant, which is different to an assistant director, of which there are five. During the cricket sequences he has been in charge of the fielders' continuity, which has involved him referring to great fistfuls of charts. These are especially vulnerable to the twisters that spring up without warning, so that the piece of paper telling him that I should be at fine leg is at least as likely to be at fine leg as I am.

Kumar – like Sanjay, his role seems to be supervisory and involve a lot of hanging around, and there is a rumour that the two of them actually collaborated with Ashutosh on the script for *Lagaan*. Unlike Sanjay, however, he doesn't grab a bat or ball the moment a scene is finished, so we have no idea whether he can play or not.

Toni – an electrician, one of the 'Sparks' team that was victorious at the tournament we saw on our first day. Huge.

Ajay – another big-shouldered, powerful-looking bloke, who lugs

the equipment about the place. Both he and Toni look capable of hitting the ball into Pakistan from here, where it would either be destroyed by army bomb disposal units or eaten by trained pigs.
Nagesh – a slender little whippet. We haven't seen him in action, but wouldn't be at all surprised if he could play a bit.
Hemant – one of the camera crew. Like Nagesh he is slightly built and something of an unknown quantity.
Nitin – a big hitter from the hair and make-up department – and I bet that's a phrase you won't find in any other books. Nitin was the difference when we lost to Raj's team a few weeks ago, hitting eighteen from a Brooks over, although he should really have been given out caught behind off his first ball.
Sherry – an all-rounder, Nitin's assistant, who has had special responsibility for Yardley's moustache over the past few weeks. I would enjoy the opportunity to pay him back for his glue-related early-morning torture, even though, of course, he's a lovely chap only doing his job (that last bit written through gritted teeth). He will play if Nitin has to return to Bombay for family reasons, so we will be facing at least one international hairstylist.

They look a formidable bunch. The lads we know about – Apu, Aamir, Saleem, Nitin – can all play, and although some of the others are not well known to us, we know some of the players who have been left out to accommodate them, so we can assume that they too will be competitive.

The England team is printed opposite the Indians on the call sheet, and we too look impressive in print. Everyone obligingly turns out to have a middle initial – essential if you are going to convince as a cricketer – and Ben and Jon have two each, which means, obviously, that I will be relying heavily on them. Even Howard, who I thought might possibly follow the Yorkshire tradition of the likes of Boycott, Illingworth and Gough and spurn the Southern frippery of the spare initial, turns out to have another Christian name, and, better still, it comes first.

In days gone by the redundant first initial was almost a

prerequisite for the England captaincy – D.B. Close, M.C. Cowdrey, J.M. Brearley – and as recently as the 3rd Test v Pakistan at Headingley in 1987 the England side could boast four gentlemen with this distinction at once, namely B.C. Broad, R.T. Robinson, C.J. Richards and C.W.J. Athey. In the nineties, however, this practice rather fell out of favour among English Test cricketers, and it has fallen to the Sri Lankans, particularly, to keep it alive, thanks to P.A. de Silva, D.P.M. de S. Jayawardene and the glorious W.P.U.C.J. Vaas. England's most recent exponent at the time of writing (if you don't count R.C. Russell, who doesn't use either of his given names)? A.M. Smith, v Australia at Leeds in 1997.

Jon, Ray and I are representing An England XI on the team sheet, and D.H. Lee is proudly proclaiming his affiliation to the Dusty Fleming International Hairstylists. The others vary wildly from the impressive – Benson, MCC, Jamie, Gloucestershire – to the rather less so – Paul, Abingdon School second XI. Paul isn't even sure that there was a school second XI, but he reckons that if there was one he was probably in it. Andrew has put down Potters Bar Crusaders as his team, and we are not a hundred per cent sure whether this is a cricket side or a twelfth-century battle recreation society.

England will line up as follows:

C.W.England (Yardley, capt.)
An England XI
D.H. Lee (Burton, wkt)
Dusty Fleming International Hairstylists XI
B.G. Hart (Benson)
Shipbourne, Paralytics, and MCC
B.J.A. Nealon (Smith)
Gaieties
J.G. Whitby-Coles (Wesson)
Gloucestershire

J.L.H. House (North)
An England XI
Aditya Lakhia (Kachra)
Ahmadabad, India
A.P. Tappin (cricketer)
Potters Bar Crusaders
R.W. Eves (Willis)
An England XI
P.B. Blackthorne (Russell)
Abingdon School second XI
S.G. Holmes (Brooks)
London Theatres

At the end of filming on Saturday the production team laid on a big party to celebrate the completion of the cricket sequences – even though we'll all be back here on Monday to do some more.

By the time we've all changed there are tables and chairs set out, and a makeshift bar is open for business as the sun sets. There is beer, rum, and whisky, and all of it seems to be real as opposed to the alcohol-free bootleg rum-flavoured beverage you can buy on the black market. The Brits, to a man, hurl themselves at this bar with the enthusiasm of travellers, lost in the desert, suddenly catching sight of a swimming pool.

Before very long there is a noticeable increase in merriness. Dance music is pounding out of the huge speakers – no need to worry about the neighbours, they're forty-five minutes' drive away. The *Ice Cold in Alex* reverence with which the first beer was treated has given way to some enthusiastic nectar-necking, and one or two are well on the way to a serious hangover. Harrison appears without the beard which has been driving him mad the whole time he has been here, and his newly shaven chin is enthusiastically toasted.

Nuella, one of the extras, does her party piece – part juggling, part martial art, swinging two big lumps of fire on the ends of two chains. They whirl around her head, around her body, carving burning orange circles into the black desert night. It is spectacular, and Howard, the born street entertainer, is not to be outdone. As soon as Nuella runs out of paraffin – allez oop! – H has a chair on his chin.

In the middle of a raucous conversation about something or other, I catch sight of Aamir, sitting on the verandah of the pavilion, watching us. A laugh dies in my throat and my blood freezes in my veins. He has the look of a Bond villain whose masterplan to take over the world is falling perfectly into place, and I can almost imagine him rubbing his hands together and murmuring to himself the single word:

'Excellent . . .'

It's actually more of a sitcom plan than a Bond film one, of course. Get the opposition drunk as skunks the night before the big game, and then knock them over easily as they hold their poorly heads and ask you if you wouldn't mind not appealing quite so loudly.

Aamir himself is teetotal. Apu is going round making sure everyone has a drink, but I haven't seen him actually drinking anything himself, and all the Indian players I can see – Sanjay, Kumar, Saleem – have clearly not been indulging either. I wonder whether it's still not too late, whether I can get a lid on my team's drinking before too much damage is done.

But then it occurs to me: these boys are English cricketers. There's not a man here who won't have played with a hangover before, countless times. In fact, it might even make us all feel more at home. I wave a bottle cheerfully at Aamir, and pretend to fall over drunk. I'm saying I was pretending – that's my story and I'm sticking to it . . .

Later on, Howard and I stroll round the boundary in the darkness, imagining the game tomorrow on this very pitch. The pavilion in the distance is brightly lit, with silhouetted figures dancing in front of it, and from a distance, surrounded by black darkness, with the thin noise of the music carried on the still night air, the whole scene has the look of a location in a horror film where something very, very nasty and unexpected is about to take place.

18
The Match – Qayamat 2000

Capt. Russell and his team are unwinding on the palace terrace. Drinks are being served.

YARDLEY
Sir, what is our plan for the match tomorrow?

CAPT. RUSSELL
If we win the toss, we'll bat and drum up a huge total!

ALL
Cheers! Cheers!

(*Lagaan* – English translation)

26 MARCH

It makes a refreshing change, after all the cricket fixtures I've organised in English summers of variable quality, not to be worried about the weather when I wake up on the morning of the Big Match. My only real meteorological concern today is whether it will be bloody unbearably hot or merely fucking hot.

Over breakfast Howard tells us all about his journey home to Bhuj from the party in the desert last night. When he wandered off to look for a lift he bumped into Aamir, who offered to get one of the production drivers to take him so he wouldn't have to wait around for the bus like everyone else. Howard gratefully accepted, and clambered into the back of one of the Sumos.

After a minute or two a driver got in and started the engine. Then, just before the car pulled away, the back doors were yanked open and Aamir and Apu jumped in on either side, sandwiching Howard in the middle. He was trapped, like

Bob Hoskins in the last shot of *The Long Good Friday*, and all the way back to town the two Indians pumped him for information about my tactics for the match.

All the Brits are hyped up and nervous, apart from Jamie, who's still asleep, and Neil, who's on his way back to Blighty despite a late scare yesterday when it seemed that his flight hadn't been confirmed properly and he might be staying after all.

Mid-morning there was a costume fitting for the ball scenes next week. All of us had to try on dress uniforms, with a silly little bib underneath instead of a whole shirt. This would have been fine, except that none of the jackets was big enough to do up, so vast acres of pale British guts were on constant wobbly display. The costume department threw its collective hands up in horror and set about making two dozen cummerbunds. Good word, cummerbunds. Good P.G. Wodehouse kind of word.

At 12.30 the team bus is waiting outside Sahajanand Tower. It quickly fills up – all my team, half the Indians (the other half are coming on the other bus from the Hotel Abha), and plenty of spectators. This is a world away from cricket at home, where half my players will understand the phrase 'two o'clock start' to mean 'leave your own house and begin long journey to match at about two fifteen'.

The bus sets off on the forty-five-minute journey to the ground, positively ahum with excitement. For the past few weeks we have been doing this drive at six in the morning, trying to grab another few minutes' sleep here and there while the road tries to bump the fillings out of our teeth. Now we are all wide awake, adrenalin pumped.

Apu comes down the centre aisle in his Indian one-day international shirt and bullish mood, the disappointment of his missed trip to Delhi banished by the excitement of playing today. He says he thinks the game will be close, but the Indians have a slight edge.

Aamir, following him, reckons the Indians are the underdogs.

Apu stops the bus and buys choc-ices for everyone. Remem-
bering the evil effects of the ice cream at the 'I.V.' the other
week, and also 1970 and Gordon Banks's Mexican beer, I
decline. This is my first international, for goodness' sake,
and I don't want to spend it galloping to the bogs every five
minutes.

As the bus rattles through the cacti deeper into the Kutchi
desert, I try to sort out a batting order. I toy for a while with
using Shady as an opener, but in the end I stick him at three
and go with myself and Johnny Player as the opening pair.
We have opened many an innings together for An England
XI, and it usually works pretty well. Howard has a Boycottian
dedication to platform-building, and if I am there as well I can
hurry him up if he grinds to a halt altogether.

Ben's repeated mentions of a century he scored last summer
persuade me to put him at four, with Jamie at five. At home I
would normally have Jon in at seven or eight, but he's in the
form of his life, as far as I can see, and I have no qualms about
making him number six. Then Adi and Andrew, followed by
Ray and Paul, while Brooksy has obligingly offered not only
to go in at eleven but also to score as well. Stout fellow.

Getting off the bus the heat hits us like a wall. Without the
gradual acclimatisation usually provided by a dawn start, the
conditions are immediately extremely oppressive. It must be
several degrees hotter than back in Bhuj, and it takes us all a
few minutes to get used to it.

Rounding the corner at the foot of the mountain, we come
to the cricket ground. It's familiar, of course – we've been
working here for five weeks – but without all the camera
equipment, and lights, and trucks, and light panels, and cranes,
and umbrellas, it suddenly looks spectacular all over again.
The pavilion gleams green and white in the desert sun, a lone
figure from the setting department is putting in a set of stumps,

it's peaceful, warm, bright, and just the most perfect setting for a cricket match.

Ray has his camcorder, and some of us set off into the middle to look at the wicket and do a pitch report for him. Jon, as Geoffrey Boycott, is in the middle of a rant about the state of the track when he discovers that the bails have been stuck to the top of the stumps with Blu-tac – fine for filming in blustery conditions, but not so clever if you're actually going to play for real.

After a bit of loosening up, I go out with Aamir to do the toss. Before the formality takes place, we agree that it will be a twenty-over game – any more in these conditions would go beyond fun – and I present him with a tiny nine-inch bat that we have all autographed, in the hope that he will be so touched that he will feel obliged to use it in the match. No such luck, though . . .

Like the fictional English captain in *Lagaan*, I win the toss, and like him I decide to bat first – '*bali basi karenge*', as Captain Russell put it. As in the film, our plan for the match is to knock up a big total and then bowl the opposition out, and I'm hoping not to piss it away like our counterparts from 1893.

We shake hands and set off back to the pavilion, where we see that there is a film camera here today after all. Satya, the sharp little production executive and table tennis demon, has been given a new responsibility, which is to produce a 'Making of *Lagaan*' documentary, and he and an assistant are wrestling with some cables, trying to get the unfamiliar equipment started up.

Suddenly, out on the field of play, the weather intervenes. A desert twister appears out of nowhere and sweeps right across the wicket, with cricketers, spectators and setting guys running for cover with their hands over their mouths. It takes a minute or two to travel boundary to boundary, and then disappears into the scrubby undergrowth. The setting guys scurry around rebuilding the boundary fence and looking for four of the stumps, which have been scattered around the outfield. Two are left standing, and remarkably, thanks to the Blu-tac, a bail is still in place. Must remember to mention that to the umpires before we start, or we might have an international incident on our hands . . .

The Indians take the field. Where my team are all more or less in white, give or take the odd pair of multicoloured Bermuda shorts, Aamir's boys are a riot of colourful leisure gear. Apu is sporting the Indian one-day international shirt with the big number 10 on the back, which he has been wearing on and off during the filming in the hope of intimidating us – not without success, I have to say – and the skipper himself is looking very dapper in a smart blue shirt and jeans.

The pair of massive speakers which were used to play the music at last night's party are still in place in front of the pavilion, and some music suddenly blares forth as Howard and I set off to open the innings. We haven't got far, though, before Ray has got hold of the DJ's microphone, and Richie Benaud's unmistakable tones hum across the desert.

'Good afternoon, everyone. You join us here at the Polo Crickut Ground in Kutch for this one-day international match between India and England. It's a maarvellous day here, and we're all set for a maarvellous day's crickut . . .'

Howard is wearing his trademark battered white helmet. We are playing with the MRI ball – local rules – rather than what we would have called 'a corky' when I were a lad, but after his painful groin injury Howard is not to be separated from his full range of safety equipment. Aamir gives the tin hat a playful knock as Howard passes.

The full international status of the fixture may have been open to question, but that doesn't stop Ray from leading a few of the Brits in a quick rendition of 'God Save The Queen' while Aamir places his field. This provokes an immediate response from the Indian spectators in the pavilion. Kiran and Priya, Apu's assistants, grab the microphone, and begin a spirited bellowing of the Indian anthem, with which their compatriots – Lakha and Goli among them – join in, standing proudly with hands on hearts. I'd say we lost that one.

The garrulous Amin takes over the commentary, displaying all the high standards of neutral impartiality that are tradition-ally associated with the job. 'Come on, India!' he yells. 'Full power!!'

1st over
Bowler: Nagesh from the Pavilion end
Not Apu. I suppose he must be opening from the Hill end.

As we suspected, Nagesh looks like he can play a bit, and his third ball is a good-length delivery just outside off stump. Howard plays and misses, the ball whistles through to Hemant, the keeper, and the whole Indian team go up for a catch. Amin, in the pavilion, screams: 'He's gone! We've got him!', and then when Jon, umpiring, is unmoved, goes on to remark with spoof bitterness: 'Well, the umpires are both Brits so we have no chance!'

The very next ball is full and on the stumps, and Howard scoops it up off the bottom of the bat straight to Apu at mid-off, who dives forward to catch it. The Indian fielders whoop and rush to congratulate the big man, Amin yells the microphone to distortion: 'He's out! He's out this time!', and I turn away to absorb the disappointment of our dread-ful start.

Hang on a minute, though. Howard's not walking, Jon hasn't given him out, and apparently it was a bump ball. Aamir's team take it very well, I must say – apart from Amin, who says: 'These guys are used to cheating, but we will fight them tooth and nail!' – and I thought it was out . . .

We pick up a couple of singles – 2–0.

2nd over
Bowler: Ajay from the Hill end
Still no Apu. Possibly inflamed by the sight of Howard's helmet, Ajay tries to knock it off and gets hooked for four. Amin is still commentating at full volume – 'Great fielding! Kick ass, guys!' – and displays a knack for not quite spotting what is going on, describing a pleasingly deft pull shot as a lucky nick – 10–0.

3rd over
Bowler: Nagesh
Another tidy over which we can't really take liberties with, but we run a couple more singles. After Howard plays a big air shot Amin cries: 'Well left!' (possibly sarcastic) – 12–0.

4th over
Bowler: Ajay
Ajay bowls a short ball and I try to cut it. It is blinking hot out there and when I miss the ball the bat slides out of my sweaty hands and flies down the full length of the wicket, narrowly missing Ajay's shins, then Howard's shins, then the stumps – 17–0.

5th over
Bowler: Apu
Here is the confrontation we have been waiting for, and possibly the first turning point of the match. Apu paces out his long left arm over the wicket run-up, and brings the field in closer except for Hemant, the keeper, who moves right back.

In a calculated gesture of disdain for their star man, Howard takes off his helmet and gives it to the square-leg umpire. In its place he puts on the maroon cap of his character, Burton, and in all the times we've batted together this is the first time I've been able to see his face.

Amin tells us, over the music, that Apu's number 10 shirt was given to him by Sachin Tendulkar.

Apu is finally satisfied with his field, and moves in to bowl – with his big wide shoulders and his billowing shirt he is like a ship in full sail. His loosener goes away down the leg side, and the English lads hoot as the wide is signalled.

Amin yells: 'Full power India! No runs please!'

Apu thunders in, beats Howard's forward defensive, and the hoots are from the other side now. Next, a leg-stump yorker is worked away for a single, and I am on strike.

I have always disliked facing left arm bowling from over the wicket. I can never manage to line myself up properly, and knowing that I am vulnerable to this type of bowling only makes it worse. I resolve to get forward and try to block Apu out.

Apu runs in, I take a big forward stride, and the ball strikes the middle of my defensive prod and runs away through the covers for four. Amin plays a burst of music to mark the boundary 'to cheer everyone up'.

Apu then beats me three times outside off stump, but I manage not to get a nick on any of them, not for want of trying. 23–0.

6th over
Bowler: Kumar
In the ten-over games that made up the tournament on our first day here, 70 was a par total, and so I am looking for a total of around 140–150. Apu seemed to have got into a groove by the end of his first over, and so I reckon we need to get after the bowling at the other end. Kumar is bowling with a large white cloth wrapped around his head and draped around his shoulders against the sun and the dust. I slog one straight to Sanjay at long on, but fortunately it reaches him on the bounce. Then I glance one to fine leg for four, whereupon Amin puts on his music 'with a heavy heart for

India, but it's not really music for the Indian spectators here, it's more like . . . torture, to us . . .' I lift the last ball over Sanjay's head for a six, and we've begun to accelerate nicely – 37–0.

7th over
Bowler: Apu
Although Apu is bowling well and beats both Howard and me, I manage to bottom-edge a four past the keeper, and we pick up four singles as well to move to 45–0. Amin, drained, takes a break from his hyperactive commentary, and Ray and Jon take over.

8th over
Bowler: Aamir
The captain has trouble landing his slow spinners, but when they do pitch the bounce is very high and awkward. We pass fifty, and then I try to slash one away square on the offside and hole out to Nagesh at point. I've made 32, and we are 51–1.

9th over
Bowler: Sanjay
Barry has come in, and finds the bounce takes a bit of getting used to, surviving a big and enthusiastic appeal for a catch behind. A couple of singles only from the over, and the score is now 53–1.

10th over
Bowler: Aamir
With a new batsman in, and Aamir's slow bowling difficult to get away, I begin to worry that we should be pushing on a bit more, especially as it is such a short game. From the boundary I give Howard a signal to hurry up, and he gives

the very next ball a big charge and is stumped by Hemant for 16. 55–2.

11th over
Bowler: Sanjay
Barry gets the message, and slaps Sanjay's first ball for four behind square leg. After that, though, Sanjay ties him up, and we reach 61–2.

12th over
Bowler: Aamir
Ben is facing for the first time, and both he and Barry pick up boundaries in this, a good over for us – 72–2.

13th over
Bowler: Sanjay
After a couple of wides, Barry tries to deposit the bowling into the pavilion and loses a bail, having made 12. Jamie comes in, and edges his first ball for four. It's 80–3.

14th over
Bowler: Saleem
Yardley's stunt bowler comes on in place of the skipper, and bowls briskly and straight. Has a good shout for lbw against Ben, but the umpire – me – is not convinced. A mixed bag of singles and wides keeps the scoreboard ticking over, but we could do with getting a move on. 85–3, with six overs left.

15th over
Bowler: Aamir
The dapper skip has changed ends, and is having a go from the Pavilion end, even though the rolled mud wicket seems to me to be absolutely uniform throughout its twenty-two yards. Jamie, the ex-pro (albeit an ex-pro number eleven), has the same difficulty as the rest of us with the high-bouncing slow

deliveries, although he does swat one of them for six. At the end of Aamir's allotted maximum of four overs we are 93–3.

16th over
Bowler: Saleem
Another eight-run over for us, with Jamie hitting one four off the poor man's Yardley. 101–3 now, with four overs to go. At this rate we are looking at only 135 or so – need to push on.

17th over
Bowler: Sanjay
Amin plays music for both sides in this over. Jamie smacks a big six into the scrubby trees, but Sanjay manages to hit Ben's middle stump and he goes for 10 at 108–4. This brings Jon to the wicket, and I know what to expect, having played with him many times. He can provide a flurry of quick runs, which is just what we need, or be out first ball, which is something of a speciality of his. On this occasion he snicks his opening delivery just past off stump and Hemant down to third man, where Goli, on as a sub fielder, lets it through his feet for four. We end the over on 118–4.

18th over
Bowler: Nagesh
The whippy opening bowler returns, and Jamie and Jon work him away for eleven runs, including a four past Apu, prowling up and down on the square-leg boundary, clearly thinking he should have been brought back by now – 129–4.

19th over
Bowler: Saleem
The stuntman has changed ends now, but he can't prevent the English team from accelerating. We score twelve more, incuding a huge six from Jon, and are looking good for our 150 now at 141–4 with one over left.

20th over
Bowler: Apu
Aamir seems to have miscalculated, and Apu is going to end up bowling only three of his four overs. Apu is not impressed, and steams in for this final over. Jamie scoops the ball in the air to Aamir at mid-on, but the producer/star/captain spills a straightforward catch and we pinch a single. Apu says nothing to his employer, but the set of his shoulders as he strides back to his mark speaks of a marked discontent. He hurtles in, determined to give it everything, and Jon whacks his second ball halfway back to Bhuj. Amin is playing 'Stuck In The Middle With You' to mark the boundaries, and by the end of the over we have heard nearly the whole record, as Jamie and Jon demolish a demoralised Apu with another one-bounce four and a huge six over mid-wicket. We close on 161–4, a very satisfactory total, with Jamie 38 not out, and Jon 30 not out – this pair have added 53 in three and a half overs.

Bakshi's production caterers lay on a lavish, spicy tea on the verandah of the pavilion. I am too preoccupied to indulge fully, but one or two of the others stuff their faces with spicy treats.

India's Reply

1st over
Bowler: Jon from the Pavilion end
Aamir opens the batting with Nagesh as his partner, clearly feeling that a captain's innings is required. Jon is a tricky bowler, though, and beats him three times as he starts with a maiden. 0–0.

2nd over
Bowler: Ben from the Hill end
Nagesh gets the innings under way with a hit behind square leg for four. Following the principle espoused by my opening

bowler at home, Tony the anti-captain, I immediately put a fielder on the boundary there. This turns out to be Nagesh's favourite shot, and we keep him quiet after this.

In the pavilion Apu grabs the microphone to do some commentary, but his style is less reflective and observant than it is actual outright coaching:

'Come on, guys! Full power! Don't forget the singles! Lots of space on the off side! You are playing very well!' Etc . . .

After two overs it's 9–0.

3rd over
Bowler: Jon
Jon's first ball to Nagesh is straight. The little opener is trapped right in front of the stumps, the ball flicks something, either his leg or his bat, and goes through to Adi, who is keeping wicket. Half of us go up for lbw – because if he hasn't got his bat on the ball he is absolutely plumb – and the other half go up for the catch behind – because if he has got the bat on it he's been taken by the keeper. Adi, meanwhile, is pointing at the leg-side bail, which is on the ground, and shouting that Nagesh is out bowled. Given these three alternative decisions to choose from, the umpire mystifyingly opts for a fourth option – not out. Hmmm (scratches chin thoughtfully) . . .

Jon bowls tidily and nearly has Nagesh again later in the over – 12–0.

4th over
Bowler: Ben
Ben traps Aamir in front of his stumps, and offers umpire Saleem the stuntman the chance to make his next few weeks a misery by giving his employer out, but Saleem the stuntman is understandably not interested, fearing perhaps that a new stunt might appear in the script which involves him throwing himself down the mountain. And it was perhaps a little too high . . . 14–0.

5th over
Bowler: Jon
Another over that Aamir and Nagesh can't get away, and the score moves on to 17–0.

6th over
Bowler: Ben
Aamir pulls a four, but even though the opening pair pick up ten runs from this over, they are still falling behind the rate they will need at 27–0. At the end of the over, Aamir takes a drink, and stands by himself in a familiar pose, one foot resting on top of the other, contemplating the situation.

7th over
Bowler: Jamie
Like Aamir, I have held back my main bowler rather than opening with him, because teams will always tend to begin circumspectly whoever is bowling. Jon and Ben have done a good job, and Jamie continues in the same vein, conceding only one run from his first over, with Aamir very watchful. 28–0.

8th over
Bowler: Barry
Apu, in the pavilion, is getting impatient. He grabs the microphone and booms: 'Twelve runs an over required!' This is not quite what they need to win, but rather what he himself wants to see, and I think he would like to shout 'Hit out or get out!', playground style. Just as I'm thinking it suits us to keep Apu in the hutch as long as possible, Barry brings Nagesh's quiet little knock to an end for 11 by knocking out his middle peg and it's 30–1. Aamir straightaway signals to the pavilion, promoting Apu to number three, and the big lefty strides out, pulling on some soft chamois leather gloves.

There's no mistaking the fact that this is possibly the turning point of the match. If Apu gets going, he is a fearsome hitter and could take the match away from us.

Paul and Andy have been fielding out of their skins, and I push them on to the square boundaries, and move Ben and Jon out in the hope of catching a straight hit. The tension cranks up a palpable notch, and everyone is on their toes. The match starts for real now.

Apu leaves us in no doubt as to what his approach will be by opening his shoulders and carving his first ball away, straight to where I've just put Paul, and he gets two runs.

9th over
Bowler: Jamie
Aamir gets a single to bring Apu on strike. The big AD is prowling nervously, clearly feeling the weight of expectation on his wide shoulders. He drives his first ball to mid-off, where it hits me on the shin. No run – pain, no gain. The next ball is short, and brings a huge flailing pull shot out to deep mid-wicket for a single.

Aamir picks up on the urgency that Apu is trying to bring to their innings. He swipes a Jamie full toss away for four, and then works the ball square for a quick single. We can feel the momentum starting to build menacingly, and see Apu checking for gaps in the field.

Jamie comes in, a little skip in his run-up, and fizzes the ball straight through Apu, flattening his middle stump. For a second none of us can quite believe what we're seeing, but then we are all mobbing Jamie and Apu is shambling back to the pavilion peeling off his gloves. It's 39–2, and we're right on top.

10th over
Bowler: Barry
With Apu gone, Aamir takes responsibility for pushing the Indian innings on. He smashes three fours in the over, and

the match is not over yet by any means. They are 52–2 at halfway where we were 55–2, but they will need to match the acceleration Jamie and Jon gave us in the last few overs.

11th over
Bowler: Jamie
Toni, the new batsman, can't get Jamie away, and some brilliant fielding by Andy and also Adi behind the stumps helps us to keep them down to 54–2.

12th over
Bowler: Barry
Aamir is trying hard, but the boundaries have dried up. We haven't heard 'Stuck In The Middle With You' for quite some time, and now India really do need twelve runs an over. 59–2.

13th over
Bowler: Jamie
An extraordinary over. Jamie loses his line completely, and his first two balls go for wides down the leg side. Aamir, looking to get a move on, drives the first legitimate ball of the over for two, and then swivels to hook the next for a sweet boundary. I am following the ball, and am just applauding the shot when I notice Ben running in from the boundary with his arms in the air. Poor Aamir has unluckily trodden on his stumps completing the shot, and is on his way for 35.

Amin is umpiring now, and we discover that he has a rather shaky grasp of what constitutes a wide. As the over progresses, it appears that any ball which the batsman has not managed to hit is going to qualify, and he signals 'wide' to six deliveries on the trot. One of these is well wide, and beats Adi behind the stumps to run away for four wides, but at least two bounce right over the top of middle stump.

Finally Saleem manages to get a bat on one, and steers it

straight into my hands at midwicket, to make it 72–4. Two balls later Toni holes out to Jon in the deep, and it's 73–5. Another couple of wides, and a fifteen-ball over is finally behind us. 75–5.

14th over
Bowler: Ray
Hemant greets Ray's introduction to the attack by whacking a full toss for six. Later in the over Ray has his revenge, as the little keeper snicks to his counterpart, Adi, for a neatly taken caught-behind. 84–6.

15th over
Bowler: Simon
Simon had a mare in one of our earlier games, conceding eighteen to the hairdresser Nitin, who is absent today. Ajay and Ijaz have to hit out, now, needing fourteen an over, and they get them, including one big six. 98–6.

16th over
Bowler: Ray
Ajay clobbers another big six, but India only get ten from the over thanks to a very dusty diving stop by Simon, demonstrating why he is nicknamed 'The Cobra' at home. 108–6

17th over
Bowler: Jon
Ijaz manages a couple of lusty blows, and the score goes up to 117–6, meaning that they need 44 off three. The way these two are hitting they could come too close for comfort . . .

18th over
Bowler: Ray
Ray bowls an excellent tidy over, conceding only six singles. Ajay pulls a hamstring and calls for a runner, and Apu grabs

a bat and jogs out to the middle. Aamir, commentating now, remarks:

'Apu, the run-out expert, is now at the crease – could prove dangerous for India!'

Of course, when the Cast beat the Crew, weeks ago now, Apu ran out no fewer than seven of his team-mates, so he seems an odd choice as a runner . . .

19th over
Bowler: Barry
India need the big hits, but they're just not coming. Apu's second stay at the crease is no longer than his first, as Barry bowls the ailing Ajay to make it 126–7.

20th over
Bowler: Ben
With India needing 35 from the last over, I am tempted to bring myself on to bowl, but you never know, do you . . .

Adi contrives to run out Ijaz, who has backed up far too far, and the final score is 134–8, meaning that England win by 27 runs.

———

The match has been played in great spirit, and Aamir congratu-lates everybody. For our part we try not to crow, but such has been the anticipation that a bit of triumphalist jigging about is inevitable. I catch sight of Barry, with a big serene grin on his face, and Ray and Howard and Ben are dancing in front of the pavilion for the benefit of Satya's documentary camera. Jon finds a precious bottle of beer, and sprays it all over everyone like a Grand Prix winner. Andy, who started the day in white clothes, is now completely beige, having fielded like a sliding demon throughout in great clouds of Kutchi dust.

As if to heighten the pretence that we have just played a full international fixture, some interviews are conducted on the verandah in front of the pavilion, and I hear Apu gloomily saying that it was the worst performance he has ever given in his life. He tries to persuade us to have a rematch after the filming tomorrow, but no one is interested in letting him have another crack at us, thank you very much.

My first – and only – venture into international captaincy has ended in success, and now that word is out I shall be sitting by the phone every time Nasser Hussain is taken off to hospital for 'precautionary X-rays' – i.e. about six times a season.

LAGAAN CRICKET INTERNATIONAL
INDIA v ENGLAND

Polo Cricket Ground, Kunariya, Kutch, 26 March 2000. Toss: England

ENGLAND			4	6
D.H. Lee	st. Hemant	b. Aamir Khan	16	1	
C.W. England*	c. Nagesh	b. Aamir Khan	32	3	1
B.G. Hart		b. Sanjay	12	2	
B.J.A. Nealon		b. Sanjay	10	1	
J.G. Whitby-Coles		not out	38	2	3
J.L.H. House		not out	30	3	2
Aditya Lakhia†					
A.P. Tappin					
R.W. Eves					
P.B. Blackthorne					
S.G. Holmes					
extras (b8, lb2, w13)			23		
Total (4 wkts, 20 overs)			161		

1–51, 2–55, 3–75, 4–108

Nagesh 3–0–14–0, Ajay 2–0–13–0, Apoorva Lakhia 3–0–34–0, Kumar 1–0–14–0, Aamir 4–0–27–2, Sanjay 4–0–29–2, Saleem 3–0–20–0.

INDIA			4	6
Aamir Khan*	hit wicket	b. Whitby-Coles	35	5	
Nagesh		b. Hart	11	1	
Apoorva Lakhia		b. Whitby-Coles	3		
Toni	c. House	b. Whitby-Coles	2		
Saleem	c. England	b. Whitby-Coles	0		
Hemant†	c. Aditya Lakhia	b. Eves	9		1
Ajay		b. Hart	25	1	2
Ijaz	run out (Aditya Lakhia/Nealon)		16	1	
Kumar Dave		not out	7	1	
Sanjay Dayma		not out	0		
Sherry					
extras (b6, lb2, w15, nb3)			26		
Total (8wkts, 20 overs)			134		

1–30, 2–39, 3–63, 4–72. 5–73, 6–86, 7–126, 8–133

House 4–0–12–0, Nealon 4–0–24–0, Whitby-Coles 4–0–22–4, Hart 4–0–22–0, Eves 3–0–22–1, Holmes 1–0–13–0.

ENGLAND WIN BY 27 RUNS

19
The Cricketer on Tour

LAKHA
I lost my mind, Bhuvan. I wanted to see you lose. So I
teamed up with the Angrez . . .

(*Lagaan* – English translation)

27 MARCH

At the end of play today there is a huge prize-giving for those involved in the match yesterday. I'll say one thing for our hosts, they certainly love a trophy – everyone gets one, whether winner, loser or caterer. I am asked to nominate a man of the match, a best batsman, and a best bowler, and so Jamie, Jon and Barry end up with two tin pots to carry home. I try to persuade Aamir to pick up the best batsman one himself, but he feels it should be someone on the winning side. He played as well as anyone, though, actually.

Much merriment is made from the parallels with the story of *Lagaan*, especially as it gives everyone the opportunity to castigate Adi as the traitor, like Lakha in the film. Actually, truth to tell, he wasn't the only one. Goli, who was spurned by the selectors and only used as a sub fielder yesterday, came up to me after the game and whispered:

'Did you see me let the ball through my feet for a four? This is because I wanted you to win.'

And, unlike in *Lagaan*, of course, the pasty-faced tea-drinkers won.

28 MARCH

An article in the paper this morning says that the Gujarati

government are to change their legislation on alcohol prohibition so that foreigners can simply pick up drink permits on arrival at airports. To promote tourism is the reason given, but Simon and Ray are convinced that this is all because of their constant harassment of the authorities in pursuit of beer.

I have come to an agreement with Reena that will allow me to take off for a couple of days to go to Agra, which I am looking forward to, although I am not, by nature, a relaxed traveller. I am afflicted by a condition which I call – in the absence of any other suggestions from the medical community – Tourist Guilt.

What this means is that whenever I am in a foreign country, working or on holiday, I cannot rest while there are landmarks to see within striking range. And I'm not just talking about nipping into the nearest town to stroll around in its ordinary little cathedral between a relaxing after-lunch siesta and a pre-dinner drink. Tourist Guilt extends your striking range to its fullest possible extent. It requires you to spend half of any available window of opportunity travelling to see something, a tiny amount of time actually visiting the place, and then the other half of your time travelling back to base.

No matter how tempting the beach, the pool, the light lunch, the siesta, the trashy novel, Tourist Guilt is always whispering in my ear: 'You might never get this close again.'

On holiday in Los Angeles, Tourist Guilt made me drive through Death Valley in a hire car to see the Grand Canyon. And Las Vegas. And the Boulder Dam.

Working in Tel Aviv once, I had a couple of days off, and Tourist Guilt made me take a coach journey down through the Gaza Strip to Cairo and back to see the Pyramids.

Following Oldham to Genoa on their one and only European venture – the 1995 Anglo-Italian Cup – Tourist Guilt had rushed me round Pisa and Florence before I could draw breath.

Here, in Bhuj, I have been working most days and on

stand-by most of the others, and so actually forbidden from leaving. This has meant that I have been able to relax here and get to know the little town. Coming up at the end of the week, however, I have four days with no filming, and I've worked out that it is just possible, provided all the connecting flights work out, to get as far as the Taj Mahal and back. I'm not sure I wouldn't rather just hang around here, but Tourist Guilt won't let me . . .

2 APRIL
Sunday morning. I am sitting in Delhi domestic airport waiting for a short flight to Agra. I worked out that I could get to see the Taj Mahal by leaving Bhuj yesterday morning, flying to Mumbai and then to Delhi last night, going to Agra today, back to Delhi and Mumbai tomorrow, and Bhuj on Tuesday. I'm getting a little concerned now, because this flight has already been delayed twice now by a couple of hours, and if I'm going to see the Taj I have to do it this afternoon because they close it for cleaning on Mondays . . .

For the last three days we were filming evening/night shoots at a place called Vijay Vilas Palace outside Mandvi. This is the maharaja's palace by the sea which Aamir told us about back in London. It is a pale stone building, topped with ice-cream-scoop domes, set in ornate little gardens, and just a few hundred yards from the Arabian Sea. The architectural style is impossible to pin down to an exact era, and it was easily masquerading as a palace taken over by the British in the 1890s, even though in fact it was built as a summer retreat by the Maharao of Kutch in 1945.

While the equipment was being set up a few of us found our way on to the roof, where there was a pavilion from which there were great views of the area in all directions. The bright blue sea twinkled away to one side, and Mandvi beach with its power station aeroplane-propeller windmills was in the distance to the south.

In the late afternoon, with the orange sun setting behind the palace, we filmed the British pulling out after their humiliating defeat in the fictional cricket match. A long train of buggies and wagons stretched across the gravel path, and Yardley was required to give the order: 'Company! Move out!'

I rather presumed that everyone needed to hear the order, so when I got the cue I gave it full RSM volume. The lad holding the microphone thought I was merely going to mutter 'Company! Move out!' to the driver sitting next to me, and he ripped his headphones off and began massaging his ears. He was far too polite to complain, however, and came over to me once he had recovered and said with a big grin:

'Sir, you have a wery loud woice!'

The night shoots covered the scenes in the ballroom, which was open to the night sky in the centre of the palace. I was happy to miss out on the actual dancing, because my feet had still not recovered from bowling, and Yardley was placed in a group enjoying a social snifter, along with Benson, Brooks and Burton.

Meanwhile, on the dance-floor, Terry the choreographer came into his own. He seemed to have an idiosyncratic sense of timing, which can only be a handicap in his line of work. The music, A.R. Rahman's waltz, was on a backing track, and Terry had to cue this in as well as the dancers, which he would do by saying:

'Five, six, seven . . . [pause of variable length, then suddenly] . . . GO!'

After a couple of takes I saw the normally unflappable Nakul, the sound man, reach over his sound trolley and mime throttling him. I'm not much of a dancer, I'll admit, but what little I know about the pleasures of the waltz leads me to believe that it is governed by the numbers one, two and three, repeated over and over again in the head in time to the music. If you find yourself five, six and sevening, I reckon you're lost.

Terry's other rather unhelpful – it seemed, to an outsider – habit was to keep up a running commentary of instructions –

'Hesitation, hesitation, half-turn, half-turn, hesitation . . .'

– each of which took longer to say than to actually execute, with the result that he would get further and further behind the music, with some of the dancers following him and others gamely trying to follow the tune.

To one side, Yardley, Benson, Brooks and Burton were told to start one scene with a big laugh. At four in the morning after eight hours of 'hesitation, hesitation, half-turn, half-turn . . .' this was easier said than done, but we eventually managed to coax ourselves into hysterical corpsing via a discussion about the fact that Captain Russell had acquired his nickname of Jack at Sandhurst because of his sexual enthusiasm for dogs. Ah, the glamour of the film business . . .

Yesterday, the last day for half the English team, we filmed until 6 a.m. and then drove back to Bhuj. I packed a bag and left straight away for the airport with Barry, Simon and Jon, who were going home, and Ray, who was going to Goa first for a holiday. I came here, to Delhi, and this damn flight has just been put back again . . .

Delhi

Once in Delhi the tourist feeder fish began to bite. There is a system whereby the visitor pays for taxis from the airport into the city in advance, in the hope of persuading the drivers to go to the places they are actually asked to go to rather than directly to the hotel which their brother-in-law runs. I bought a voucher from the prepaid taxi kiosk for a lift to Connaught Place, where I'd booked a hotel, and climbed into the first taxi on the rank.

I told the driver where I wanted to go – he nodded and sped off into the traffic. Fifteen seconds later he came to a juddering stop outside a ramshackle, peeling establishment and said:

'You want hotel? This very good hotel.'

I don't think we'd even left the airport. The obvious cracks in the structure of the very good hotel could have been caused by the repeated shock waves of the aircraft passing about eight feet above the roof every couple of minutes. I told him I already had a hotel booked in Connaught Place.

'That very bad hotel. This hotel better hotel.'

I explained that, nonetheless, I'd like to go to the one I'd booked, and that if he didn't take me there, I wouldn't give him the voucher that would mean he got paid. He shrugged and headed into the city.

By the time he dropped me off outside the hotel I wanted I'd already had quite a close look at at least four others. The taxi-driver must have had quite a large family. Or maybe just one extremely entrepreneurial brother-in-law.

Between getting out of the taxi and going in through the front door of the hotel, I was warmly greeted by two separate gentlemen, each of whom knew of better hotels than the one I was planning to stay in, and by the time I reached the reception desk I was half expecting the desk clerk to say:

'Welcome . . . you know, I know of a much better hotel than this one. Follow me . . .'

As it was, however, he contented himself with squinting at my passport in puzzlement and disbelief, before checking me in as Mr Christopher William from England.

I didn't bother to correct him. I was too keen to get to my room, as, appropriately enough, given that I had now arrived in India's capital, I could feel the distinctive stirrings of an attack of Delhi belhi. Many travellers find that the transition from one style of cooking to another will disturb their gastric equilibrium, and for me the shift from film production unit catering to airline food proved particularly provocative.

Once I'd settled down I went out again. I'd been up for about thirty-six hours by this time, but Tourist Guilt wouldn't let me sleep, and I strolled out into Connaught Place, the huge circular hub of New Delhi. As I walked, I wondered idly whether a stomach complaint caused by a previously undiscovered bug might be christened New Delhi belhi. Or possibly Mumbai tumbai . . .

After the tightly packed bustle of Bhuj, the lofty façades and colonnades of Connaught Place were quite a culture shock. I strolled around the wide curving boulevard past a range of expensive-looking tourist-goods shops, without looking in any, and then crossed to the park in the middle. While I was trying to make sense of a work of modern art in the centre, made out of different-coloured concrete blocks like a children's toy, two men came running over. I had already successfully deflected a variety of street hawkers, even though I'd only been out for a few minutes, managing not to buy any wooden elephants, framed illustrations torn from old books, training shoes or airline tickets, but these guys wrong-footed me.

'English! English!' one of them was bellowing as they tore across the grass to greet me. I toyed with pretending to be German, but wasn't quick enough.

'English! Lovely jubbly!' the talkative one shouted. 'Hunky-dory!'

This made me laugh, and they were in. Shouty man grinned, showing a full row of brown-stained teeth, and his silent mate thrust a small notebook into my hand. I thought for a moment that they wanted me to explain something for them, but when I looked in the book I could see it was full of oddly phrased testimonials from tourists whose feet the silent one had massaged. While I glanced through these – the most recent seemed to be about five years ago – the chap ducked down and tried to take my shoes off.

If I was honest, I'd have to admit that my feet were in a bit of a state after all the bowling I'd done in the desert in my hideously inappropriate costume cricket shoes, and I was wavering in my determination not to let this fellow touch them.

'Lovely jubbly!' his mate bellowed again, thrusting his own notebook of recommendations into my hand. Clearly they worked as a pair. Shouty Man's book was not so easy to make out as his pal's. The pages seemed to be covered in the spidery scrawl of the seriously unhinged.

I looked up to see if I could ask what service he was offering, to see him unwrapping a hideous leather packet filled with long pointy instruments of torture, like something Laurence Olivier might have carried around in *Marathon Man*.

'Hunky-dory!' he yelled, lurching for my ears with a great waxy brown crochet hook in each hand.

'Bloody hell!' I shouted back. 'Not hunky-dory!'

I tried to back out of this maniac's reach, but the foot masseur had hold of my shoelaces and I sat down hard on a low wall. Both of them seemed to take this as the cue to begin work, and it was only by throwing their precious notebooks back over their heads that I was able to distract them long enough to make my getaway with my feet unfondled and my lugs unscoured.

Looking back, it's hardly surprising that the ear cleaner's testimonials were all in the telltale purple felt pen of the truly unbalanced – what sort of person lets a bloke who comes running up to him in a park shouting 'Lovely jubbly' fiddle around inside his ears?

Tourist Guilt then made me jump into a taxi and go to take a look at old Delhi. Once the spacious multi-lane carriageways of New Delhi ran out, the traffic came to inching near-gridlock in the tight warren of the old town. As the sun set I found myself alongside the vast red sandstone battlements of Lal Qila, the red fort. The main entrance, the Lahore Gate, was reached via a narrow dogleg of a path, from which the red walls thrust sheer into the evening sky. A death trap – any army mad enough to try an assault on this gate could have been held at bay by a small child with a bucket of rocks.

Even in the increasing gloom, the scale of the red fort was

impressive. Inside the defensive ramparts behind the gate there was a covered main street with all manner of gift shops set into the arches of the walls. It wasn't busy at this time of day and I was able to browse around for a while in relative peace. The shopkeepers had had a long day, and seemed mostly haggled out.

I watched some of a *son et lumière* presentation in a vast open yard by the banks of the River Yamuna. Three huge residential palaces sit side by side there, protected by the fort on three sides and the river on the fourth, and they were all lit up in turn as crackly voices told the tale of the place to the accompaniment of old BBC Sound Effects records. 'Hoofbeats approaching' I remembered from a misspent youth making spoof radio shows. 'Hoofbeats departing' featured almost exactly as prominently, along with a 'hand-to-hand combat' effect which they may have cobbled together themselves with a couple of bin lids and a stick.

The history of the fort, surprisingly enough given its formidable walls, was of it being overrun and captured time and time again. The Moghuls, the Persians and the British all galloped up to the speakers on the left-hand side, had a bit of a hand-to-hand scrap in the middle, and galloped away again to the right. The current occupants – apart from the thriving military colony based inside the walls – were several hundred mosquitoes, who made their own sound effects and drove me out, scratching and cursing, before the show reached the twentieth century.

Once back at the hotel I nipped over the road to McDonald's for something to eat. Ordinarily I wouldn't indulge, except to get my sons free plastic models from whatever Disney film is out next, but I was fascinated to see what might be on sale, given that this outlet of the world's most prominent marketer of beef and beef-related products found itself in the land where the cow is revered and allowed to do much as it pleases. McMutton, perhaps, or McHenNecks, or maybe

Ronald McDonald would have gone native and be offering McDall, McRoti, McOkra, McBhaji, and McPrawn Dansak.

In the event I had a McChicken McSandwich with McChips, and then caught up on two nights' sleep.

———

This morning I found that the *Times of India* is splashing a huge story about Hansie Cronje, the South African captain. Evidently someone has got hold of a recording of a phone call between Cronje and a crooked bookie who is under investigation for something else altogether, in which the South African skipper seems to be discussing arrangements for throwing cricket matches, and the whole thing is breaking right now, right here in Delhi.

Reading it through it seems so unlikely. Apart from anything else the South Africans have been kicking our arses all winter long. And how do you go about throwing a cricket match, especially against an England side who are even more determined to lose it than you are? Other names are mentioned in the story in the *Times of India,* particularly Herschelle Gibbs, Nicky Boje and Pieter Strydom. Strydom in particular is an odd thought. He's only just broken into the South African side, and barely done anything to suggest he deserved to be there, so why would he deliberately underachieve? What's in it for him? Unless the culture of corruption is so widespread that he was merely being an over-enthusiastic newcomer:

'Yippee! Here I am! I've finally made it into the Test team! Now I can *really* start to throw some matches! Come on! Kick *my* arse!'

I suppose it makes a twisted sort of sense. You can imagine his team-mates having a quiet word:

'Hey, Piet, man! Take it easy, just try and get your head down, and make a few twenties and thirties, and then once you get settled, get a bit of confidence, you can start knocking out some really big noughts . . .'

The trouble with a story like this is the old one of mud sticking. Once you start to think that Cronje might be bent other things start to make sense. Of all the Test captains England have come up against in recent years, he has seemed one of the most gracious in victory or defeat – of course, if he's not necessarily trying to win, he's not feeling the elation or the pain, he's just feeling the wedge, and the satisfaction of a result secretly engineered. And of all the Test captains England have come up against in recent years he's practically the only one we've beaten at all.

The recent series against England featured Cronje in a truly terrible trough of form. Perhaps this was because the England side was so poor he had to go to extreme lengths of self-sacrifice to keep them competitive in the games. And what about that declaration in the last Test, when he and Hussain forfeited an innings apiece? In hindsight that doesn't half look generous, although England were obligingly weedy enough to make it a close call.

Agra

The short flight from Delhi to Agra, when it finally got itself together, was an unnerving experience. The plane, a small jet of the size you might expect to travel from Liverpool to the Isle of Man on, looked as though it had been in constant service for at least forty years, without anything being changed, or mended, or even cleaned. Bits of sticky-back plastic peeled off the backs of the seats and the walls, and, as it juddered alarmingly along the runway, all around me people instinctively grabbed hold of the seats in front.

It's common, of course, for people to be a little apprehensive about flying, and once the plane had lurched into the air and they'd started handing out cups of tea the stewardesses looked a lot calmer. During the actual take-off I had the distinct impression that one of them was mouthing prayers.

The landing at Agra was hardly less nerve racking. The ancient plane dipped and swooped towards the ground, finally hitting the runway with a bone-jarring crunch accompanied by a noise like someone dropping a bag of spanners. A sudden draught on the back of my neck made me think they'd got the air-conditioning working – it was a hundred and fifty simultaneous sighs of relief.

This was an aircraft perilously close to reaching the end of its useful life. If it was a dog you'd have bopped it on the head as an act of mercy.

Outside the airport I got a taxi into the city. The driver, Sami, asked me if I was a film star, and, like a fool, I started to answer him before I realised that he said that to all the tourists. At the hotel he introduced me to his friend, Athar, who was an official tourist guide. He said he was official, anyway, and he had a badge.

When I visit a new place I'm usually happiest wandering around on my own, but it was clear that the only way I could avoid being bombarded with offers from guides and taxi-drivers was to hire a couple, and I thought why not these two – they seem friendly enough . . .

It was a good decision, as it happens. Athar was entertaining and informative company, and he had a Masters degree in History from the University of Agra, where, it seems, he specialised in the history of Agra.

He also has a house which overlooks the grounds in which the Taj Mahal sits, and he said that during the state visit by President Clinton a couple of weeks ago the American secret service occupied it. No advance warning – although I suppose if they gave you advance warning they wouldn't be a secret service, would they? – they just turned up at his front door and poured past him into the upstairs rooms without so much as a by-your-leave, whatever that is. But *with* high-powered surveillance equipment and big guns.

And on the day Clinton was in town his motorcade of

sleek black tinted-windowed limousines were the only vehicles allowed on the streets. All the locals were kept indoors by a curfew so as not to hold him up as he whizzed from the Taj to the fort and back, which seems a bit much.

That must be something you really notice once you stop being President of the United States – the traffic suddenly gets so much worse.

Athar led me to the entrance where I bought a ticket which cost exactly fifty times as much as my India guidebook suggested it was going to. Evidently the price was put up recently in the hope of reducing the damage and pollution caused by the millions of visitors tramping through every year, but I don't think that many people, brought here by Tourist Guilt, are going to turn on their heels and give the old Taj a miss just because the ticket price has gone up, even by a factor of fifty.

To offset any discontent, however, the authorities now allow you to approach the Taj through the main gate, rather than the little side gate that was used until the recent price hike. This means that the first view you get of the magnificent marble monument is absolutely square on, the classic trademark shot that has appeared on innumerable guidebooks and travel brochures, showing the perfect symmetry of the building and the gardens, with the gleaming white domes and minarets reflected in the surface of the ornamental pools.

I have become pretty blasé about well-known tourist sites, but I have to say the Taj Mahal is breathtaking. The image is so familiar – partly because the absolute symmetry of the design is such a remarkable feature that everyone takes their photographs from the same place, bang in front – that the mind struggles for a moment or two to grasp that it is real, that one is really there.

Athar told me all the trivia as we walked up to the Taj Mahal, but the bare facts seem almost insignificant compared to the sheer spectacle of the place.

It was built by the Moghul ruler Shah Jahan to contain the body of his favourite wife, Mumtaz Mahal, who died in 1631 after giving birth to her fourteenth child. Shah Jahan was heartbroken, and set out to build a matchless eternal monument to his lost love, and you have to say he made a pretty good fist of it.

A workforce of twenty thousand men took twenty-one years to build it – it shouldn't perhaps have taken quite so long, but there was a problem with getting the marble from the suppliers, and many of the lads slipped away to do the odd driveway in Delhi. The marble actually came from Makrana, near Jodhpur, and the precious stones which were used in the fantastically intricate marble inlay decorations – onyx, lapis lazuli, turquoise, jade, amethyst, malachite – were brought to Agra from what must have seemed then like the ends of the earth – Persia, China, Afghanistan, Russia and Tibet.

As you approach, two other buildings – which don't usually make the photographer's cut – emerge from behind the screen of trees. To the west side there is a red sandstone domed mosque, with another building that is its mirror image opposite. This second one is not a mosque – it can't be because it's not facing east – it's a *jawab*, a dummy, built solely to complete the symmetrical effect.

Everywhere consideration has been given to subtly satisfying the eye. The four minarets at each corner have been made deliberately leaning inwards slightly, which means that the naked eye perceives them as being absolutely perpendicular. The arches on each face of the main mausoleum are decorated with text from the Koran in black inlay, and the lettering is designed so that it appears to be the same size at the top as at the bottom to anyone standing at ground level.

Before you are allowed up to the square marble platform on which the tomb sits, you have to take off your shoes and put on some silly little cloth foot covers. The temptation to slide along the perfectly smooth floor going 'Wheeee!' is almost irresistible, and many people were not bothering to resist it.

Close up, you can see that the Taj Mahal is not as uniformly white as it appears from a way off. Dazzlingly intricate little floral patterns writhe over the surface, with leaves and petals inlaid into the marble. Each of these leaves and petals, Athar told me, could consist of as many as fifty or sixty separate fragments of precious stone.

We shuffled inside in our hired cloth shoes, into a high octagonal chamber. Marble screens, intricately carved from single slabs, allow a dappled light to fall on a replica of Mumtaz Mahal's sarcophagus, with that of the tragic Shah Jahan alongside and off centre. So demanding was Shah Jahan, apparently, that the smallest defect in one of these screens meant that the whole block was smashed up and the job begun from scratch.

The positioning of Shah Jahan's coffin to one side represents the only asymmetric discord in the place, and is explained by the end of his story. Before the end of his life he was overthrown by his son, Aurangzeb, a more austere ruler, less given to vast and expensive romantic gestures, and less concerned to maintain the perfection of his father's creation when it came to dumping Dad's corpse.

Athar said: 'Walk around by yourself, take as long as you like – five minutes, ten . . .'

I took three hours. I found a spot round the back, in the shade of the Taj Mahal itself, where it was not too hot and I could watch small boats being steered across the Yamuna towards the lush meadows opposite, where farm workers moved slowly between the rows of green. Nothing like watching other people working . . .

In the distance, to the left, the outline of the Agra fort was silhouetted against the bright afternoon skyline. This is where the mournful Shah Jahan was imprisoned during the last years of his life, allowed to gaze downriver at the monument to his long-lost love, and at the big empty space on the other side of the river where he had planned to build an exact replica for himself in black marble. Now that really would have been something.

When I finally emerged Athar hurried me off to the car, saying there was something else to see. He was charging me 50R – about 75 pence – for his hugely overqualified services, and I now discovered how he makes his real dosh. He took me for a tour of the grandly titled Uttar Pradesh Handicrafts Palace to 'find out more about marble inlay work'. And, he was hoping, to buy a shitload of the stuff.

At the 'palace' I was introduced to a fat bloke with a tubercular cough, who had a way of looking over my shoulder while he was talking, as though he expected someone richer to walk in at any minute. I'm used to this – it was like talking to any comedian in any bar during the Edinburgh Festival, as they keep a weather eye out for the commissioning editor (broken comedy) of Channel 4.

The tour consisted of about two and a half minutes of demonstrating the techniques of marble inlay work, how the intricate patterns are created by tiny flakes of coloured stone, and then a lengthy parade of all the many objects I could buy.

Cheese boards, chess boards, table tops – the coughing man showed me dozens of hefty items, using a torch to demonstrate the gorgeous translucence of the marble. This seemed to me a dubious quality, though, as I very rarely find I need to illuminate the underside of a piece of cheese.

He also wheeled out some large glossy framed pictures of himself with President Clinton a fortnight earlier. It seemed that my phlegmy companion had been put forward by the city fathers as the foremost exponent of this local craft – that was his story, anyway – and so I asked what Clinton had bought.

A cloud darkened the man's features, and he spat bitterly

on the floor behind his gloriously translucent marble-topped desk.

'Rugs!' he barked, spitting again. 'The fool bought rugs! And then he tried to buy my shirt!'

'So he didn't buy any marble at all, then?'

'My own shirt, right off my back!' (spit)

Clearly a raw nerve. Not wanting to be lumped together with Arkansas Bill in the man's curses I did actually buy something – a small box. With a lid. Actually he caught me at a vulnerable moment – it was my wedding anniversary, and I'd just spent the afternoon alone at the world's greatest monument to married love. I don't know what Susan will do with a translucent inlaid marble box. Perhaps she could put a little torch in it.

Back at the hotel I had a splendid dinner, with beer, and then, thinking of Howard enduring another evening meal at Sahajanand, I faxed him a picture of the Taj Mahal, with a caption saying that this was what I'd just had for dessert.

In the morning Athar reappeared with a different driver, whose name was Godu. Apparently Sami had gone down with some sort of stomach bug in the night. Perhaps he'd picked up a touch of English belly from somewhere.

I had time before the lunch-time return flight to Delhi to look around the Agra fort, which was almost as massive as the red fort in Delhi. It was more of a residential palace, though, and the main attractions were the cool pavilions on the riverside from which the imprisoned Shah Jahan could gaze wistfully at the Taj Mahal in the distance.

I was also taken with a novel defensive moat which was filled with jungle rather than water, in which the Moghul rulers would keep man-eating tigers, and a huge black marble slab of a throne, which overlooked both the grounds within the fort and the town and river outside. This had a huge crack in it which, it was alleged, was caused by a British cannonball during an attack in the nineteenth century, although judging by the size of the arses of two American tourists who were perched upon it the damage could have been much more recent.

After a pleasant couple of hours wandering the grounds of the fort in the morning sunshine, Athar offered me the 'opportunity to learn more about local handicrafts', and I picked up a lot more information about the price of rugs, shawls and various jewellery without really gathering much about how they came to be made. While I was looking at some ferociously expensive bits of silverwork, Athar suddenly said:

'I'd better just go and check whether your flight has been cancelled.'

Which seemed an odd thing to say. I kept an eye on the car with my luggage in it while he went to use the telephone. Sure enough, a moment or two later he reappeared and said: 'Your flight has been cancelled.'

I must say I was a little suspicious of Athar's remarkable prescience, and wanted to check for myself, and so Godu took us to the Indian Airways office. There a shrugging shambles of a clerk confirmed that the flight had been cancelled.

'Why?' I asked.

'The plane has been declared unfit to fly,' was the reply, which certainly carried the ring of truth.

Now, I thought, I'm shafted. I have to get to Delhi this afternoon, to get a flight to Mumbai this evening, so I can get back to Bhuj on the one daily flight in the morning in order to be available to film tomorrow afternoon. Tourist Guilt had finally overreached itself.

As it happened I needn't have worried. The flight which had been cancelled was a daily 'hopper', which was scheduled to do short hops from Delhi to Agra, to Khachchuro and to Varanasi, before turning round and doing the same trip in reverse. The plane was such an old crock that it failed its airworthiness test four or five days a week, and I'd been lucky to get a go on it at all the day before.

There was nothing sinister about Athar's seeming to know the flight would be cancelled – the fact is it usually was. The result being that he knew I'd probably need someone to drive me to Delhi. Sami hadn't fancied it so Godu had stepped in, and his overnight bag was in the car already.

The five-hour drive was not without its compensations. We had time to take a quick look at Akbar's mighty tomb at Sikandra – Tourist Guilt would not let me just drive past – and a little later pulled in at another huge red sandstone building, sprouting domes and minarets like some vast ancient palace.

Amazement and wonder in my voice, I asked Godu: 'What is this amazing place?'

He said: 'It's a service station. Do you want a sandwich?'

By five o'clock in the afternoon we were driving through Faridabad, an industrial city which occasionally hosts one-day internationals. Suddenly we heard a huge klaxon going off nearby.

'Uh-oh!' said Godu, and tried to step on the gas, but he was too late.

Within seconds hundreds of people burst out of small low-slung factories on either side of the road, all running as fast as they could. Many of them were trying to run and leap on to bicycles at the same time, and the traffic came to a steaming standstill in clouds of dust.

Everyone had huge beaming smiles on their faces – it was knocking-off time at North Western Steel Wrenches, like it was in the days of *The Flintstones*. Yabba dabba doo. One moment it was a lazy late-afternoon crawl along a quiet main through road – the very next second it was rush hour.

I made the flight to Mumbai with a few minutes to spare, and thus – phew! – the one to Bhuj in the morning.

8 APRIL

Finished my work on the film with two very tedious hot days at Vijay Vilas Palace. One good thing was that I was used entirely in the background, so I was able to say goodbye to my constant companion for the last few weeks – the Yardley moustache. I didn't like to make a big-deal farewell out of it – we'd hardly been on speaking terms for at least a month.

Midway through the last afternoon I was summoned to the location and an announcement was made that I had finished, whereupon I was given a round of applause from the crew, which was nice of them. Many of them – Ash, Apu, Nitin and Sherry the moustache-wranglers, Jogi, Sanjay, Kumar, Hassan, Yogesh – took the trouble to come over and shake my hand, and I was quite touched.

I think the Indians have been pleasantly surprised by how agreeable, on the whole, the English actors have been. We, for our part, have found that this production has certainly not lived up to Bollywood's reputation of being gung-ho and disorganised – it has been efficient, effective and harmonious, and I'm sure many of us feel we have made friends that we will remain in touch with out here.

There was time to wander through the grounds of Vijay Vilas to the private beach for a last dip, as the late-afternoon sun glistened on the warm Arabian Sea. Fish leaped out of the water right in front of our faces, and ten flamingos – one for every week I have been in Kutch – flapped lazily overhead.

9 APRIL

I left Sahajanand Tower after breakfast, leaving a handful of Brits still in residence. Paul, Ben and Rachel had more scenes to film, including a classic romantic Bollywood song-and-dance number for Rachel to mime along to. At least there was a good chance that she'd know the tune, since

A.R. Rahman has been staying in the next room to her, arranging and composing at all hours of the day and night in his studio, which had been transported up here wholesale from Chennai.

Howard's girlfriend, Sue, had just arrived from England, and the two of them were going off round India to see the sights, while Jamie and Katkin were planning their wedding the following weekend. They have arranged to have a ceremony in the fake temple in the fake village of Champaner, and Aamir is going to conduct the proceedings himself. Charlotte is also staying on a little longer, having struck up a rapport with Amin, the highly chatty Indian actor who is playing a dumb mute in the film in what appears to be an elaborate in-joke for everyone who knew him, so there'll be some in-laws in attendance on the wedding day.

At the airport I was separated from one piece of hand luggage – the Tusker, which I had eventually agreed a price for – presumably in case I bashed the pilot on the head with it.

The plane took off smoothly and banked slowly to the left, giving me one last long lingering look at Bhuj. The whole compact little town fitted neatly in my window, with all its landmarks picked out by the bright sunlight. The reservoir, the Hamirsar tank, twinkled away on the western edge of town, its water level having shrunk and dwindled even further away from its old walls during my stay.

Next to it the clock tower of the Prag Mahal, a slightly darker brown than the ubiquitous sandy beiges or off-whites of the other buildings, dominated the old city and the faded grandeur of the Aina Mahal alongside it. The tower, a brown finger pointing skywards, was easily the largest building in the place, apart from . . . where was it . . . ? There, alongside the pale ribbon of the Mandvi Road. Sahajanand Tower, only seven floors high, but a mighty skyscraper by Bhuj standards. On the ground floor, Mahesh the don or sex-obsessed Omar

Sharif would be manning the telephone office, while the apartments on the top three floors would be mostly empty, their occupants busy filming down at Mandvi.

A little further round, we flew over the Jubli cricket ground, in constant use, with tiny white figures scurrying around as ever on its dry dusty outfield. From there I could make out the main drag into town, and the neon sign of the I.V., the restaurant whose proud boast was that it had put at least two of us in hospital. Further down, One-piece Cricket Bat Man had probably whittled at least a dozen new bats since sun-up, and the roadside toilet-bowl salesman no doubt still had his weather eye open for his annual sucker to pass by.

Then over the other edge of the old part of the city, nestling in the shadow of what was left of the old city wall, the cramped shopping streets and alleyways where the only gridlock is bovine. Somewhere in there was the curving, narrow little lane where I had bought my new bat, and Micky's ancient printing press.

The broad strip of Station Road bustled out to the east of town, where Purvesh Ganatra dodged the street cattle to open up his internet office, and where my 2p piece was Sellotaped into his mother's diary.

As the plane nosed away south and east towards the sea, and beyond that Mumbai, I could make out the vast stretch of desert to the north of town, where somewhere in the near-distance there was Champaner, the *Star Trek* village, and a brand spanking-new Victorian cricket ground in the middle of nowhere. To the other side, the lush coastal plain towards Mandvi and the inhospitable white salt flats of the Rann of Kutch, which I only saw from the air.

Behind the wing now the little town twinkled in the desert sun, and a place that had seemed so alien ten weeks ago now felt almost like home, and I wondered if I'd ever be back.

10 APRIL

Mumbai

On the way home I have another overnight in Mumbai. At Mumbai airport there is a driver from the production waiting to take me to the hotel, and I see that the subcontinent has found one last way to mangle my name. He is holding up a big piece of cardboard on which is written:

'MISTER CHRIST, ENGLAND.'

It seems almost blasphemous to accept the lift.

The hotel is right by the beach so I go for a walk along the shore. It is a very different coast to the Kutchi one of yesterday. The sea looks brown and smells appalling when the wind catches it, and you are certainly aware that one of the most crowded and populous cities in the world is nearby. You could imagine someone floundering in the breakers in an episode of the lifeguard drama *Bombaywatch*. David Hasselhoff would gallop up to the water's edge in his orange trunks, man-breasts rippling, and say:

'Fuck right off, I'm not going in there . . .'

Aamir is in town, having left Bhuj for a break while I was in Agra. I call him to make my farewells, and he very kindly invites me over to join him and his extended family for dinner. His driver picks me up and takes me to Aamir's apartment in Bandra, and this turns out to be the very same building in which the Khan had grown up.

He shows me where he learned to play cricket, in a wide space between two buildings, in the days when his childhood playmates included little Mohammed Azharuddin. Local rules meant you were out if you hit the ball above a certain line and threatened the windows of the apartments. I can only remember breaking one window playing cricket as a lad – with a hook shot so extravagant I lost hold of the bat which smashed through the window of my father's garage – although a friend once broke a vase playing air cricket indoors with an entirely imaginary bat and ball (it was quite a shot).

I spend a very enjoyable evening with Aamir and his family – a sister, a brother, a brother-in-law, a nephew, a son, a daughter, and a cousin. At one point they are chatting about some famous Indian film actors, and I am particularly taken with the sound of a comic called Govinda (I think). He was once filming a shot in Bombay in which he had to drive away from the camera in his car. The first time he did this they shouted 'Cut!', but he was driving and couldn't hear, so he just kept going. After a minute or two he disappeared from view, and his crew assumed he would just turn around and come back, but after half an hour there was no sign of him. Another half-hour passed, then another hour, until eventually, three hours later, they got a telephone call from Govinda. He had finally stopped in Poona, the next city, and wanted to know: 'Well? How was the take?' Top man.

The trip back is pretty uneventful. During the stopover in Dubai I read my first British newspaper for weeks, and ascertain that Oldham have done enough to keep them clear of the relegation scrap for another year. I also buy some presents for Peter and John – I got them some little embroidered elephants in Bhuj at the craft fair, but I know they'll be more interested in the toy cars that are on offer here in the duty-free shop.

Susan and the boys are waiting at Heathrow, waving some home-made 'Welcome Home Daddy' flags, which is very sweet. Good to be home.

20
Aftershocks

A deep blue sky – cloudless. A harsh afternoon sun.
Yashodamai stands on a parched landscape looking
skyward, her hand shading her eyes.

HARI
What are you gazing at, Mai?

YASHODAMAI
When will the sky darken with clouds? How I long to see
it. A month of the rainy season is gone by. Not a drop of
rain yet . . . !

(*Lagaan* – English translation)

Shortly after I returned to London I read an article in a
newspaper about the terrible drought that had stricken part
of India. Villagers were being forced to walk miles to find
water, and farmers were driving cattle further and further
from their farms in a constant battle to find the wherewithal
to keep them alive. With a sudden start I realised that the
drought-hit region was Kutch, and that all the time I had
been there the local people had been struggling with this
severe shortage of water.

I remembered the water level in the Hamirsar tank in Bhuj,
and how very much lower it was than in pictures of the town.
I vaguely remembered seeing women slowly swaying along the
roadside with huge water jugs on their heads, as we rode in
cocooned comfort in the unit bus to and from the location,
and huge herds of cattle with their ribs showing being driven
along, presumably, in retrospect, in search of water.

With a wince of embarrassment I recalled the huge water pipes that were used to create the rainstorms for the end of *Lagaan*, and the mud for the splashabout fun on Holi. The gigantic tankers of precious water must have rumbled along the tracks to the location through any number of villages that were literally gasping with thirst, and many local people had been used as extras to dance on the cricket pitch welcoming the fake rain, all the while taunted by the continued absence of the real thing. Looking back, it must have seemed like rather a cruel joke to them, but it just goes to show how enormous and self-contained an operation a film unit is. A serious local crisis like a drought simply didn't impinge on my consciousness at all until I got home.

Then I heard that the heavens had opened in the week after the filming finished, bringing relief to the area. Many of the farmers whose lands had been used in the filming of *Lagaan* were all right, in any case, as the production had agreed to compensate them for the crops they would have grown on the land if we hadn't been on it, and so the fact that they wouldn't have been able to grow anything because of the drought was rendered irrelevant.

When the cricket season started, just a couple of weeks after we got back, Ray, Jon, Howard and I discovered that our respective eyes were well and truly in, after our prolonged winter nets at the PCG, and An England XI swept all before them. Well, almost all. We did lose to Howard's Yorkshire Invitation XI, for whom young Jamie scored 112 not out in a total of 152.

Jamie was a married man by that time. He and Katkin had a ceremony in the temple at Champaner, the *Star Trek* village, a week after I left to come home. Katkin wore red, as is traditional, and Jamie wore a *sherwani*. All the cast and crew attended, and Aamir himself conducted the proceedings, performing Katkin's *kanyaadaan*. As a result they have some of the most exotic wedding photos imaginable, dazzling reds, whites and oranges, faces lit by fires, with the Kutchi night sky as a backdrop.

In the summer a director called Rajiv Rai, known as the 'Bollywood Spielberg', came to film his latest movie in Scotland. It was to be called *Pyaar Ishq Aur Mohabbat,* which, rather oddly, translates into English as 'Love, Love, Love'. The benefits of filming north of the border for an Indian film are twofold – lush green yet mountainous scenery, and the sort of anonymity it is impossible to find back in India itself. And it's cheaper than Switzerland, which is another favourite Bollywood location, and they sell deep-fried Mars bars there.

Howard read about *Pyaar Ishq Aur Mohabbat* in the paper, and cheekily rang up the production to ask if he could get a part in it. They were polite but dismissive, as they would be to any crank call, and said that all the parts were cast. Until, that is, Howard mentioned that he had just been working with Aamir Khan on *Lagaan,* whereupon they whisked him up to Glasgow, transformed him into Lord Something-or-other's butler, and wrote him into the background of some scenes in the film.

Satya let us have a copy of the videotape of the Big Match at the PCG, which he had shot in case he could use any of it in his 'Making of *Lagaan*' documentary. I was able to make a brief highlights package, also using footage from Ray's camcorder, which we showed at the next An England XI/Dusty Fleming International Hairstylists XI AGM dinner and dance in December. The highlight of these highlights was the incontrovertible evidence that Howard had in fact been legitimately caught out in the first over – not a bump ball after all – and when he saw it Howard had the decency to cover his face and howl like a dog in pain.

It turned out that I had misjudged Hansie Cronje, who had been trying to fix matches after all. He was banned, having admitted to working with an Indian bookie to contrive results, although it has never really become clear quite how or to what extent he actually managed to do this. A wider investigation into corruption in the game mentioned some other big names, including Mohammad Azharuddin and Manoj Prabhakar, who were alleged to have been involved in some chicanery, and Alec Stewart and Wasim Akram, who have been exonerated.

———

Friday, 26 January 2001. I was driving to play football, exactly as I had done on the equivalent Friday a year before on the day I left to fly out to Bhuj. On the car radio, a reporter started to talk about 'the huge earthquake which has rocked western India', and my ears pricked up.

There was a split second in which I remember thinking: 'Oh, I wonder if they felt that in Bhuj . . .', before the report went on to say that the epicentre of the quake was actually just outside the town, on the desert plateau to the north.

At first the only information coming out of India concerned the damage to Ahmadabad. This was bad enough – many killed and injured, and buildings reduced to rubble – but the epicentre was near Bhuj, and so I knew that Ahmadabad was many miles from the heart of the disaster. It seemed that the towns closest to the quake – Bhuj, Surat, Anjar – were currently completely cut off from the outside world. No phones, no electricity, no news in or out.

When I got home I discovered that I could get Star News, the Indian channel, via my satellite dish, and so I stuck myself in front of that, waiting for news.

The statistics were first. The earthquake hit at 8.46 in the morning, local time, and lasted for forty-five seconds. At first it was reported to have registered 6.9 on the Richter scale, which would have made it the strongest in the region for half a century. Later, Chinese and French scientists agreed with the US Geological Survey that it had reached 7.9 on the scale, and you would have to go back to 1819 to find a more powerful quake than that.

Kutch, it seems, is an area of particular seismic risk, right at the edge of the Indian shelf/plate. When this moves slowly against the main Asiatic landmass tension builds up where the two tectonic plates meet, and this earthquake occurred when the land along the Indian side of the line suddenly shifted to catch up with the rest of the Indian landmass, which had been moving minutely but inexorably for decades. This explains why the devastation was so much greater to the Indian side of the epicentre than on the Pakistani side, which was on the other plate which had remained still.

To the west, tremors were felt in Mumbai, in Delhi (600 miles away), and in Nepal and Bangladesh, well over 1,000 miles away. We felt shock waves here in London, too. The quake was described as striking with a force 30,000 times greater than the Hiroshima bomb, that landmark event which has now become a universally accepted unit of destructive power, it seems.

First estimates suggested 150 dead in Bhuj. By the end of the day it was 1,500. By the next day 10,000 were feared dead, which was the number killed in India's previous worst earthquake, in Maharashtra in 1993.

When I did finally see something on the news from Bhuj itself, it was a piece of film shot from the window of a relief plane as it came in to land at the air force base. It was an eerie sight, heaps of grey and beige rubble as far as you could see. It was impossible at first to work out what had been where, but then the plane circled over the Hamirsar tank and I was able to orientate myself. There was the old city, with hardly a building left standing, and further out the suburbs had fared no better.

I couldn't help thinking back to my last sight of the town, from the window of the plane as I was leaving, the whole place bathed in bright sunlight, all the landmarks which had become so familiar to me clearly visible. I had wondered if I would ever go back to Bhuj. Now I wondered if there'd ever be a Bhuj to go back to.

Reports said that there had been between thirty and forty thousand buildings in Bhuj, and engineers were currently of the opinion that none of them were safe, even the ones that were still standing. The talk was of razing the whole town to the ground and starting again.

By Sunday, forty-eight hours after the quake, newspaper reports began to feature places that I knew.

The Aina Mahal, Bhuj's only real tourist attraction, had been badly hit, and one paper mentioned the local maharaj's cousin, who had saved himself by leaping from his bath and standing under a door frame. I wondered which of the brothers that was.

The receptionist at Hotel Prince, where we had changed money and bought our small alcohol allowance, described the desk shaking under his pen as he prepared bills. At first he thought it was the army letting off an explosive cracker in the hills outside the town, as they were wont to do, but then the whole building started lurching from side to side and he ran out into the street.

Cricket had finally stopped at the Jubli Ground, which had become a huge field hospital, covered in tents and makeshift shelters. Doctors were giving what rudimentary treatment they could to hundreds of patients, without the supplies or equipment to do the job properly.

The entire five-hundred-year-old walled city, with its bazaars and markets, that was once a bustling stop on the mediaeval trade routes from India to the western world, was now reduced to rubble. The streets were so narrow that when the buildings collapsed they simply filled the streets up with concrete and stone, and an area of around five square miles was now virtually impassable.

The entire remaining population of the town was sleeping in

the streets, for fear of further aftershocks collapsing unstable buildings. Temperatures were falling to 7°C at night, and Bhuj from the air in the dark was a twinkling bedspread of bonfires, which reminded me of the painstakingly embroidered mirrored cloths on sale at the craft fair a year before.

Despite the fact that Prime Minister Atal Behari Vajpayee declared that India would meet this emergency on a war footing, the rescue seemed to be co-ordinated mainly by neighbours pulling at rubble with bare hands.

There was a widespread feeling that the authorities were simply unable to cope with the magnitude of the disaster, the collapse of local administrations, and the complete breakdown of communications with the outside world, and who can really blame them? There were also accusations that local officials were too involved with preparations for a forthcoming visit to the disaster area by the Prime Minister, though, which did seem depressingly likely to be true.

A charismatic Hindu leader, Narayan Swami, mobilised his disciples from all over India to fill the administrative vacuum, and doled out rice and tents from distribution centres they'd set up to those who waded through the local government red tape to get the appropriate vouchers.

The national government's chief concern seemed to be to play down the seriousness of the disaster wherever possible, in the hope of preventing a large-scale exodus from Gujarat, which would mean refugees putting economic pressure on the rest of the country. Charming.

Every day terrible stories emerged. The baby saved after God knows how many hours under a collapsed house, saved by the warmth of his dead mother's body. The school that fell on top of dozens of small children, who were only there to rehearse for their Republic Day pageant. I saw one poor fellow being interviewed alongside the wreckage of a concrete staircase which had buried his mother-in-law. Her hand could clearly be seen sticking out from the rubble. A relief worker grimaced as he explained that decomposing bodies were distracting sniffer dogs from finding anyone left living.

As the smoke from dozens of cremation fires billowed out over the desert, hundreds of vultures circled overhead while planes and helicopters arrived as part of the relief operation.

Distressing tales: the relief effort was focusing on Bhuj itself, to the exclusion of the outlying villages, many of which had been utterly destroyed. Military planes brought in supplies and doctors from Ahmadabad and Mumbai, but everything was used up immediately in Bhuj, and villagers either had to make their way there or try to leave Kutch altogether. This led to aid trucks heading for the town being waylaid and pillaged by desperate people on the roadsides.

The army had to cordon off the walled city to prevent looters from trying to reach the old silver market. Large amounts of gold and silver remain buried there, apparently.

Then, after ten days, a middle-aged brother and sister were found still alive. The houses on either side fell against theirs, giving the impression that it was just a pile of rubble. In fact, underneath it all their kitchen was intact, and they had biscuits and bottled water to keep them going. Fortunately their faint cries were heard just before their whole street was to be dynamited and bulldozed.

The estimates began to agree that the final death toll for the whole of Gujarat would be somewhere in the region of 30,000, three times that of the previous worst India had suffered. Thirty thousand people. That's the entire population of Worksop, the town I grew up in. Half a million at least had been made homeless, and it was thought that the bulk of these would still be living in tents in two years' time.

Within a week, the bulletins from Bhuj had dwindled away to almost nothing. I realised how very small our capacity is for empathising with the victims of a disaster like this. Television news editors and newspaper journalists know we can only take so much, and even a catastrophe on such a mind-boggling scale as this one simply loses its topicality within a few days.

We did hear further news in the form of an e-mail from Reena, Aamir's wife and his co-producer on *Lagaan*.

I was aware that all the filming on *Lagaan* was finished, and so most of the people involved with the production would now be back in Mumbai, either busy with post-production or working on other things. Adi, I knew, lived in Ahmadabad, and I sent him an e-mail in the hope that he would be able to reply and let us know he was all right, and happily he did that fairly quickly. His family's home was still standing, evidently, but the houses on either side had fallen over.

Aamir and Reena were obviously deeply affected by the disaster, having lived and worked with the people of Bhuj for so many months the previous year, and they quickly sent Mr Rao and Satya from the production to assess the situation, and to try if possible to locate and help the people we knew. They found that 90 per cent of the people associated with the film were alive and well, with the rest unaccounted for. Some of these had lived in the old walled part of the city, which was now just a pile of rubble.

Kotai, the village near the film's location, had provided many people who were involved in *Lagaan*, some in front of the camera, some lending animals or transport or helping to build the sets for Champaner or the cricket ground. The village, which was, if anything, even closer to the epicentre of the quake than Bhuj itself, was completely flattened, but miraculously not one person was killed or injured there. The houses were all only one storey high, and so everyone had managed to get out before they collapsed. Everyone was homeless now, and living in the open, but Mr Rao and Satya found them in remarkably good spirits. The villagers were regarding the episode as a great escape as much as a great disaster.

Their most urgent need was for shelter, so the production

sent five hundred tents right away, and committed to rebuilding the houses as soon as possible.

Back in Bhuj the story was less encouraging. Sahajanand
Tower had collapsed into its bottom two floors, and what
was left had split down the centre. Twenty-two people had
lost their lives there, including the two daughters of Bapu,
the watchman, and the building was far too precarious to
approach.

The Prag Mahal, which served as the British HQ in the
film, had come down in parts, as had the Aina Mahal, and
the Maharao had decamped to the Mandvi palace, which was
undamaged.

Mr Rao and Satya described a chaotic situation. Relief was
arriving steadily from outside, but there was no real distribution network being set up at all. They met the film's unit
doctor, who was terribly upset, having performed countless
emergency amputations in the first forty-eight hours after the
disaster without anaesthesia or the proper instruments. When
they saw him, days later, he was just being tentatively asked
whether he needed these things.

The e-mail that Reena sent us all detailing their findings
included a list of names of Bhuj-based people involved with
the production who had been found and who were safe. I was
happy to note that Zaki, the lad who'd helped me berate the
local cable company when ESPN had disappeared, was OK,
but there was no mention of Mahesh and Omar Sharif, the
chatty chaps who operated the telephone office on the ground
floor of Sahajanand Tower. Perhaps, though, they weren't
actually part of the production, and anyway, the office would
not have been open at 8.46 in the morning, which was when
the whole tower collapsed on top of it, so maybe they were
safe. I certainly hope so.

It is easy – too easy – to become blasé about major disasters
striking some distant part of the world. An earthquake in
Chile, or Turkey, or China – they all look pretty much

the same on the news. Shots of rubble, despairing survivors scrabbling with their bare hands in the forlorn hope of finding loved ones alive, experts in orange jump suits flying in with specialist equipment after a day or so, the faces of people unable to comprehend the scale of what has happened to them, the grief intruded upon, leavened by the occasional heart-warming rescue story of someone trapped for days and believed perished.

It's all terribly familiar, somehow, as any catastrophe any-where in the world goes through the news mangle and comes out the same. When it happens to a place you know it is very frustrating when a disaster's topicality expires. You know that people are still suffering and still need help, but somehow the world has moved on, and the overwhelming feeling is one of horrible impotence. I did briefly wonder if there was any point in going out to Bhuj, thinking that at least I would know my way around, but then the place that I knew my way around had gone forever. Howard and Sue took charge of organising all of us, setting up a proper fund that we could all contribute to, which would supplement Aamir's rebuilding of the Kotai village, and also collecting clothes and stuff to send out to Gujarat via Willesden temple, where many of the regulars come from Bhuj. Paul put on a splendid exhibition of his photographs in Soho, with the proceeds going to Gujarat.

And when *Lagaan* was ready, in June 2001, Aamir, Paul and the whole of the Indian cast took it to Bhuj for its world première. They had considered erecting a big outdoor screen in the desert, but in the event the town's cinema was one of the few buildings to survive more or less intact. The movie received a rapturous reception, and, for a night at least, some of the quake survivors were able to put their troubles behind them.

21
Bowled Over

Bhuvan blinks once again and his face hardens as Yardley reaches the crease with his hand coming round to deliver the ball. Bhuvan pulls the ball with his eyes shut for a huge six . . .

(*Lagaan* – English translation)

For months rumours fly around about the opening of *Lagaan*. Perhaps there will be a première in London, or perhaps in Mumbai, or maybe in Johannesburg. At one point Aamir is supposedly planning back-to-back opening nights in all three places, with a further trip to New York for a gala screening there, before returning across the International Date Line, getting home the day before he set off. Once the première has taken place in Bhuj, however, the more extravagant plans to take over the world seem to be put on hold.

Then, out of the blue one June afternoon, I get a call. Could I make a screening in Leicester Square?

'Well, let me see, it depends when it is . . .' I say, getting snow blindness looking at my utterly blank wall planner.

'Seven o'clock,' comes the reply.

'What? Tonight? I . . . er . . .'

'Yes or no? I've got two hundred more people to ring.'

'Well . . . yes, all right, I'll be . . .'

Click.

Knowing that it would take at least a week to get the second-hand-shop smell out of my dinner jacket, and anyway not having had time to ask the voice on the phone, I decide not to go formal. Baby Michael, a recent arrival at England Towers, is too tiny to be left with a sitter, and so Susan, sadly, can't come along. By the time I've narrowed my fantasy film première companion short list down it's time to go and get the Tube, and there's no time to call Kylie or Cathy Zeta.

At the Leicester Square cinema there are no crush barriers holding back the movie-glamour-crazed fans, but luckily there are no movie-glamour-crazed fans either. My name gets me into something, for once, and I am shown up towards a private reception in one of the cinema bars.

As I reach the top of the escalator I am suddenly faced with a bank of paparazzi and a couple of television cameras. The snappers instinctively yank their big-lensed machines up to eye level as I appear, and then, to a man, allow them to drop slowly without even wasting a flashbulb on me.

All of the English cricketers have turned up to see themselves on screen, apart from Neil, who I presume was off being Barney somewhere in the world (excluding America), and Jamie, who is with Charlotte and Katkin visiting Amin in India, and who went to the Bhuj screening.

We mingle with a smattering of London's Asian celebrities. 'Oooh, look!' somebody says. 'There's Sanjay off of *East-Enders*, and the girl from *The Thin Blue Line* . . .'

Suddenly there is an ecstasy of flash-popping, and Aamir has arrived. Ashutosh is with him, and so is Paul, who has been in India with them doing the publicity thing. All three of them look a little hollow eyed with travel, and apparently they are off to Johannesburg in the morning.

I grab a quick chat with Paul, who says that he left the Bhuj première in the middle to go and have a look around the town. He says that the Jubli cricket ground is covered with tents, and where the seven-storey Sahajanand Tower was there is now just a single broken sink, a pipe and a tap sticking up out of the ground. It seems incredible that when a whole town is so utterly destroyed people still try and live in it.

Once we are all seated inside the cinema, which is large and almost full, Aamir and Ash make short speeches of welcome, and we settle down with our complimentary popcorn to watch the film.

As the opening titles roll, over languid shots of maps and other paraphernalia, I suddenly realise that I don't quite know what to expect. It's difficult, sometimes, to watch something you've worked on, because the whole thing can feel like a lavish home movie, and you have to suppress the impulse to point and say 'Oh look! I had a piss behind that bush!' (for example). And there is always the nagging fear that your proper critical faculties have become disarmed by your proximity to the project, and it might just turn out to be crap . . .

Lagaan begins with a sonorous voice-over by Amitabh Bachchan, the legendary star of Bollywood. Once the angry young man of Indian cinema, he is now the host of *Kaun Banega Crorepati*, the Indian version of the hit show *Who Wants to Be a Millionaire?* (Imagine if instead of Chris Tarrant we had Albert Finney . . .)

A group of British soldiers gallop at breakneck speed around a corner, led by someone who is clearly wearing my moustache, and I offer up a silent thank-you to Ash for not making me do that particular shot.

Then we are in Champaner, the *Star Trek* village, and it is sunshine bright, and vivid, and lively. Everywhere there is a familiar face, and wild man Guran is taking the early comic honours. Clouds then darken the sky, threatening the much-longed-for rains, and we are into the first musical number. It is massive. Mind boggling. Villagers leap from every building and street corner, and fill the screen with perfectly synchronised colour and movement. The music is thrilling, driving, captivating, and . . .

I glance around, and about a third of the audience – which is mostly Asian, I would say – is taking the opportunity to head for the toilets. This strikes me as a little odd, walking out on the most lavish and extravagant sequence so far, but it certainly seems that those cinema-goers who are used to the Bollywood experience have developed the habit of bailing out on the songs. Could it be, I wonder, that the whole genre has come about because of the necessity of providing toilet breaks in these marathon epics, as well, don't forget, as an interval in which the audience can stock up their bladders to bursting point once again?

The story begins to unfold properly after the cricket-bet confrontation between Paul's outstandingly sneery Captain Russell and Aamir as Bhuvan, our hero, and there is a hilarious scene in which the baffled villagers try to get the hang of the game of cricket. When Bhuvan describes what he knows about the game to Elizabeth, reducing it to its absolute basics, there is a comic monologue which should, if there was any justice, appear on tea towels at seaside resorts everywhere, supplanting that ghastly 'first you're in then you're out' item which has been cranking out its ponderous wit since the dawn of time itself.

I catch my first sight of Yardley, in the middle distance, flicking an elegant-looking four to fine leg – could have done with a close-up, I reckon – and then being run out like a fool, but the Brits don't figure much in the first half.

During the interval, about two hours in, people are mostly talking about two things. Firstly how absolutely gorgeous the film looks. It has been beautifully shot and is simply fabulous to look at. Then there is the performance of Gracy Singh as Gauri, Bhuvan's jealous village girlfriend. I barely met her during the filming – she was there, but tended to stay in her room and keep herself to herself – and she seemed extremely quiet and shy. On-screen, though, she is a little fireball, and definitely one of the best things in the movie.

For me, though, the acid test of *Lagaan* would come in the second half. Sport on film is a tricky thing to pull off, as anyone who has seen *Escape to Victory* could tell you. Why is it, I wonder, that we are so unwilling to suspend our disbelief when it comes to watching actors playing sportsmen? I'm so used to watching Oldham players trying to pass themselves off as the genuine article that it ought to be a doddle. The fact is, you can't simply learn to act that special quality that sets a top-class player apart, or fake it with special effects, nor can you choreograph the little sequences of action that unfold spontaneously in the course of a game.

Then there is also the constantly nagging thought that the result of the game has been decided upon in advance by a writer rather than genuinely being played out by the participants, and so a sport film never quite engages you in the same way as actually watching the sport. There's an element of the unknown missing, and even if you don't know how the story is going to play out, you know that somebody knows, and has worked it all out beforehand.

I needn't have worried. Once the climactic cricket sequence begins it has something of the feel of a classic spaghetti western confrontation. Yardley even has a special twangy little musical sting whenever he comes on to bowl, and I hear one or two murmured boos.

There is no disguising the fact that Jamie is a far superior player to everyone else, but then we are only supposed to be a bog-standard army team, and the village side are absolute beginners, so the match play actually appears pitched at the perfect level. The two hours plus of storytelling building up to the game invest it with so much emotional significance for the characters that it really becomes like a matter of life and death. The cricket match takes an hour of screen time to unfold, and well before the end I start to watch it in the way I would watch a real game, getting involved in the twists and turns. Ashutosh keeps it visually fresh throughout with a dazzling array of unexpected camera angles, and I can safely say I have not seen sport done better in a film. He even manages to make me look like a bowler, which is cinematic magic of the highest order.

Afterwards we go to Ashutosh and Aamir's hotel for a small

drinks do, and I congratulate them on their fantastic creation. They are modestly pleased with how it has turned out, and both of them seemed to sense that they might have something big on their hands . . .

Some weeks later. I was much better informed about Bollywood films than I had been a year and a half ago, but even so I was surprised by how big a splash *Lagaan* managed to make.

When it went on general release in this country, *Lagaan* went into the top ten in the UK box office charts, despite the fact that it was only being shown on twenty-nine screens, while those alongside it on the list were typically appearing on three or four hundred. Over the next few weeks the movie made steady progress towards becoming the most successful Bollywood film in the UK, chasing *Kuch Kuch Hota Hai*.

The distributors, emboldened by *Lagaan*'s early success, decided to broaden their approach. Typically Bollywood films released in the UK are aimed at a traditional niche Asian audience. They are promoted in Asian newspapers and magazines, and advertise on the Asian-oriented satellite television channels which offer them their core audience on a plate. Few of the prints that circulate are subtitled, and little attempt has so far been made to break into a crossover market and attract non-Asians in any sort of numbers. The huge critical, Oscar-winning and box-office success of the subtitled *Crouching Tiger, Hidden Dragon* suggested that it might also be possible for a high-quality Bollywood film to appeal to an English-speaking audience. Fine reviews from *Time Out*, Radio 4 and the *Guardian*'s excellent film reviewer Peter Bradshaw – who described the movie as having 'a dash of spaghetti western, a hint of Kurosawa, with a bracing shot of Kipling . . .' – all seemed to hint that *Lagaan* could be the film to take the first big step. As a result a broader marketing campaign was tentatively launched, and adverts started to appear for the film in English newspapers.

In purely commercial terms, you could argue that the three-hour, forty-five minute *Lagaan* would be better off at half the length, making it easier to fit into non-specialist cinema slots. To cut it down, though, would be to rob it of the richness and life that set it apart from, say, a Hollywood film, which can run at that length only with the sort of colossal budget usually reserved for a Kevin Costner vanity project.

In Bollywood's home market *Lagaan* was doing outstanding business, and was heading for the title of their biggest-ever blockbuster. The soundtrack CD, which we were all sent, went straight to number one in India and stayed there. And if there was any doubt that Aamir is one of the biggest stars in world cinema, there was a story about the crowd of fans waiting to greet his personal appearance in New York when *Lagaan* opened there stopping traffic in Times Square.

And no self-respecting international smash hit goes entirely ungarlanded. There were audience prizes at international film festivals in Locarno and Leeds, and no doubt many a Bollywood gong will ultimately come the film's way. There is even a rumour that a best foreign film Oscar nomination is in the offing.

The production have also mounted a lavish website, with production details, some of the music, and interviews with Aamir. There was a mention of us all playing cricket, but strangely no mention of the result. Funny that . . .

22
Following On

CAPT. RUSSELL
Englishmen make jolly fine sportsmen. The best in the
world, don't you think?

PURAN SINGH
Absolutely the best!

(*Lagaan* – English translation)

After the screening in London I explained my idea for *Lagaan*
2 to Ashutosh.

It is a couple of years later. Bhuvan has hung up his bat
and vowed never to play *gilli-danda* again. Back in England,
in disgrace, Captain Russell becomes broody and obsessed
with the defeat he suffered at Bhuvan's hands. He returns
to Champaner with his sidekicks Yardley and Burton and
forcibly kidnaps all eleven of the original village team. They
are taken to England and obliged to take part in a rematch for
their passage home to India.

The parallel between our match and that in *Lagaan* is thus
complete when I receive an e-mail from our old chum Apu.
Broody and obsessed with the defeat he suffered at our hands,
he is coming to England with his cricket team on a summer
tour, and he wants a rematch.

Then, one evening, stretching my legs, I pass the Indian
video shop where I bought my bootleg Aamir Khan films
all those months ago. On an impulse, I nip in, and ask the
guy behind the counter if he knows when *Lagaan* is released
on video. There are big glossy posters all over the walls for
dozens of other Bollywood films, but none for *Lagaan*, so I

assume it's not out yet, but he says, under his breath so that another customer doesn't hear:

'I have this film.'

Oh really? He puts his finger to his lips, and then goes off to make the other customer a snack at a food counter he has set up at the far end of his shop since I was last here. I browse, trying not to look suspicious. When this other man leaves, the video-shop man beckons me over, reaches under the counter, and shows me a tape.

'*Lagaan?*' I ask.

'*Lagaan,*' he says. I reckon it was worth asking, as it has a home-made label on it which reads '*Laggan*'.

'And it is subtitled?' I ask, before I hand over my seven quid.

To confirm this, he puts it in his video machine. The tape is at the end of the film, as he has evidently just finished copying from the DVD version which has already been released in India. He winds it back a few minutes and presses 'play', and suddenly his wide-screen television is filled with the fat whiskery jowls of good old 'Hardly' Yardley. It is the last over of the cricket match, and the ferocious pace bowler turns in slow motion at the end of his run-up, and snarls.

I look back at the video-shop man to say that this is the right film, and his mouth has dropped open in a cartoon expression of astonishment.

'It . . . is you . . .' he murmurs, unable to tear his eyes from the screen.

'Ah . . . umm . . . yes, it is . . .' I mumble. Clearly the moustache and sideboards are nowhere near as effective a disguise as they felt like they were at the time. 'Could I . . . erm . . . ?'

Still in a zombie-like trance, he ejects the tape and hands it over. As I leave his shop he comes to, and calls after me.

'What is your name?'

'England.'

As I step into the street, I add quietly to myself: 'And what is your country . . . ?'

Acknowledgments

This whole thing – the trip to India, and the book about it – was only possible because of my wife Susan. First of all her enforced ten-week stint of single parenthood looking after Peter and John, and then the subsequent months keeping Peter and John – and latterly baby Michael as well – out of the study while I wrote about the experience, represent a sustained and heroic piece of cricket widowhood.

My special thanks are due to Ashutosh Gowariker, whose brilliant script for *Lagaan* is quoted in these pages, and to Aamir Khan, who is a star.

Thanks to everyone who supplied photos: page 1: top right, Barry Hart; bottom, Paul Blackthorne. Page 2: top left, Paul Blackthorne. Page 3: middle left, Paul Blackthorne. Page 4: bottom, Paul Blackthorne. Page 5: middle and bottom, Paul Blackthorne. Page 6: top left and top right, Paul Blackthorne, middle, Umpire Roy; bottom, Howard Lee. Page 7: middle left and middle right, Paul Blackthorne; all others Ben Nealon. Page 8: top, Paul Blackthorne; bottom, Howard Lee.

I would also like to thank Paul Stevens at ICM, Angela Herlihy for first showing an interest in the idea, and Rupert Lancaster for pointing out some of the bits that were crap and insisting that I get rid of them (apart from this bit, which he wanted me to leave in).

And Jonathan Maitland, Arthur Smith and Nick Hancock. And Dusty Fleming.

Streatham Common (near Balham), September 2001

Glossary of Names

No cricketer's tour diary would be complete without a guide to help the reader through the morass of nicknames and aliases that any team builds up. During the making of a film there are so many people for the production to keep track of that it is commonplace for actors to be addressed by their character names most of the time, and these appear in italics below.

Me – *Yardley*, bristling-moustache-wearing all-action fast bowler – aka Christopher William – aka Mr Christ

Aamir Khan – *Bhuvan*, star and producer
Adi – *Kachra, the untouchable*, and my table tennis partner
Akhilendra – *Arjan, the blacksmith*
Alex – *Flynn*, cricketer
Amin – *Bagha, the mute*
Andrew – *extra*, cricketer
Anil – director of photography
Anupam – *Namdeo*, and our sometime flatmate
Apoorva – first AD – aka Apu
A.R. Rahman – composer
Ashutosh – director, writer – aka Ash
Bakshi – unit catering
Barry – *Benson*, cricketer – aka Shady
Ben – *Lt Smith*, cricketer
Cecil – *extra*, Hergé professor
Charlotte – Jamie's sister, *extra*
David – *Major Warren*
George – *extra, Boyer's stand-in*, India-based Brit from Bangalore
Guran – *wild-haired village madman*
Howard – *Burton*, cricketer – aka Johnny Player – aka Mr Spill-it

331

Ijaz – stuntman, cricketer
Jamie – *Wesson*, cricketer
Jeremy – *Major Cotton*
John – *Colonel Boyer*
Jon – *North*, cricketer, and acoustic guitar
Katkin – later Mrs Jamie, *extra*
Kumar – co-writer and director's assistant
Mahesh – telephone monitor at Sahajanand Tower
Micky – local journalist
Nakul – sound, and harmonica
Neil – *Harrison*, cricketer – aka Barney the Dinosaur
Nicole – make-up
Omar Sharif – telephone monitor at Sahajanand Tower
Paul – *Captain Russell*, cricketer, swine, and photographer
    extraordinaire
Pina – *hair*
Pradeep – *Deva, the noble Sikh*
Rachel – *Elizabeth*
Raj – *Ismail*, and Aamir's brother-in-law
Ray – *Willis*, cricketer
Reena – Mrs Aamir Khan – co-producer
Rob – *extra*, not cricketer
Ronit – unit security, former pin-up
Saleem – stunt co-ordinator
Sanjay – co-writer and director's assistant
Sherry – moustache-wrangler, cricketer
Simon – *Brooks*, cricketer – aka Brooksy
Terry – camp choreographer
Tipu – *the child actor*
Umpire Noel – *extra*
Umpire Roy – *extra*
Yashpal – *Lakla, the traitor*
Zak – hairdresser
Zakir/Zaki – odd-job man at Sahajanand Tower

The Oxfam Relief Effort in Bhuj and Gujarat

Oxfam in Emergencies

The earthquake which hit Gujarat on Friday 26th January measured 7.9 on the Richter scale and affected over one million people. This earthquake is said to have been the largest for 50 years.

Oxfam was already working in this area, and immediately sent trained personnel to assess what was needed. We provided temporary shelter, food, blankets, warm clothing, and cooking and eating implements to 65,000 people. We also provided clean water and sanitation in the Kutch region to help prevent the spread of disease.

However, once the TV cameras had left and the disaster became yesterday's news, there was still much work to be done. Recovery from an earthquake of this scale can take years, so Oxfam stayed to put in place longer term solutions. Some examples of this work include:

- After an emergency, many people living in cramped conditions are vulnerable to disease. To promote good hygiene practice, Oxfam trained over a dozen trainers and nearly 400 volunteers across the region.

- Drought had already lowered the water table and this was exacerbated by earthquake damage to dams and embankments. Oxfam instigated 'food and cash for work' programmes assisting communities with repair and construction of check dams to ensure regular and safe access to water.

- Rebuilding programmes are using local skills and construction materials to benefit 7,500 of the most vulnerable families.

- Other labour opportunities were reduced significantly with many of the main sources of employment, such as the salt pans, destroyed. Oxfam provided seeds, tools and agricultural support to allow people to grow their own food.

We are only able to respond quickly to emergencies such as the earthquake in Gujarat with the support of many thousands of people who donate to us on a regular basis. If you would like to make a donation to our work, you can:

- call our credit card line on 01865 313131

- log onto our website at www.oxfam.org.uk to make a secure online donation

- post your cheque to Oxfam, 274 Banbury Road, Oxford, OX2 7DZ

- drop into any Oxfam branch

Oxfam GB is a member of Oxfam International.
Registered charity no 202918

Index

Figures in italics indicate character names in *Lagaan*;
'CE' indicates the author.

335

Index